QUEER BURROUGHS

Queer Burroughs

Jamie Russell

palgrave

First published 2001 by
PALGRAVE™
175 Fifth Avenue, New York, NY 10010 and
Houndmills, Basingstoke, Hampshire, England RG21 6XS.
Companies and representatives throughout the world.

Palgrave is the new global publishing imprint of St Martin's Press LLC
Scholarly and Reference Division and Palgrave Publishers Ltd (formerly
Macmillan Press Ltd).

ISBN 0–312–23868–1 hardback
ISBN 0–312–23923–8 paperback

Library of Congress Cataloging-in-Publication Data is available at the
Library of Congress.

Design by Letra Libre, Inc.

First Edition: July 2001
10 9 8 7 6 5 4 3 2 1

Printed in the United States of America.

Contents

Acknowledgments

My interest in Burroughs' work developed over the course of many years, first as an M.A. dissertation and then as a Ph.D. thesis. Throughout this time I have been fortunate to receive invaluable advice and guidance from Professor Andrew Gibson and Dr. Tim Armstrong of Royal Holloway College, University of London. I am indebted to their insight and enthusiasm.

I am also deeply grateful to James Grauerholz for suggesting revisions and for alerting me to additional biographical information regarding Burroughs' sexual history and to my doctoral examiners—Dr. Oliver Harris of Keele University and Dr. Carol Watts of Birkbeck College, London University—for offering advice on preparing the thesis for publication.

The patient ears of my fellow students and friends ensured that I could always find someone willing to listen to my interminable conversations about Burroughs. I would particularly like to thank the following: Jenny Bavidge, Chris Boughton, Brian Holmes, Jon and Helen Macmillan, Ling Eileen Teo, Elizabeth Wells, and David Whittaker. I apologize to all of them for the boredom they have suffered at my hands. Without the constant optimism of all of these friends, the last four years would have been much more difficult. I would also like to thank John and Anna Maria Groombridge for their enthusiasm and encouragement since the very beginning. Finally, my greatest thanks go to my mother and grandparents for their constant love and support.

An earlier version of chapter one appeared as "William Burroughs' Talking Asshole: Negotiating the Effeminate Model of Homosexuality in 1950s America" in *European Journal of American Culture* 19.2 (2000).

"Burroughs is a real man,"

—*Norman Mailer* [1]

QUEER BURROUGHS

INTRODUCTION

QUEERING THE BURROUGHS CANON

By the time of his death on 2 August 1997, William S. Burroughs had established a formidable reputation as one of the key figures of late twentieth-century art. He had been at the forefront of the popular drug scene from its genesis with American junkies in the postwar years, and subsequently rode the tides of the beat era, the counterculture, punk, and nineties cyberculture.[2] In his later years he was transformed into an unlikely elder statesman of American letters, passing on his words of wisdom to a generation that constituted the cultural equivalent of his grandchildren, with appearances in several feature films, on the *Beavis and Butthead* cartoon show, and in Nike Airmax advertisements. Canonized as both literary innovator and postmodern saint, Burroughs seemed to have firmly established himself as one of the dominant figures of twentieth-century American culture.

The obituaries that followed his death were precise in their replication of the usual Burroughs legend: junkie, wife-killer, novelist, homosexual. But suggestions of his standing as a *gay* novelist were virtually nonexistent. In the favorable obituaries, the main emphasis fell on his iconoclastic status as one of the leading *avant-garde* writers of the postwar period. In the more acerbic pieces he was styled, as is often the case with the *avant-garde,* as a boring, nonsensical, and overrated charlatan. With the exception of the U.K. magazine *Arena,* who reached for the sensational in the claim that he was a pedophile, Burroughs' sexuality was mentioned only in passing and not once in relation to his novels.[3] Despite his having produced a queer fiction that is unabashed in its sexuality, unafraid of its explicit lusts, and uncompromising in its condemnation of the oppression and restriction of sexual freedom undertaken by the heterosexual dominant, not one of Burroughs' obituaries bothered to consider the possible impact his work has had on gay literature or gay identity.

Such silence over Burroughs' literary output as *queer* has been a consistent feature of his reception. Norman Mailer, a vocal and loyal supporter of Burroughs' work throughout the years, claimed: "Burroughs may be gay, but he's a man. What I mean is that the fact that he's gay is incidental. He's very much a homosexual but when you meet him that's not what you think of him [. . .] that's not somehow the axis."[4] Burroughs wrote about gay characters, themes, and issues from the publication of *Junkie* in 1953 until his death. Yet in three casual sentences, Mailer reduces all of this to nothing: Burroughs isn't queer, he's one of the boys—a "real" man. He doesn't write that pansy stuff, he's interested in real issues, *masculine* issues. Many fans of Burroughs might well agree with this kind of sentiment. After all, Burroughs was always keen to present himself as occupying a position that was antithetical to the effeminacy of the "sissy" or the "fag."[5] Whether brandishing machetes and firearms, disappearing into the Amazon in search of exotic drugs, or advocating violent revolution, Burroughs always presented himself as exactly the "man" that Mailer applauds. Indeed, as the sixties passed he frequently seemed more like an aging redneck than a (sexual, political, or moral) subversive.

As David Cronenberg's adaptation of *Naked Lunch* illustrated, the Burroughs mythology is, to some extent, always dependent on his being other than gay. Blending the novel with the biography, Cronenberg's film produces a Burroughs-like protagonist who isn't queer, just confused, stuck in a moment of sexual ambivalence, or, as he calls it, "sexual ambulance." The play on words is significant, for such "ambivalence" produces "ambulances" throughout the film as Bill Lee repeatedly shoots his wife in a grim parody of the death of Joan Vollmer.[6] Cronenberg, an ardent admirer of Burroughs' work, considers his cinematic version of the novel as nothing less than a synthesis of Burroughs and himself, not least in the film's sexuality: "One of the things I said to [Burroughs] was 'You know, I'm not gay and so my sensibility, when it comes to the sexuality of this film, is going to be something else. I'm not afraid of the homosexuality, but it's not innate in me'."[7] However conscious Cronenberg is about the problems that his handling of the text's sexuality produces, he fails to prevent the film from becoming a narrative about a heterosexual man suffering the agonies of repressed homosexual drives.[8]

The American literary tradition has similarly managed to overlook, ignore, or shun Burroughs' queer status. The texts are styled as beat, cult, or *avant-garde,* but never queer. His acceptance by the gay press has one glittering moment: his appearance on the cover of *Gay Sunshine* in 1974.[9] Even then, the black-and-white shot of his gangly naked torso that graces the cover is shockingly out of step with the increasingly macho physiques of the 1970s gay scene. But Burroughs has always been sanguine about his strange relationship with the gay press; as early as the 1950s he was aware that the extreme imaginary of his texts was out of step with the nascent gay movement. In "Lee and the Boys," a short story that is thought to date from his time in Tangier, he notes the problem faced by gay reviewers when confronted with his literary persona:

He was sure the reviewers in those queer magazines like *One* would greet Willy Lee as heartwarming, except when he gets—squirming uneasily—well, you know, a bit out of line, somehow.

"Oh, that's just boyishness—after all, you know a boy's will is the wind's will, and the thoughts of youth are long, long thoughts."

"Yes, I know, but . . . the purple-assed baboons . . ."

"That's gangrened innocence."

[. . .]

"So they are . . . and the prolapsed assholes feeling around, looking for a peter, like blind worms?"

"Schoolboy smut."

"Understand, I'm not trying to belittle Lee—"

"You'd better not. He's a one-hundred-percent wistful boy, listening to train whistles across the winter stubble and frozen red clay of Georgia."[10]

Expecting exclusion, Burroughs tries to rationalize the extreme (queer) imaginary of his texts in terms of his status as a good ol' boy of the Deep South, excusing his texts as locker-room smut. But the tactic is half-hearted. Burroughs knows that his texts can never be accepted by the gay community because they are always prone to get "a bit out of line" and become "somehow" unclassifiable. In the conservative climate of the 1950s, the gay community's hesitancy over accepting Burroughs seems more than understandable. Yet even the more recent blossoming of queer history, literary studies, and theory has rarely accepted Burroughs as a gay novelist, leaving his appropriation into the heterosexual tradition unchallenged. On the few occasions when Burroughs' sexuality is briefly discussed, he is usually attacked for not being gay enough. Unlike Allen Ginsberg, Burroughs has never been seen as a heroic gay icon; when not just simply ignored, he is adopted as exemplifying all that politically committed queer literature ought to avoid. As Gregory Woods suggests:

Whether one should unhesitatingly describe William S. Burroughs as a "gay novelist" is open to debate. Of his homosexuality there is no doubt. That it is a crucial element of his fiction, where it plays a major and explicit role is also certain. The problem comes with the casual and all-too-easy use of the word gay in its post-Stonewall senses, to describe the writer and his work. There are many readers who would argue that Burroughs is not gay at all, but a rather old-fashioned kind of homosexual who has never contributed, or sought to contribute, to the momentum of social change.[11]

Wood's assassination of Burroughs is so complete that the editor of the sourcebook in which the article appears suggests that issues of gay identity occur only "repressedly" in Burroughs' texts.[12] Such a reading is endorsed by one of Burroughs' publishers, John

Calder, who claims that homosexual readers "often dislike what [Burroughs] writes and his reasons for doing it. Burroughs is no apologist for militant homosexual causes, keeps his private life strictly private and writes to put over a world view that has no partisan bias."[13] As we will see, such comments are quite mistaken.

In a similar fashion, Burroughs' main critics have remained largely uninterested in the texts' possible status as pieces of gay literature. Eric Mottram, Jennie Skerl, and Robin Lydenberg generally downplay the texts' status in this respect, maintaining a remarkable degree of silence over issues of gay sexuality. While such critics are quite prepared to consider the role of misogyny, sexual dualism, and body horror in Burroughs' texts discussions of male-male sexuality are consistently slighted and ignored. Ihab Hassan's belief that "despite the elaborate depiction of homosexuality in Burroughs' work, there is no attempt to understand or justify the homosexual" is indicative of this blind refusal to engage with the explicit gay thematics of the texts.[14] Even in the rare moments when homosexuality is briefly considered as a valid issue of textual discussion, it is always read as a reference to something other than itself—body horror, the "Algebra of Need," addiction, power relationships, and so on.

More recent studies of the novels benefit from the explosion of postmodern theory in academic departments on both sides of the Atlantic and, in particular, the more vocal presence of queer studies in cultural criticism. Timothy S. Murphy, for instance, is not afraid to discuss the texts' queer thematics; yet he does so only in passing. Murphy offers a general reading of the texts' political commitments that might silence critics such as Woods but does not focus extensively on the texts as gay literature.

Interestingly, when Murphy does discuss the relationship of Burroughs to the gay literary canon, he suggests that one of the reasons for the texts' gay invisibility is the fact that their author "has always been 'out' and spends little time narrating how he got there."[15] Implicitly relegating queer literature to the status of confessional narrative and failing to note that it long ago matured beyond such a limited scope, Murphy claims that queer cultural productions are always obsessed with the narrative norm of the in/out dialectic of the closet.[16] The fact that Burroughs has always been vehemently "out" of that closet is taken as an indication that his texts might not best be read as pieces of gay literature. In addition, Murphy claims that Burroughs' "discontinuous" treatment of the social repression experienced by the gay subject "radically undermines all gestures of narrative or phenomenological closure."[17] Expanding upon this, Murphy suggests that Burroughs' aim is to attack all systems of social repression, regardless of issues of sexuality. Thus the texts are denied any queer status.[18]

Ignored or castigated by queer critics while being actively appropriated by their heterosexual counterparts, the novels fall into a strangely oppositional position vis à vis other works of gay American literature. The aim of this book is to redress the balance by offering the first extensive reading of Burroughs' novels in terms of their queer thematics, gay political commitment, and gay social concern. Although Burroughs was never a key figure in the gay liberation movement of the 1950s onwards (not in its initial Mattachine Society incarnation, or its later post-Stonewall Gay Liberation Front radicalism, or post-AIDS concern with self-empowerment through social visibility and social rights), it will become apparent that his texts feed off the progressive expansion of the American gay rights movement and in many ways subvert that expansion for their own political project.

Although out of step with the gay rights movement, Burroughs' texts do offer a complete (as opposed to *discontinuous*) pronouncement of a radical gay subjectivity that is in stark opposition to the heterosexual dominant's stereotypes of gay identity. Reacting against the social repression of the 1950s, drawing energy from (and simultaneously analyzing) the explosion of "out" gay identity from the 1960s and 1970s, and offering a fantastic vision of the end of the body in the post-AIDS world, Burroughs' texts are predominantly concerned with articulating a masculine gay identity that is often at odds with the prevailing mainstreams of both hetero- and homosexual culture. As the gay male body is transfigured into a "body of light" in Burroughs' texts of the 1970s, 1980s, and

1990s, the extent to which his identity politics transgresses the orthodoxies of queer literature becomes apparent.[19] It is this uncompromising refusal (or, perhaps, inability) to center his texts within the gay or straight mainstream that ensures their invisibility.

The aim of this book is not to establish a niche for Burroughs in the queer literary canon (although this may well be one outcome), but rather to chart the progression of the novels' gay thematics, in particular the ways in which they respond to the gay movements that intersect their forty years, and the means by which they attempt to imagine a radical gay identity that builds upon the social gains made by the gay civil liberties movement. The moments at which the texts transgress the aims of the agendas that comprise that movement, in favor of more outlandish visions of social transformation, will illustrate the reasons why Burroughs' work has remained so resistant to assimilation into the gay mainstream.

It is not the aim of this book to produce a new exclusionary dynamic in Burroughs criticism by concentrating only on the queer politics of the texts. However, the dominant critical silence over the sexual politics of Burroughs' fiction makes it necessary to focus attention on those queer politics in order to counter previous heterocentric readings. I do not wish to replace the current pigeonholing of Burroughs as "beat," "cult," or "postmodern" with the equally restrictive label of "queer." Rather, what I hope to demonstrate is the manner in which the silence over the texts' sexual politics results from the strategies of resistance used within the texts themselves. In other words, Burroughs' gay invisibility—his continuing presence on the "cult" shelves of the bookshop rather than on those of the "gay writing" section—is a direct result of the strategies of passing that his texts employ. Rather than re-brand Burroughs as "gay" or "queer," my predominant intention is to delineate the manner in which Burroughs' gay politics attempt to ape the dynamics of a masculine, heterosexual dominant that ultimately can never accept them. That an analysis of the texts' gay politics has been so long delayed is indicative of how effective Burroughs' passing is.

As a final note it is important to define my usage of the terms "gay," "queer," and "homosexual." Throughout this book I have used "gay" and "homosexual" interchangeably to signify male same-sex desire. While the term "homosexual" is predominantly related to medical and psychoanalytic models of same-sex desire, "gay" is used rather less formally, drawing on its occurrence in American subcultural slang from before World War II to signify same-sex desire. The term "queer" has been employed in two senses: the masculine-focused identity that Burroughs' texts explicitly define and, more contemporarily, the body of philosophy and literary criticism that emerged at the end of the 1970s, "queer theory." It is an indication of the semantic complexity existing with regard to the term "queer" that on several occasions it comes to possess contradictory meanings (for instance, Foucault's use of "queer" to denote a set of oppositional practices is quite different from Burroughs' relation of "queer" to gay masculinity). I have highlighted such redefinitions of the term within the text itself where necessary.

CHAPTER ONE

RESISTING THE PARADIGM

BATTLING THE DISCOURSES OF EFFEMINACY IN *JUNKIE,* *QUEER,* AND *NAKED LUNCH*

QUEER AUTHORS, STRAIGHT PUBLISHERS

Writing to his friend, literary agent, and former lover Allen Ginsberg in 1952, Burroughs laments his publishers' decision to call his second novel "Fag" instead of *Queer*. Speaking in characteristically forthright terms, he instructs Ginsberg to lay down the law to the editors at Ace Books:

> Now look you tell [Carl] Solomon I don't mind being called queer. T. E. Lawrence and all manner of right Joes (boy can I turn a phrase) was queer. But I'll see him castrated before I'll be called a Fag. That's just what I been trying to put down uh I mean *over,* is the distinction between us strong, manly, noble types and the leaping, jumping, window dressing cocksucker. Furthechrissakes a girl's gotta draw the line somewheres or publishers will swarm all over her sticking their nasty old biographical prefaces up her ass.[1]

The passage's strict dichotomies of gender behavior are startling, yet simultaneously the tone is playful, almost parodic. Burroughs differentiates between what he sees as two very different kinds of gay identity: the "fag" and the "queer."[2] The hints of effeminacy in the "leaping" and "jumping" manner and "window dressing" preoccupations of the fag lead only to sexual passivity (as he becomes a sucker of cocks rather than one whose cock is sucked).[3] In comparison, Burroughs' definition of the "queer" suggests a gay identity that lays claim to a heritage of masculinity stretching back to T. E. Lawrence's adventures and beyond. Such resignification, though, entails a certain degree of radicalism. Lawrence of Arabia and "all manner of right Joes" may well have been masculine-identified gay men, but openly acknowledging their queer potential is in itself a subversive act, as Burroughs himself self-consciously indicates—"boy can I turn a phrase." Is he merely commenting on his literary skills, or noting the "turning" (resignification) of the all-American "Joe Public" into a queer "right Joe"? In postwar America the "turning" produced by the suggestion that gay men could ever be masculine was a radical challenge to gender stereotypes that had held sway since the end of the nineteenth century.

For all his outrage at Solomon's suggestion, Burroughs' own role as "strong, manly and noble" is undermined by this camp self-consciousness. The fake hesitation—substituting "put down" for "put over"—and the description of himself as a "girl" seem far more in keeping with a register of effeminate theatricality than efficient masculine communication. This undermining of masculine standing culminates in the metaphorical position of sexual passivity that he assumes as he is anally raped by his publishers. The hierarchy of gender identifications this relies upon is explicit; the 'girl' will always be a victim unless she stands up for herself (becomes a man). The feminizing rape can only be avoided through violent (masculine) retaliation.

The biographical preface with which he fears he may be assaulted is a point of contention earlier in the same letter. Burroughs' remarks indicate that the problem he has with Solomon's request is that he is uncertain quite how he should fix his identity upon the page:

Now as to this biographical thing, I can't write it. It is too general and I have no idea what they want. Do they have in mind the—"I have worked (but not in the order named) as towel boy in a Kalamazoo whore house, lavatory attendant, male whore and part-time stool pigeon. Currently living in a remodelled pissoir with a hermaphrodite and a succession of cats [. . .]"— routine like you see on the back flap? (*Letters*, 119)

As with the semiotic challenge about gay identity, the problem centers on the different registers that exist in the gay subculture and the straight world; with a title as forthright as *Queer* (or, one could argue, "Fag") would have been in 1950s America, the biographical sketch would have to be quite sensational in order to satisfy the public's expectations about the author. The hyperbolic antagonism of Burroughs' suggested draft indicates his awareness that readers would likely create their own vision of this queer author, a vision that would no doubt be as inaccurately exotic as his own parody. The rape by the publishers is thus revealed to be an attempt to regulate identity: Solomon's naïve handling of the title and his insistent demands for a back-cover biographical sketch are construed as bovine attempts by a heterosexual publisher to deal with the rare commodity of an openly queer author.

The argument over the title and biographical sketch suggests that Burroughs is caught between two conflicting visions of himself as a homosexual man: his own belief that he is a "strong, manly, noble" queer, and the stereotypes of homosexuality upon which his publishers' reactions are based. This sense of instability is exacerbated by Burroughs' own epistolary discourse; in spite of his professions of masculinity, the language he employs in the letter to Ginsberg is the antithesis of that belonging to any heterosexual, masculine register: he calls Ginsberg "sweetheart," writes "PLUMMM. That's a great big sluppy kiss for my favorite agent" (*Letters*, 119), and asks him to "Translate me into all languages if you can. It makes me feel so delightfully international" (*Letters*, 121). Thus the letter simultaneously offers a seemingly strict definition of the gender differences that constitute the two supposedly oppositional labels of "fag" and "queer," while confusing both positions by repeatedly shifting between their two extremes.

Contemporary gender and queer theory would read such fluidity as a deliberate act of political resistance to the fixed categories of gender identity imposed upon the gay subject by the discourses of the heterosexual dominant. Judith Butler, for example, reads appropriations of the feminine by the masculine (or *vice versa*) as emancipatory subversions of two signifiers that have no prediscursive reality:

> When the neighborhood gay restaurant closes for vacation, the owners put out a sign, explaining that "she's overworked and needs a rest." This very gay appropriation of the feminine works to multiply possible sites of application of the term, to reveal the arbitrary relation between the signifier and the signified, and to destabilize and mobilize the sign.[4]

From such a perspective, Burroughs' repeated shifts from masculine to feminine registers and identifications could be read as just such a destabilization of heterosexual gender constructs, a deliberate act of political resistance that challenges the myth of gender and sexuality as prediscursive "signs" through a playful appropriation and performance that collapses sex/gender stability. However, what will become apparent is that the gender fluidity of Burroughs' early texts of the 1950s is not a precursor of contemporary notions of "genderfuck," but is rather a sign of the confusion faced by the gay subject during a period in which homosexual identity was closely regulated.

To approach Burroughs' texts of the 1950s in this manner marks a break with the predominant emphasis of recent readings—such as those by David Savran and Timothy S. Murphy—that suggest that the fragmented male subject of the texts is a product of late capitalism. Whether reading this schizophrenia as the outcome of a masochistic giving up of the self or as a liberatory desire to multiply subjectivity, these critics consistently ignore the importance of recognizing the fact that the Burroughsian male subject is always homosexual in orientation. In reading Burroughs' texts through the lens of queer history and theory, it will become apparent that the fragmentation of the male subject that the texts of the 1950s so consistently depict is not a positive, pleasurable act or a strategy of political resistance. Rather, this schizophrenic fragmentation is the very mark of the regulation of the gay subject by the heterosexual dominant.

The confused registers of Burroughs' letter to Ginsberg are symptomatic of the extent to which 1950s American gay culture defined and expressed itself in terms of the effeminate paradigm of male homosexuality. The widespread deployment of the effeminate model by the heterosexual dominant in the postwar period— through popular, legal, medical, and psychoanalytic discourses— attempted to render the gay male subject "schizophrenic," as his masculine identity was usurped by the demand that he act as a woman. Burroughs' hatred of effeminate gay men is indicative of his dissatisfaction with the effeminate model itself and his awareness of its role as a tool of regulation and marginalization. The slippages of his letter, though, suggest the problems faced by gay men of the period who believed that their identity was oppositional to that of the "fag"—the masculine gay identity toward which the "queer" reached was yet to be established.

In what follows in this chapter, the centrality of the relation between the "fag" and the "queer" in Burroughs' texts of the 1950s will be demonstrated. The regulation of homosexual identity indicated in the semiotic dispute over the title of *Queer* is what his texts of this period attempt to outline, sidestep, and negate. In contextualizing Burroughs' presentation of homosexuality against postwar American discourses on sexuality, the extent of the frustration played out in his letter to Allen Ginsberg will become clear.

NEGOTIATING THE MARGINS:
THE CONFUSED GENDER IDENTIFICATIONS OF QUEER

One of the most striking factors of William Burroughs' career is his late start as a novelist. Publishing his first novel at the age of

39, Burroughs was much older than any of his Beat Generation friends and contemporaries. One result of this unusual situation has been the comparative lack of biographical documentation surrounding Burroughs' early years. Nowhere is this more apparent than with regard to our understanding of his sexual history. Burroughs' biographers have done much to reclaim this uncharted territory, yet the fact remains that Burroughs himself always remained remarkably silent about the modes of gay existence that existed in 1930s and 1940s America—something particularly disappointing given the richness of American gay life between the wars.

Even without extended authorial discussions of gay life in the years before the World War II it is apparent that Burroughs was aware of the extent to which his desires operated outside of the "normal" scope of American sexuality. Consider for instance, his autobiographical short story "The Finger," which recounts the amputation of his little finger with a pair of garden shears.[5] Burroughs had played out this "Van Gogh kick" of self-abuse in 1940 in a desperate attempt to win the affection of his lover Jack Anderson. In "The Finger" Burroughs' alter ego Lee replays this act. Significantly, however, Lee's version of the story transforms Jack Anderson into a girl "so stupid I can't make any impression."[6] The reader is left to wonder whether the resignification of unrequited gay love into a conventional boy/girl story is suggestive of Burroughs or Lee's discomfort at the homosexual basis of the story's origin.

There is a definite sense throughout Burroughs' early work that the America of the 1940s and 1950s was one that did not permit the way of life that he desired. The history of Burroughs' expatriation from the United States begins at the end of the 1940s as Burroughs and his family moved across the border from East Texas into Mexico. This crossing of the border was to initiate a period of exile that would see Burroughs travel through South America, into North Africa, and across Europe during the following decades. The letters of this period indicate the extent to which Burroughs was in search of a kind of freedom that he self-consciously conceived in terms of the American frontier but that was significantly not available to him in America itself.

Writing to Kerouac and Ginsberg in 1950, Burroughs laments the state of his homeland: "The way things look from here, don't know as I'll ever want to go back to the States. [. . .] What ever happened to our glorious Frontier heritage of minding ones own business?" (*Letters*, 61). Praising the "general atmosphere of freedom from interference that prevails" in Mexico (*Letters*, 62) Burroughs explicitly and repeatedly links his experience of self-reliant entrepreneurship with the bygone American tradition of the frontier: "This country down here (I mean the whole of Mexico and points South) is about where the U.S. was in 1880 or so" (*Letters*, 78).

As Oliver Harris has suggested, the most important impetus for Burroughs' expatriation was his increasing awareness of the "untenable social position of the addict and the homosexual" in the United States.[7] However, while much critical energy has been expended on outlining and documenting Burroughs' experience of drugs and addiction during the postwar years, the extent of the "untenable social position" of the homosexual and its relationship to Burroughs' work has rarely been discussed. The letters themselves indicate just how important the ideal of sexual freedom was to Burroughs. Describing his sexual encounter with a boy in Lima in 1953, Burroughs tells Ginsberg: "Now you must understand this is an average, *non-queer* Peruvian boy. [. . .] They have no inhibitions in expressing affection. They climb all over each other and hold hands. If they do go to bed with another male, and they all will for money, they seem to enjoy it. Homosexuality is simply a human *potential* [. . .] and nothing human is foreign or shocking to a South American" (*Letters*, 176).

In this manner, the geographic space of South America serves Burroughs as a zone in which it becomes possible to objectify and discuss the restrictive social regulations of the United States. However, what is so interesting about this search for sexual freedom is the extent to which Burroughs remains unable to divorce himself from the restrictive nature of American social morality. As we will see, it is these distinctly American sexual mores that repeatedly encroach upon Burroughs' search for sexual self-reliance, ultimately limiting the scope of his quest since they continue to define his (homo)sexual self even though he has ostensibly left the sphere of their influence.

There are a number of reasons why these American sexual values continue to impinge upon Burroughs, the most obvious of which is the manner in which Burroughs' epistolary contact with Ginsberg, Kerouac and others, means that he remains deeply involved in the politics, culture and social happenings of his former homeland. Most importantly, though, Burroughs remains acutely aware of the "untenable social position" of the American homosexual even when in exile. Throughout a range of letters Burroughs discusses Ginsberg's attempts to cure his homosexuality through experiments with psychoanalysis and also comments on Donald Webster Cory's book *The Homosexual in America*. Furthermore, as the letter concerning the titles *Queer* and "Fag" demonstrated, Burroughs was unable to escape the psychological impact of the regulation of homosexuality that was occurring in America during the 1940s and 1950s, internalizing its influence. The extent of this regulation from afar is, as we will see, best exemplified in *Queer*, in which Lee finds himself trapped within an expatriate community that replicates—in microcosm—the repressive sexual and gender politics of the world he has fled.

Burroughs' literary career began with a largely autobiographical novel documenting his heroin addiction during the 1940s entitled *Junkie*. By the time the novel was published in 1953, Burroughs had begun work on a second text, intended as a sequel. The publishers had originally considered the possibility that this second text—*Queer*—could be published with *Junkie* in one volume.[8] However, these plans fell through and *Junkie* appeared as part of Ace's "Double Book" series, joined together with Maurice Helbrant's similarly autobiographical *Narcotic Agent* in an attempt to cash in on the postwar obsession with drugs and addiction.[9] As a result, *Queer* remained unpublished until 1985, over thirty years after its completion. Burroughs has always been quite dismissive of the text and reputedly released it only as part of a lucrative publishing package.[10] Regardless of this lack of authorial endorsement, the novel (if only because of its title) has to mark the beginning of Burroughs' status as a gay writer.[11]

Despite the thirty-year time lag that separates their publication, *Junkie* and *Queer* remain companion pieces. Much of this is a result of their strange status within the Burroughs corpus; in comparison with the texts that would follow, the first two novels are the nearest that Burroughs ever came to producing realist fiction. He had, however, originally envisaged *Queer* as "neither joined nor separate to" *Junkie*, an accurate description of the final relation of these two texts (*Letters*, 119). While both novels operate within a realist mode as they follow the experiences of Burroughs' alter ego William Lee on the cultural margins (as drug addict and homosexual), there is actually little else that they can be said to hold in common.

The hard-boiled milieu of *Junkie* is an obvious borrowing from the pulp fiction writers of the period—Hammett, Spillane, Chandler. This world of drug deals, robberies, and entanglements with the police is so intensely masculine that there is little mention of homosexuality, or indeed of any kind of sexual desire. However, at one of the few points when Lee does let his desire for boys overcome his desire for drugs, he is careful to make sure that the reader realizes that he considers himself "masculine" in his dealings with other gay men (something further emphasized by the brief references to his wife). He rants vehemently against queer bars: "A room full of fags gives me the horrors."[12] In *Queer*, though, Lee has kicked his habit and is a radically changed man. No longer is he the single-minded protagonist of the earlier novel simply looking for his next fix; suddenly he has become a needy, desperate individual in search of contact with the external world. This is exacerbated by the shift away from the first-person narration of *Junkie* into the omniscient third-person of *Queer*. Burroughs explains the change in the preface to the novel: "In my first novel [*Junky*] the protagonist 'Lee' comes across as integrated and self-contained, sure of himself and where he is going. In *Queer* he is disintegrated, desperately in need of contact, completely unsure of himself and of his purpose."[13]

Burroughs links much of this with acute opiate withdrawal symptoms, a return of the repressed in which emotional and sexual responses suddenly overwhelm the ex-addict in an uncontrollable rush: "everything that has been held in check by junk spills out" (*Q*, xiii). The reader is warned that the shift in Lee's personality must be understood in terms of his previous addiction, otherwise "it will appear as inexplicable or psychotic" (*Q*, xiii). The novel pays little attention to the actual withdrawal from heroin; rather, Burroughs is interested in the psychosexual effects of the post-withdrawal state.

In spite of Burroughs' suggestion that Lee's disintegration is a result of his withdrawal symptoms, it quickly becomes apparent that Lee's confusion is predominantly a result of his homosexual status. In many respects, *Queer* establishes itself as part of the quest tradition, with Lee searching for a sense of himself in the post-junk world. Yet it is a quest that seems doomed to failure, characterized by repeated frustration as Lee's relationships with other men undermine his ego stability. With the return of his (homo)sexual desire, Lee experiences the fundamental issue that characterized gay experience in 1950s America—that is, the popular conception of the homosexual male as effeminate. This cultural stereotype demanded that all gay relationships conform to a parody of heterosexual couplings in which the confirmed gay man played a feminine, passive role while his more ambiguous, self-styled "masculine" partner (the hustler, the punk, or the otherwise hard-up "straight" man) indulged in homosexual acts without compromising his masculine/straight status and without becoming open to accusations of effeminacy.[14]

Throughout *Queer*, Lee is caught between his fear of being branded effeminate and his desire for a masculine partner. At the opening of the novel these two points are illustrated as Lee frantically searches for sex. Within the first 35 pages he is rebuffed three times: by Carl, the straight but mother-dominated Jewish boy (*Q*, 1–3), Moor, the sexually "border-line" hypochondriac (*Q*, 4–7) who could "out-bitch any fag" (*Q*, 26), and Allerton, the masculine, seemingly straight boy whose attention is diverted from Lee by a young girl (*Q*, 16–19). In his attempt finally to find a willing sexual partner, Lee ends up in a "fag bar" (*Q*, 19) where he picks up a young boy.

Though Lee finally does find sex, this opening narrative of frustrated desire ends with a whimper. Despite having lambasted fag bars in *Junkie*, he is forced to visit just such an establishment in order to find a partner. This decision is a contradiction of his regular subcultural identifications; he pointedly chooses the Ship Ahoy bar over the Green Lantern and its "screaming fags" (*Q*, 35). The names of the two bars are suggestive, one a reference to the masculine camaraderie of the sea voyage, the other a sickly green beacon of gender deviance and exhibitionism. Yet since all of Lee's primary sexual objects have rejected his advances, he finds himself placed in the position of a "detestably insistent queer" (*Q*, 9), an appellation that implicitly feminizes him as he takes on the stereotypical role of a desperate, needy, and near-hysterical suitor. Long departed is the Lee of *Junkie* whose voice drawled with the self-assured masculinity of a Chandler hero.

In order to rediscover this masculine identity (without renouncing homosexuality) it is clear that Lee must take an effeminate partner, thereby retaining an active, dominant role for himself. But his "effeminophobia" prevents him from taking this step.[15] Lee is so disgusted by the very idea of a man pretending to be a woman that he searches for a partner who is as masculine as he believes himself to be. Watching a group of young boys, he asks:

> "What have they got that I want, Gene? Do you know?"
> "No."
> "They have maleness of course. So have I. I want myself the same way I want others. I'm disembodied. I can't use my own body for some reason." (*Q*, 99)

By refusing to play the effeminate role or take on an effeminate partner himself, Lee is clearly in search of a mode of gay identity and relationship that would fulfill the definition of "queer" given in his letter to Ginsberg. Yet the "queer" position he seeks is consistently denied him since it contravenes all preconceived ideas about the limits of gay identity.

Embarking on a relationship with the straight but curious Allerton, Lee hopes to create a utopian traffic in masculinity, a narcissistic relationship in which each of the participants reflects the masculine status of the other. However, these hopes are quickly dashed; the effeminate paradigm of homosexual identity is too deeply ingrained within this community of expatriates. Allerton approaches the awkward relationship with his own set of prejudices. Since he equates queerness with "at least some degree of overt effeminacy," he is appalled as the relationship with Lee becomes sexual (*Q*, 27). Lee attempts to appease him by indicating his own awareness of the stereotype created by the conflation of effeminacy and homosexuality: "I shall never forget the unspeakable horror [. . .] when the baneful word seared my reeling brain: I was a homosexual. I thought of the painted, simpering female impersonators I had seen in a Baltimore night club. Could it be possible that I was one of those subhuman things?" (*Q*, 39). Yet such expressions of effeminophobia are not enough to prevent Allerton from quickly becoming dissatisfied with the arrangements.

Lee may not present himself as a "painted, simpering" fag, but the fact remains that the relationship transgresses the conventional (heterosexual) boundaries of masculine friendship/bonding. However curious Allerton may have been, he quickly becomes recalcitrant and aggressive as his confusion over his own status mounts. Neither of these two men is willing to play the passive, feminine role. Increasingly, though, it is Lee (as the confirmed gay man within the relationship) who is forced into this position. Allerton's detachment and his lack of emotional ties to Lee once again places the latter in the position of the "detestably insistent queer." Indeed, Lee's emotional attachment to the boy frequently leads to his symbolic castration: "Allerton had abruptly shut off contact, and Lee felt a physical pain as though a part of himself tentatively stretched out towards the other had been severed, and he was looking at the bleeding stump in shock and disbelief" (*Q*, 58).

The relationship stays locked in this pattern of oscillation throughout the course of the novel. Far from being a meeting of two mutually masculine men, it becomes a fight for dominance in which the loser is forced into a position of effeminacy. Allerton is quick to adopt the traditional role of hustler to Lee's confirmed homosexual, accepting financial reward for his company—the rescue of the camera from the pawn shop (*Q*, 58)—which leads to Lee's apt description of him (in gay slang) as a "punk" (*Q*, 48). In an attempt at retaliation, Lee tries to style the relationship in terms of father and son, masculinizing his own position by relegating Allerton to the position of the boy in older paradigms of homosexuality such as pederasty, in which the youth is (stereotypically) always passive and "feminine," the receiver of an older, masculine man: "All I ask is be nice to Papa, say twice a week" (*Q*, 72).

The affair between the two men increasingly renders Lee not only effeminate but, more importantly, schizophrenic. Caught between his own masculine identifications and his awareness that he is being forced into the role of the "painted, simpering" fag, Lee is torn between his view of himself and the stereotype that society demands he play out. The end result of this oscillation is the gradual disintegration of Lee's psychic stability, something that is underlined by the imaginative projection of himself into the bodies of other men and, more importantly, the composition of a series of insane monologues he terms "routines."

In an attempt to experience his own masculinity, Lee increasingly relies upon that of others, feeding off them in a futile attempt to regain stability. Whether watching a group of adolescents (*Q*, 96–97) or in the cinema with Allerton (at a screening of Cocteau's classic exploration of narcissism, *Orpheus*), Lee consistently experiences the desire "to enter the other's body, to breathe with his lungs, see with his eyes, learn the feel of his viscera and genitals" (*Q*, 36). This desire to usurp the masculine status of others is clearly a result of his fear that he is being made to adopt an effeminate position as a result of his sexuality. Savran suggests that the desire of the Burroughsian subject "to *become* the other" is "doubtlessly part of what makes Burroughs' writing so queer."[16] Yet, clearly it is exactly the opposite: Lee fails to be "queer"—in Burroughs' own definition of the term, at least—for as long as he needs to act out this fantasy of becoming. The stable masculine queer subject would not need to invade, usurp, or steal.

In a similar fashion, Lee's (and Burroughs') reliance on a salacious narrative mode dubbed "the routine" suggests a disturbing psychic collapse. The routine emerged as a narrative form during Burroughs' relationship with Adelbert Lewis Marker (the real-life model for Allerton in *Queer*). Later, in his long-distance love affair with Allen Ginsberg, Burroughs developed and expanded the format. Burroughs was aware of its value in seducing potential partners: "Whenever I encounter the impasse of unrequited affection my only recourse is in routines" (*Letters,* 204). As Oliver Harris suggests, the routines have a multiple function as "an act of threatening courtship, love-letters, black-mail" (*Letters,* xxiii). The register of the routine form is one of ever-increasing outrageousness; it marks entry into an extreme imaginary that is at odds with conventional narrative, being comprised of bawdy, violence, deviant sexualities, and camp while retaining a tone which is essentially comic.

We have already seen the way in which Burroughs (in his letter to Ginsberg) possesses an authorial voice that frequently oscillates between masculine and camp registers. In many respects, the routine form employed in the letters and by Lee in *Queer* encapsulates that oscillation for it repeatedly moves between a masculine and a camp tone. Writing to Ginsberg, Burroughs relates the routine— rather offhandedly—to ideas about gay identity: "I've been thinking about routine as art form, and what distinguishes it from other forms. One thing, it is not *completely symbolic,* that is, it is subject to shlup over into "real" action at any time [. . .] In a sense the whole Nazi movement was a great, humorless, evil *routine* on Hitler's part. Do you dig me? I'm not sure I dig myself. And some pansy shit is going to start talking about *living* his art" (*Letters,* 216).

Both fantastic and realistic, the routine is monstrous. Its schizophrenic oscillation between opposed registers (real/fictional, comic/terrifying, masculine/feminine) threatens to overwhelm the teller, turning him into a mere ventriloquist's dummy like Lee in *Queer,* who receives the routines "like dictation" from an unknown source (*Q,* 66). In this respect, the routine feminizes the receiver, throwing him into a camp hysteria that is likely to tear him apart, bringing about his psychic disintegration. At the same time, however, the subject who survives the telling of the routine gains a certain amount of masculine credibility through confronting the danger of losing the self and by reveling in the form's scatological, smutty bawdiness. The routine is thus a performance—like camp—that involves a giving up of the self; the danger is that one might not be able to regain full autonomy. It is thus an appropriate narrative mode for Lee (and his creator) to employ, for it symbolizes the schizophrenic fragmentation of the gay male ego. It is important to note that it is only in Burroughs' texts of the 1950s that the routine dominates. When employed in the later texts it is remarkably less dangerous and less hysterical, a fact that has much to do with the shift in Burroughs' methods of textual production in the post–1959 period.

In *Queer*, Lee's routines are fantasies that are generated in an attempt to woo Allerton. The four routines of the novel—the Oil Man (*Q*, 30–33), the Chess Players (*Q*, 64–65), the Used Slave Lot (*Q*, 66–70), and the Skip Tracer (*Q*, 123–124)—are all transparent fantasies of control and manipulation. In each of these narratives there is a central figure who is able to bend others to his will through a combination of performance and persuasion. As such, the routines are clear metaphors of Lee's relationship with Allerton, his attempts to style the affair as one in which he is in a dominant position, successfully wooing his young lover without compromising his masculine identity. Each routine thus marks an attempt by Lee to salvage some degree of ego stability through fantasy; however, the very nature of the routine—in particular the way in which it overwhelms Lee as he dictates it and drives Allerton away—leads to Lee's further collapse. The routines culminate with the phantom figure of the Skip Tracer, who marks the total disintegration of Lee's sense of self.

In many respects, this reading of *Queer* is in opposition to that produced by most recent critics of Burroughs' work, who have been united in their attempts to read the texts of the 1950s in relation to postmodern discourses on madness, masochism, and schizophrenia. Both David Savran and Timothy S. Murphy claim that the disintegration of Lee can be interpreted as indicative of the fragmentation of the male subject brought about during the postwar period. Savran, for instance, suggests that the hipster is always a "schizoid" subject:

Unlike the normative middle-class working man/husband/
father, the hipster is a hybridized subject, a product of cultural miscegenation, a cross-dresser, neither completely white
nor black, masculine nor feminine, heterosexual nor homosexual, working class nor bourgeois. Rather, as I will demonstrate, his oscillation between these different positionalities
produces him as a schizophrenic, self-defeating—and
masochistic—subject.[17]

Timothy S. Murphy follows a similar line of argument, reading
Burroughs' texts through the lens of Deleuze and Guattari's work and
their vision of the radical schizo. Murphy's reading of *Queer*, for instance, centers on explaining the disintegration of Lee's stable subjecthood as part of a progressive, revolutionary movement towards a
telepathic community. He suggests that the routines of *Queer* are
signs of a "radical otherness"[18] and mark the beginnings of Lee's entry
into a telepathic community in which he will find "the ability to fragment (or what amounts to the same thing) multiply his subjectivity
in order to experience other subjectivities and perspectives."[19]

For Murphy, such contact with Otherness is always positive, a
transformation of the self that challenges stability, coherence, and
order through forcing the subject to adopt other positions antithetical to his original one. However, this glamorization of the
schizophrenic confusion of Lee in *Queer* is problematic since it ignores the ways in which the text itself strives to represent such
fragmentation as the unwelcome result of the impasse into which
"queer" affection (that is, male-male, masculine-identified relationships) has been forced through the deployment of the stereotype of gay male subjectivity as effeminate.

Consider, for instance, Murphy's reading of the final routine of
Queer, Lee's dream of himself as the Skip Tracer for a company
called Friendly Finance (*Q*, 132–134). Having lost Allerton, Lee
fantasizes tracking him down to remind him that the sexual contract still needs to be fulfilled: "Haven't you forgotten something,
Gene? You're supposed to come and see us every third Tuesday.
We've been lonely for you in the office" (*Q*, 132). Murphy reads
this as a progressive image:

the finder of missing persons dramatizes the potential for real subversion and new community grounded in the proliferation of ghetto subcultures. He works at the edges, in the liminal and underdetermined spaces that can harbor, for a time, the opponents of control, trying to bring people of different spaces together. But the missing persons he finds are not simply people who are lost, have been abducted, or have gone underground; more importantly, they are people who have not yet come into existence [. . .] Lee's telepathic "virtual" community is such a people, a community to come, and both the subject and the object of his open-ended concluding promise are this community, as figured in Allerton: "We'll come to *some* kind of agreement."[20]

This attempt to style the Skip Tracer as an image of liberation is disingenuous. Rather than subverting or resisting power by bringing "people of different spaces together," the Skip Tracer is an instrument of control (and therefore part of the capitalist, consumer hierarchy) unleashed when a debtor tries to escape the control machine. Burroughs presents his pursuit of Allerton as unwarranted, since it is based upon a spurious legality; the clause in the contract that is the point of contention is one that "can only be deciphered with an electron microscope and a virus filter" (*Q*, 132). The fact that he works for Friendly Finance is an obvious irony, for the Skip Tracer is both *un*friendly in his persistence and *over*friendly in the sexual nature of his demands. His final comment that Murphy makes so much of—"We'll come to *some* kind of agreement"(*Q*, 134)—seems less a promise of a utopian community than a terrifying threat. The image of the Skip Tracer suggests that Lee has actually traveled full circle; once again he is the "detestably insistent queer" (*Q*, 9) that he was at the beginning of the narrative.

The epilogue serves only to underline Lee's total failure in establishing Murphy's community, or even the stable identity promised in the novel's title. Trapped in the dead zone of Panama, surrounded by the hostile, paranoid telepathy from which he hoped to escape, Lee's gender identity remains in flux. He returns to his earlier tactic of appropriating the masculinity of others. In Panama he takes photographs of a masculine fisherman, with the camera serving as a mediator between self and (desired) other: "In my mind I was running a finger along the scar, down across his naked copper chest and stomach, every cell aching with deprivation" (*Q*, 124). He cruises a bar full of servicemen, but they are either straight (buying drinks for the parasitic local girls) or suffering from the end result of hostile telepathy, the "light concussion Canal Zone look" (*Q*, 125). Back in Mexico City, Lee flicks through "*Balls: For Real Men*" at the magazine stall but finds only articles about violent emasculation, the hanging of Sonny Goons (*Q*, 130). Having failed to establish his own autonomous gender identity, Lee is still trying to usurp that of others.

This dubious ethical relation to the Other is highlighted by Oliver Harris, who suggests that Lee's "sadistic aggression towards racial others" throughout the text "seems to be an act of hysterical compensation for the impotence in his sexual relationship."[21] As Harris continues:

> In *Queer*, Lee's identity is destabilized by desire: he tries to shore up the walls of his psyche by aggressively policing the borders of his national identity, attacking the body politic's enemies without in a defensive reaction designed to deal with an enemy within. It is in the context of relations of power, more particularly the *frustration* of power, that Lee now takes on an identity so emphatically based on class, race, nationality and money.[22]

The intersection of sexual inadequacy, ego disintegration, and American nationalism can be related to the broader issue of Lee's masculinity. The "*frustration* of power" that Lee experiences is also a frustration of his masculine identifications. Excluded from a position of masculine mastery and stability, Lee is driven to create increasingly disturbing fantasies of violent domination of the Other (whether the Latin American populace of *Queer*'s setting or Allerton). As we will see in the following chapters, this problematic movement toward the reactionary becomes an index of the conformity inherent within Burroughs' masculinization.

What these fantasies alert us to is the degree to which Lee is terrified of losing his masculine self. It is vital to realize that Burroughs' early texts are deeply opposed to valorizing any fragmentation of gay identity and—instead—are overtly concerned with criticizing the way in which gay identity in 1950s America is consistently forced into a position in which it is unable to remain stable, coherent, whole. What both Savran and Murphy overlook is that the texts are self-conscious in their discourse on the schizophrenic subject and quite clear in their belief that the gay subject's experience of schizophrenia is intimately tied to issues of both gender identification and the influence of the (heterosexual) dominant's discourses on homosexuality. Burroughs' understanding of gay identity is sophisticated enough to recognize the role of the heterosexual dominant in constructing that identity and regulating it by rendering the gay subject schizophrenic.

Burroughs' explicit discourse on schizophrenia begins in the second half of *Queer* as Lee and Allerton enter the Amazon jungle in search of the hallucinogen *yagé*. For Lee, this quest is an attempt to escape the schizophrenic gender identifications that have plagued him throughout the novel. Worried that both the CIA and the KGB are researching the drug's reputed effect of increasing the user's telepathic ability in order to facilitate mass mind control (*Q*, 91), Lee hopes to prepare himself through proactive self-experimentation. Interestingly, his paranoia over McCarthyite social regulation leads him to suggest a link between *yagé*, telepathy, and schizophrenia: "In some cases of schizophrenia a phenomenon occurs known as automatic obedience [. . .] synthetic schizophrenia produced to order [. . .] Incidentally there is some connection between schizophrenia and telepathy. Schizos are very telepathically sensitive, but are strictly *receivers*. Dig the tie-in?" (*Q*, 91). Such power could offer Lee one means of establishing a level of dominance in his relationship with Allerton, as he jokes: "Think of it: thought control. Take anyone apart and rebuild them to your taste. Anything about somebody bugs you, you say, 'Yage! I want that routine took clear out of his mind.' I could think of a few changes I might make in you, doll" (*Q*, 89).

In Lee's hands, *yagé* might be a useful tool for creating a utopian queer relationship, allowing him and Allerton finally to "establish contact on the non-verbal level of intuition, a silent exchange of thought and feeling" (*Q*, 58) as he has always desired, or more worryingly allow him to finally achieve dominance over his young partner through brainwashing him. In the service of the government, though, Burroughs suggests that *yagé* might well be used to usher in a new order of complete social regulation, rendering the population politically impotent by forcing them into a state of schizophrenia and automatic obedience.

Interestingly, Burroughs' own experience of *yagé* illustrates the manner in which schizophrenic dissolution is closely tied to issues of gender identification. On experimenting with the drug in South America, Burroughs described it as an "overwhelming rape of the senses" and claimed "complete bisexuality is attained" (*Letters*, 180). Significantly his response to its effects was somewhat ambiguous. The clearly terrifying paranoiac visions of the "Composite City" are offset against the potentially liberatory dispersal of the self that the drug brings about.[23] As Burroughs notes, *yagé* effects the fragmentation of the white male as racial, gender and, most importantly *homosexual* identity is ruptured: "It was like possession by a *blue spirit* [. . .] a tremendous sexual charge, but *heterosex*" (*Letters*, 171); "I could feel myself change into a Negress complete with all the female facilities [. . .] Now I am a Negro man fucking a Negress" (*Letters*, 180). When Allen Ginsberg followed Burroughs' path through South America and found the drug in 1960, he reported a similar experience of bisexual dissolution in which he saw everyone as "an eternal seraph male and female at once—and me a lost soul seeking help" (*YL*, 54).

Burroughs is quite aware of the subversive possibilities of such a powerful hallucinogen: "This is the most complete negation possible of respectability. Imagine a small town bank president turning into a Negress and rushing to Nigger town in a frenzy to solicit sex from some Buck Nigra. He would never recover that preposterous condition known as self-respect" (*Letters*, 180–181). However, at the same time, it is important to recognize the extent to which *yagé* must also be understood as a dangerous weapon of control and regulation. Schizophrenic dissolution is a powerful tool of self-creation if employed at the subject's own behest, but does it remain inherently liberatory if imposed upon an unsuspecting and unwilling subject by external forces? The fact that both the CIA and KGB really were experimenting with *yagé* during the 1950s in the attempt to produce a "Manchurian Candidate"—a brainwashed citizen programmed to carry out covert assassinations unwittingly—adds an important dimension to the theme of schizophrenia in Burroughs' texts of this period.[24] From the marginalized position of the American homosexual, schizophrenic dissolution was a dubious goal—its usefulness depended upon who was responsible for inducing such fragmentation of the self.

As we will see in chapter two, Burroughs' interest in producing this schizophrenic dissolution of the self reached a peak in his textual experiments of the 1960s. However, it is important to acknowledge the extent to which this kind of self-induced schizophrenia differs from the loss of the masculine self experienced by Lee in *Queer*. Increasingly important in Burroughs' fiction after *Queer* is the fact that the situation Lee imagines of *yagé*-induced schizophrenia, mass obedience and brain washing is not the product of some future dystopia, but is actually a parallel of the experience of the gay subject in America during the postwar period. In this respect, Lee's search for *yagé* becomes as fruitless as Cotter's own experiments on isolating curare, since the conditions of total regulation he hopes to escape are already in place; his efforts are "already superseded" (*Q*, xvii). Trapped in a restrictive culture that refuses to countenance the possibility of the homosexual male being masculine, the gay subject is forced into a position of gender confusion or schizophrenia like that experienced by Lee. It is not a conscious fantasy or decision; he experiences no pleasure (masochistic or otherwise) in his fragmentation. Rather, Burroughs shows it to be the end result of the social regulation of homosexual identities by an aggressively homophobic heterosexual dominant (one that cannot even be escaped through voluntary exile). In order fully to understand the extent of the regulation of

homosexuality in postwar America and the form that it took, it is
necessary to place Burroughs' work within a historical context, especially since, after the writing of *Queer,* he begins to use his narratives directly to address contemporary medical discourses on
homosexuality.

CONTEXTUALIZING QUEER:
DISCOURSES ON SEXUALITY AND EFFEMINACY

Burroughs' belief that the gay man is rendered "schizophrenic" as
his masculine identifications are consistently denied by the discourses of the heterosexual dominant is hardly without historical
precedent. The effeminate paradigm dominated Western discourses on homosexuality throughout the first half of the twentieth century. An awareness of this is crucial in understanding the
texts' belief that effeminacy is a signifier of difference, disempow-
erment, and marginalization. Furthermore, an understanding of
the discourses from which the effeminate paradigm emerges will
explain why it is that the overriding fear that Burroughs' texts of
this period consistently replay is that of the man who mimics (or,
in the most nightmarish moments, actually *becomes*) the female.

The origins of the effeminate model of male homosexuality that
dominated popular, medical, and psychoanalytic discourses in
America in the 1950s can be traced back to the explosion of sex-
specific research that occurred at the end of the nineteenth century
and created the "category" of homosexuality. The work of researchers into sex and sexuality such as Ulrichs, Krafft-Ebing,
Hirschfeld, and Havelock Ellis marked both the beginnings of
what might now be considered (via Foucault) the era of regulated
sexuality and, in addition, the establishment of a gay identity that
would last well into the twentieth century. As Foucault claims in
The History of Sexuality, the nineteenth century's classification of
sexualities and sexual acts led to "a new *specification of individuals*"
that made sex between males not just an act (sodomy) but the basis
of an identity (the homosexual): "Nothing that went into [the ho-

mosexual's] total composition was unaffected by his sexuality [. . .]
The sodomite had been a temporary aberration; the homosexual
was now a species."[25]

The original aim of Ulrichs and his contemporaries had been
the classification of sexualities; the researchers, whatever their
personal leanings, became increasingly aware of the sheer diversity
of sexualities and accompanying identities. With regard to homosexuality, there was a general acceptance of the fact that any given
gay male subject's gender identity could be ultra-masculine, ultra-
feminine, or some point in between. Ulrich's notion of *anima
muliebris in corpore virili inclusa* [a feminine soul in a male body]
was just one category of gay male identity, yet it was this category
that came to achieve popular dominance in discussions of homosexuality. The model of inversion or gender deviance in which the
subject's sexed body did not coincide with his or her gender performance even overcame ideas of homosexuality as an expression
of virile masculinity (as espoused by theorists such as Benedict
Friedländer).[26] Gert Hekma's historical reevaluation of this period concludes that patriarchal culture had much to gain from this
conflation of homosexuality with effeminacy: "The suggested effeminacy of gays was a forceful social strategy that marginalized
homosexual desires and thus prevented the deployment of gay
identities."[27] Effeminacy became a visible signifier of deviance,
abnormality, inversion, and perversion.

The effeminate paradigm, as Hekma suggests, insisted on a
single, regulated identity in place of the *identities* that were
steadily accumulating. Homosexuality became a fixed state of
mind and body with fixed cultural codes. Alan Sinfield argues
that the effeminate model established itself as *the* culturally conditioned and legally sanctioned homosexual identity at the precise historical moment of the Oscar Wilde trials. Before 1895
effeminacy was not a sign of homosexuality. What Sinfield convincingly argues is that the "dominant twentieth-century queer
identity" emerged "mainly out of the elements that came together
at the Wilde trials: effeminacy, leisure, idleness, immorality, lux-
ury, insouciance, decadence and aestheticism."[28] The effeminate

paradigm (which had, of course, been gathering momentum since the sexologists' categorization of sexual identities during the late nineteenth century) would be solidified in the popular imagination—on both sides of the Atlantic—during the Wilde trials, and furthermore defined in the legal and media discourses that surrounded them. The construction of the effeminate paradigm as the only mode of tolerated gay identity was virtually complete.

Although Freud argued against the inadequacies of the third sex model, his work ultimately found itself battling against a cultural stereotype that had ingrained itself in late-nineteenth-century discourses. In his theory of the polymorphous perverse, Freud was effectively challenging the kind of moralistic arguments that read homosexuality as a deviation from the normal (heterosexual) course of psychic and sexual development. If we each shared a universal psychic heritage of primary bisexuality, then homosexuality could be read as a difference in object choice rather than a sinful, degenerate act of indecency. Furthermore, Freud argued against the effeminate paradigm as the key to homosexual identity: "A man in whose character feminine attributes obviously predominate [. . .] may nevertheless be heterosexual."[29] Such findings meant that "the supposition that nature in a freakish mood created a 'third sex' falls to the ground."[30]

Despite this relatively liberal approach to homosexuality and gender deviance, the cultural discourse of effeminacy proved too much for the Freudian school to overcome. The Schreber case offers an interesting example of this while also setting a historical precedent for the conflation of homosexuality, gender inversion, and schizophrenia that we have seen in Burroughs' texts.[31] Freud's analysis of Schreber's memoirs concluded that Schreber's paranoid schizophrenic state was a result of the eruption of homosexual libido. Schreber's repressed desire for his doctor, Flechsig, leads him to believe that he is being emasculated, his body literally transforming from male to female. In his attempts to resist this change, his mental disturbance increases as he substitutes God for Flechsig and attempts to style the metamorphosis in transcendent terms.

Freud oedipalizes his plight (Flechsig=brother; God=father), yet this does not extirpate the general assumption at the core of Schreber's discourse that homosexuality must entail effeminacy. The voices that Schreber hears taunt him with the appellations "Miss Schreber" and "the person who lets himself be f-d!," while demanding "Don't you feel ashamed in front of your wife?"[32]

Schreber's predicament (and much of his schizophrenia) thus emerges from his belief that homosexuality and masculinity are incompatible and, concomitantly, that being overwhelmed by homosexual desire always entails the refashioning of the body and soul—he conflates the two through his vision of the nervous system—by some external force. Interestingly, Freud is aware of Schreber's own subjection to the discourse of the third sex model and alerts the reader to this: "It is not to be supposed that he wishes to be transformed into a woman; it is rather a question of a 'must' based upon the Order of Things, which there is no possibility of his evading, much as he would personally prefer to remain in his own honorable and masculine status in life."[33] From this perspective, the inevitability of the resignification of the gay subject as effeminate is made clear, the dominance of the third sex model means that there is no possibility of conceiving of male homosexuality as anything other than a feminized subject position. Such assumptions about homosexuality as an abdication of maleness and masculinity are at the core of Burroughs' discourse on Lee's sexuality in *Queer*.

Between the historical moments of Schreber's autobiography and Burroughs' vision of Bill Lee, a significant shift in understandings of homosexuality had occurred. Whereas Freud's discourse on effeminacy had been restricted to a narrow audience, the psychoanalysts who followed him, particularly in 1950s America, created a model of homosexuality as gender deviance that was not only disseminated through popular texts on sexuality but was also being used as a tool for social regulation.

Queer historians have only recently reclaimed the 1950s. While every student of gay history is familiar with the watershed of Stonewall—a moment of triumphant gay empowerment and

liberation—the immediate postwar period has been generally af-
forded far less attention. In many ways this is surprising since the
1950s not only saw an aggressive, state-led policy of homophobia
that was without precedent, but also marked the beginnings of gay
political resistance to marginalization by the heterosexual dominant. Before World War II the American authorities were largely
tolerant of gay life. According to George Chauncey, a culture of
laissez-faire existed from the 1890s to the 1940s, with the result
that in a metropolitan center like New York, gay life "was *less* tolerated, *less* visible to outsiders, and *more* rigidly segregated in the
second half of the century than the first, and that the very sever-
ity of the postwar reaction has tended to blind us to the relative
tolerance of the prewar years."[34]

One indication of this shift from tolerance to the outright homophobia of the McCarthy years was the work of the American
psychoanalysts. Whereas Freud had tried to take a liberal view of
homosexuality (without resorting to Victorian notions of morality
and degeneracy), the rising tide of psychoanalysis in America
throughout the 1930s, 1940s, and 1950s was interested in offering
a more conservative reworking of the Vienna school, coding homosexuality both as a pathology and a deviation from the heterosexual norm. Rejecting the pessimism that Freud displayed in his
"Letter to an American Mother" over the possibility of reversing
homosexual tendencies through psychoanalysis, the American
Freudians began to push for a cure.[35]

Sandor Rado's adaptational school of psychoanalysis was at the
forefront of this movement during the 1940s. Rado rejected
Freudian theories of bisexuality, refusing to regard homosexuality
as the outcome of an imbalance between masculine and feminine
drives and instead placing the majority of his emphasis upon environmental forces. The belief in homosexuality as an essential identity was replaced by theories of its social construction in which it
was characterized as a phobic flight from heterosexuality, a mental
sickness that Rado's "positive therapeutic stance" aimed to cure.[36]
Significantly, the effeminate paradigm remained at the forefront of
Rado's thinking on homosexuality:

The desire to fulfill the male-female pattern is a sexual characteristic shared by all members of our civilization. Fear and resentment may drive this desire underground, but neither these feelings nor any other force, save for schizophrenic disorganization, can break its strength. Individuals with mates of their own sex are impelled by this underground desire to generate a spurious male-female pattern that will achieve for them the illusion of having, or being themselves, a mate of the opposite sex.[37]

Rado's comments—with their startling, heterocentric logic—offer an illuminating insight into the presuppositions about homosexual relationships that cause both Lee and Allerton so much misery. For Rado, the order of things demands that all sexual relationships conform to the dynamic of the heterosexual pattern: one partner is male-masculine-active; the other, female-feminine-passive. All homosexual relationships must therefore be a parody of the originary authenticity of the male-female pattern. Any gay man who attempts to break out of this culturally sanctioned pattern and demand a male-masculine/male-masculine coupling must be in the throes of a "schizophrenic disorganization" in which he is uncertain of his own sex and gender status.

The sickness theory of homosexuality deployed in the 1950s drew upon the work of Rado and his contemporaries, emphasizing "sickness" as a combination of perverse desire, gender deviance, and moral weakness. By viewing homosexuality in such terms, the emphasis was placed on the gay man himself to change his proclivities through therapy. In such a manner, the effeminate paradigm's castigation of the gay subject as deviant (in terms of sexuality and gender) meant that social regulation was justified in order to keep the "sickness" from contaminating the wider populace. The extent to which the effeminate paradigm was deployed as a means of marginalizing the gay community was clearly evident in the postwar years.

The shift that occurred between the prewar and postwar period had much to do with the mass mobilization of men and women after Pearl Harbor. For many gay men and women the displacement from rural to urban areas as a result of military service marked the first moment in which they were able to articulate a gay identity amongst other like-minded individuals. The empirical data that Colin Spencer catalogues in *Homosexuality: A History* indicates the possibilities that the war created for gay relationships and encounters. As one lesbian claims, "it was such a lovely war. What went on was no one's business . . . it was a riot."[38]

Yet the authorities far from tolerated this explosion of sexuality. The problem of homosexuality in the armed forces had already been a major issue during the 1920s and 1930s; indeed, in the years before World War II, the American naval authorities decided to use Portsmouth Naval Prison in New Hampshire as a prison for "moral perverts"—by the 1930s over 40 percent of new admissions had been convicted of fellatio or sodomy.[39] When mobilization began, the military became increasingly obsessed with restricting the admittance of homosexuals into the forces. It was at this moment in the 1940s that American culture first began to construct a popular discourse about homosexuality that reached a mass audience. The military's screenings were run by psychiatrists who claimed that they had devised a series of tests and evaluations that could quickly reveal whether the recruit was a homosexual or not. John D'Emilio notes the shift that this produced:

> The medical model played only a minor role in society's understanding of homosexuality until the 1940s. Before then, it was elaborated upon primarily in the pages of specialized journals. However, psychiatric screening of inductees ordered by the federal government during World War II catapulted the psychiatric profession into the lives of millions of Americans [. . .]
>
> Increasingly, Americans came to view human sexual behavior as either healthy or sick, with homosexuality falling into the latter category. Medical guides aimed at a lay audience expounded the phenomenon of same-sex orientation and the possibilities of curing it.[40]

But what exactly were the ideas upon which the medical model was founded? Spencer states that the psychiatric professionals

drafted in by the army to aid them with the screening of new recruits believed that there were three possible signs for identifying
male homosexuals: "feminine bodily characteristics, effeminacy in
dress and manner and a patulous or expanded rectum."[41] The cru-
dity of this model in detecting proclivities for deviant sexuality is
suggested by the military discharge figures that D'Emilio cites:
discharges for homosexuality rose from one thousand a year in the
late 1940s to two thousand a year in the early 1950s.[42] Yet the negative effects of the model were widespread; the image of homosexuality that was disseminated through these screenings and that
would soon reach the wider audience of the American public was
of gay men (and women) as perverts whose sexual identity was
characterized by gender deviance. The effeminate paradigm was
thus given further social, medical, and legal acceptance as *the* homosexual identity.[43]

In the postwar years, of course, homosexuality was becoming
even less tolerated. The military discharge figures cited above
have much to do with the increasingly antagonistic attitude of
the state, particularly during the McCarthy period. The entanglement of homosexuality and the red scare meant that gay men
and women were put under increased pressure from regulatory
bodies such as the FBI and found themselves hounded out of the
army and government positions. There were mass purges of the
civil service and—at a grass-roots level—the police began to
crackdown on cruising areas, bars, and clubs, often carrying out
random venereal disease inspections. Meanwhile, the FBI cata-
logued arrest records from vice squads across the country regardless of whether or not convictions had resulted, and encouraged
post office workers to monitor suspect pen-pal clubs and recipi-
ents of physique magazines.[44]

The medical model of homosexuality as sickness and disease
was central to the beginning of a far-reaching moral panic over issues of sex and sexuality. The relative tolerance of the 1930s collapsed as the state increasingly used discourses on sexual normality
to marginalize "undesirables," a policy that peaked in the 1950s as
McCarthy and Hoover both used moral panic over the intersection

of sexuality and politics to consolidate their political positions.[45] The 1950s marked the beginnings of an unprecedented medical, legal, and social regulation of homosexuality, all of which occurred with widespread popular awareness and acceptance.

There were, of course, other discourses on homosexuality attempting to challenge this new conservatism. Sympathetic researchers were questioning both the need for a cure and the usefulness of the medical model's emphasis on the gay subject as schizophrenic gender-deviant. The 1948 Kinsey Report—*Sexual Behavior in the Human Male*—did much to counter the notion of heterosexuality as "normal" development. Kinsey's figures indicated that 50 percent of American males acknowledged erotic responses toward their own sex and that one out of eight males had been predominantly homosexual for a period of at least three years.[46] The data suggested that homosexuality could hardly be an indication of psychopathology since it was such a widespread phenomenon.

In a similar vein, Clellan Ford and Frank Beach's work of 1951—*Patterns of Sexual Behavior*—studied sexual activity in non-human primates and noted that there was often concurrent hetero- and homosexual behavior in their relationships. They concluded that human homosexuality was part of our mammalian heritage and that we, like the primates they studied, were in possession of a primary bisexual nature. Evelyn Hooker's 1954 experiments with gay men and Rorschach tests revealed that there was little to suggest that homosexuality was a psychopathology in itself.[47]

Outside the psychoanalyst's consultation room and the sex researcher's lab there was a concurrent attempt by some gay men to counter both the repressive climate of the 1950s and the popularization of the effeminate paradigm as the sole model of homosexual identity. This program of resistance began with the establishment of America's first sustained gay movement, the Mattachine Society, set up in 1948 by Harry Hay. Growing out of the relaxation of social restrictions that occurred during World War II, the society soon found itself operating in a period of outright homophobia. Nonetheless, by 1953, its yearly convention could boast an audience of five hundred people, an unprecedented mobilization of gay power.

Operating during the McCarthy years, the society and its affiliated organizations such as the Daughters of Bilitis and ONE Inc. were diplomatic in their policies of resistance, organizing themselves more in terms of a network of gay self-support groups than an oppositional voice against the unchecked homophobia of the House Un-American Activities Committee. The power of HUAC was such that vocal opposition was inconceivable. Instead, the Mattachine leadership focused on normalization, a cautious policy that aimed to promote heterosexual tolerance and effect the full integration of homosexuality into American life. As one of the Mattachine slogans proclaimed, the society was determined to seek its goals "through EVOLUTION not REVOLUTION."[48] John D'Emilio notes, though, that such a policy set the Mattachine Society's leadership radically at odds with many of its members: "Again and again [the Mattachine leadership] minimized the differences between heterosexuals and homosexuals, attempted to isolate the 'deviant' members of the gay community from its 'respectable' middle-class elements, stressed the responsibility of lesbians and gay men for their second-class status and urged self-reformation."[49]

This gentrification of the gay community revolved around the issue of homosexuality as deviance and, in particular, gender deviance. The effeminate model was increasingly plaguing the emergent gay movement, something that the Mattachine Society's emphasis on normalization desperately tried to counter. Many of the Society's leaders believed that the policy of normalization and assimilation that they were actively pursuing could be achieved only if the gay community rejected the effeminate stereotype. Gender politics had suddenly become the main issue of Mattachine debate. Bayer claims that "the Society saw it as of vital importance to educate homosexuals regarding the appropriate forms of public behavior. Integration could not proceed if decorum was not maintained." He cites the following lament as typical of the society's policy during the period: "'When will the homosexual ever realize that social reform to be effective must be preceded by personal reform?'"[50] Many members, though, were dissatisfied with such effeminophobia. D'Emilio quotes the following comments from *ONE* (which was rather less conservative than the *Mattachine Review*): "'When we are led by our life-long fear of being considered a sissy into contempt for effeminate homosexuals, we cease to be able to respect ourselves,' one man declared. Another deplored the tendency to 'excommunicate any homosexual who belies the . . . thesis that we aren't different.'"[51]

To the Mattachine leadership, however, it seemed that normalizing homosexuality could become a possibility only once the stereotype of effeminacy was eradicated. The argument was that gender deviance could never be accepted into mainstream (heterosexual) American culture and, furthermore, that such deviance was the very mark of difference, the pink triangle that would guarantee persecution. Effeminate identity would always be marginalized since it was the heterosexual establishment's dominant understanding of homosexuality and was conflated with ideas of sickness, deviance, and perversion. Simultaneously, it was also a *visible* mode of gayness. The Mattachine leadership despised the physical nuances of effeminacy—which had previously served as one strategy for negotiating male-to-male encounters—because they drew unwanted and dangerous attention toward the gay man.

Effeminacy was regarded as a beacon that would alert an aggressively homophobic state to the sexuality of the individual/group. If gay men wanted to enjoy the increased social freedom of the heterosexual world, they had to fulfill the promise of the society's name and remain masked and closeted.[52] Such a policy of normalization was problematic since it argued for a reentry into the closet at the very moment that the gay community was finding its own voice. The Mattachine Society's emergence signaled a moment of escape from the closet, the organization of gay men into a political minority group, but then compromised this by relying on a series of cautious tactics. In addition, the effeminophobia that the desire for acceptance created meant that gay men were increasingly internalizing the power of state regulation, branding their fellow gay men "deviant" and "marginal," in exactly the same terms that the heterosexual dominant used itself. The extent of the effeminate paradigm's influence as a means of denying gay men a political voice was thus to be seen even at the first peak of their political mobilization.

Donald Webster Cory, who produced one of the central tracts of the Mattachine Society, *The Homosexual in America: A Subjective Approach*, was a committed supporter of this policy of normalization and carefully argued against the effeminate model:

> Actually, the effeminate invert usually forms a subgroup within the group, for he is *persona non grata* among the more virile. "I am no better than they are," a homosexual of the more virile type will say, "but I just couldn't afford to be seen in their company." If a homosexual must wear the mask, he cannot associate with those who have discarded it.[53]

The alignment of virility with masculinity against effeminacy is striking. The effeminate homosexual is branded as counterrevolutionary, an exhibitionist whose body is the site of deviance and whose confrontational tactics are dangerous for those who want evolution rather than revolution. Indeed, Cory's espousal of cautionary evolutionary change leads him to suggest that gay men should gladly accept their oppressed status and reach toward the beatitude of martyrdom:

> The sympathy for all mankind—including groups similarly despised in their own right—that is exhibited by so many homosexuals, can be a most rewarding factor, not only for the individual, but for society. The homosexual can—and often does—demonstrate that he harbors no bitterness, for he learns of necessity, the meaning of turning the other cheek. He is forced by circumstance to answer hate with love, abuse with compassion.[54]

For Burroughs, Cory's liberal, Christian martyrdom was not only sickeningly accepting of the status quo, but also a dangerous tactic of accommodation. In a letter to Ginsberg written while he was working on *Queer*, Burroughs claims that Cory's book is

> Enough to turn a man's gut. This citizen says a queer learns humility, learns to turn the other cheek, and returns love for hate. Let him learn that sort of thing if he wants to. I never swallowed the other cheek routine, and I hate the stupid bastards who won't mind their own business. They can die in agony for all I care. (*Letters*, 105–106)

Clearly Burroughs feels that Cory's sentiments are enough to offend any "man"; furthermore, the derogatory use of "citizen" (in contrast to, one supposes, the hip, beat cat) suggests that Burroughs is wary of the accommodationist position that Cory is adopting. Against this, Burroughs argues for an aggressive policy of active confrontation, equating cheek-turning passivity with femininity (or effeminacy) and his own anti-accommodationist position with masculinity. Interestingly, Burroughs turns Cory's argument back upon itself. Arguing for normalization, Cory rejects the effeminate paradigm; Burroughs lambastes Cory's text because he feels that the accommodationist position is in itself effeminate. He styles himself as more masculine than the Mattachine author because of his willingness to demand respect and autonomy rather than accept emasculating humiliation. Cory's liberal text thus occupies a middle ground in the gender debate (at least when juxtaposed with Burroughs' comments).

Viewed alone, Cory's book may appear somewhat reactionary in its attempts to make effeminacy a crime against the liberation movement; yet Burroughs accuses Cory of not going far enough, suggesting that cheek-turning acceptance is an overly passive (and thus unmanly) program. A hierarchy thus emerges (in ascending order): the effeminate gay male; the gay man who accepts his second class status but tries to minimize it by acting "normal"; the gay man who claims a "masculine" position that is confrontational towards the heterosexual dominant and unforgiving of any other mode of gay identity. Between the "schizophrenia" of effeminacy and the "blank," genderless identifications of Mattachine policy,

Burroughs inserts a more radical claim to *masculine* identity. However, before he can imagine a truly masculine gay identity, the nature of effeminacy needs to be fully understood in terms of its role as a state-regulated identity designed to produce a marginalized, schizophrenic subject.

SATIRICAL RESISTANCE TO EFFEMINACY IN *NAKED LUNCH*

Despite its forthright title, *Queer* is a somewhat timid novel that consistently avoids describing the sexual aspects of the relationship between Lee and Allerton. Although the reader is under no doubt that their relationship is physically consummated, the novel is coyly reticent about the form that this takes. The shift from *Queer*'s chaste textuality to *Naked Lunch* is startling. In place of reticence, *Naked Lunch* offers the reader a pornocopia of sex and sexualities, an orgiastic explosion of fantasy that led to the Boston obscenity trials in 1965 and secured Burroughs' status as an *avant-garde* author (to such an extent that it is still *Naked Lunch* for which he is best known).[55]

While *Junkie* and *Queer* are documentary accounts of life on the cultural margins, *Naked Lunch* is a savagely satirical attack on the dominant that produces those marginal spaces. The main aspect of this attack—and one that has been consistently overlooked by critics of the novel—is concerned with homosexuality and in particular the state's creation of a homosexual identity that is schizophrenic. What I want to suggest is that the text is obsessed with the deployment of the effeminate paradigm by the heterosexual dominant, and it is this cultural formation that Burroughs seeks to expose in order to undermine the creation of gender-schizoid gay subjects.

Although critics have tended to ignore the possibility of reading *Naked Lunch* as a *queer* satire/social protest novel in which the overriding emphasis is on the role of sociopolitical power in the regulation of identity and marginal sexualities, Burroughs' original

conception of the text makes this theme perfectly clear. In a letter
to Ginsberg, he writes: "Briefly the novel concerns addiction and
an addicting virus that is passed from one person to another in sexual contacts. The virus only passes from man to man or woman to
woman, which is why Benway is turning out homosexuals on as-
sembly-line basis" (*Letters*, 365).

While *Queer* only tentatively suggested a link between Lee's
fears about a dystopian near-future of state-produced schizophrenia, *Naked Lunch* explicitly links schizophrenia with the state's deployment of the effeminate paradigm of homosexuality. The main
conspirators of the novel are the group of scientists, psychiatrists,
and surgeons headed by Doctors Berger and Benway, whose overriding aim is the creation of a technique by which the population
can be regulated and controlled. Sexuality emerges as the key to
total state control. In a grim parody of the nightmare of Mc-
Carthyism run amok, the novel depicts a society in which guilt by
association leads not to denunciation as a "red," but rather marginalization and regulation as a homosexual.

The lobotomized homosexual subjects such as the "cured swish"
and "tired old brainwashed belles" paraded by Dr. Berger as symbols
of "health incarnate" in a television commercial to promote his new
therapies have not so much been cured as conditioned through various tortures such as the "switchboard and the pail."[56] Berger's
grotesque, brainwashed creations indicate the lengths to which the
state is willing to go in order to rob the gay male subject of his autonomy. Similar attempts to "cure" non-heterosexual desire through
invasive methods were, of course, being regularly used by the American medical establishment. In the 1930s, convulsive shock therapy
was a common treatment used on institutionalized homosexuals,
augmented by hormone medication in the 1940s and lobotomy in
the 1950s. By the time of *Naked Lunch*'s publication in 1959, a report on patients at the New York Pilgrim State Hospital concluded
that lobotomy had little effect on sexual behavior, but this was after
large numbers of irreversible experiments on institutionalized gay
men had been undertaken.[57] Aversion therapy such as that employed by Berger was also prevalent during the period.[58]

Dr. Benway, Berger's colleague, is also shown to be interested in regulating sexuality. His goal is the complete eradication of his patients' autonomous identities, as is made clear in his interview with Carl (*NL,* 178–188). Summoned to the doctor's office, Carl is tacitly accused of being homosexual. His fearful reaction indicates that in a (sexually) repressive society, even the mere threat of being branded a homosexual is an effective means of regulation. Carl's desire to ignore the interview as a mistake is tempered by his belief in the absolute omniscience of the state: "But he knew they didn't make mistakes . . . Certainly not mistakes of identity" (*NL,* 178).

Carl's recognition of the state's power leads him to confess everything to Benway with very little prompting. The examination is as psychical as it is physical: Benway simultaneously plays the role of psychoanalyst, policeman, and priest. He accepts Carl's admission of hustling while in the army (*NL,* 187–188) but warns against the supposed eugenic crisis that will emerge from latent homosexuals marrying and procreating. His aim is total exposure.[59] His insinuations continue while Carl remembers his experience with Hans, the confession (if only to the reader) of which comes as something of a surprise after his indignant response to the summons and Benway's leading questions; however, what it serves to underline is the fact that "mistakes of identity" are not made by the state when such a well-oiled system of categorization exists. The categorization of the individual by the state allows identity to be fixed, frequently reducing it to its lowest common denominator, allowing it to be forced into predefined pigeon holes that, in Burroughs' terms, limit and restrict the individual's choice of self-expression.

The reader is left wondering, though, just how gay Carl actually is. Does his relationship with Hans indicate a homosexual nature, bisexuality, or a simple sexual experiment? To an extent, Benway's Kafkaesque "interview" has branded Carl "homosexual" in both his own and the authorities' eyes, although little evidence exists. Benway, as in Burroughs original conception of the novel, is thus able to mass-produce homosexuals simply through insinuation: the medical establishment categorizes the subject as gay or straight.

The advantages of such mass production of "deviant" sexualities during the 1950s are illustrated in Harry Hay's description of the factors that prompted him to establish the Mattachine Society:

> The post-war reaction, the shutting down of open communication, was already of concern to many of us progressives. I knew the government was going to look for a new enemy, a new scapegoat. It was predictable. But Blacks were beginning to organize and the horror of the Holocaust was too recent to put the Jews in this position. The natural scapegoat would be us, the Queers. They were the one group of disenfranchised people who did not even know they were a group because they had never formed as a group.[60]

Such aggressive regulation of sexuality by the state adds an additional resonance to Lee's opening words in the novel. Trying to escape from a narcotics agent who is tailing him, Lee runs into the subway: "I can feel the heat closing in, feel them out there making their moves" (*NL*, 7). The primary signification of the words is that Lee is the fleeing junkie; the secondary meaning, though, must be that Lee is the fleeing homosexual. This additional register is complemented by the agent's disguise: "imagine tailing someone in a white trenchcoat—trying to pass as a fag I guess" (*NL*, 7). Burroughs thus conflates two underworlds of 1950s America: the drug world and the gay world.

As in *Queer*, regulation of sexuality (particularly homosexuality) in *Naked Lunch* leads only to gender confusion since the dominant always deploys the effeminate paradigm. Even the authorities themselves seem uncertain about the reality of gender and sexuality, having been duped by their own propaganda; narcotics agents tracking Lee burst into a room he has long moved out of, surprising a newlywed couple: "[They shout] 'All right, Lee!! Come out from behind that strap-on! We know you,' and pull the man's prick off straightaway" (*NL*, 13). Since Lee is a known homosexual, the police consider him a "fag," his body signified as female and hence without a penis. He can never be anything more than a male impersonator. As the passage indicates, though, state regulation can make even the most heterosexual masculine man (here the bride-groom) lose his sex/gender identity as he is castrated by the police. A real penis becomes as detachable as a strap-on dildo, illustrating that both hetero- and homosexual men can be castrated, femi-nized, and categorized by the authorities.

Such gender confusion continues throughout the novel. It is re-peatedly shown to be the end result of social regulation, as the Lee/Allerton relationship of *Queer* suggested. The power of the state is such that, as Benway remarks, agents can be made to be-lieve their own cover story:

> "An agent is trained to deny his agent identity by asserting his cover story. So why not use psychic jiu-jitsu and go along with him? Suggest that his cover story is his identity and that he has no other. His agent identity becomes unconscious, that is, out of his control; and you can dig it with drugs and hypnosis. You can make a square heterosex citizen queer with this angle . . . that is, reinforce and second his rejection of normally latent homosexual trends—at the same time de-priving him of cunt and subjecting him to homosex situation. Then drugs, hypnosis and—" Benway flipped a limp wrist. (*NL*, 32)

This creation of "experimental schizophrenia" (*NL*, 30) illustrates Burroughs' fear that identity is a malleable attribute that can be al-tered with alarming ease. Furthermore, Benway's comments indi-cate the way in which the effeminate paradigm is deployed: the gay man who uses the effeminate paradigm as a strategy of negotiating male-to-male relations is likely to be told that that "cover story" is actually his only identity. As in Benway's technique, his agent identity (masculine identification) becomes unconscious and can be eradicated at will, leaving the agent to continue believing the cover story of effeminacy that he adopted only temporarily and out of necessity. Thus, the role of effeminacy as a secret code—as a set of signifiers that could indicate sexual preference—is transformed into the defining characteristic of the individual who loses, by de-fault, all opportunity of returning to his original masculine state.

The dangers of this loss of the self through mimicry or impersonation are given a nightmarish gloss in the most famous passage
of the novel, the Talking Asshole routine (*NL*, 126–128). Significantly, it is an episode that has rarely been considered by critics in
terms of gay politics and never in terms of gay gender identity. This
is surprising, since it is a very obvious morality tale that warns
against the mimicry of the feminine that is the basis of the effeminate paradigm and camp. The hideously comic image of an anus
talking on its own makes it easy to overlook the fact that the "carny
man"—as Robin Lydenberg terms the unfortunate protagonist—
actually uses his skill as part of "a novelty ventriloquist act" (*NL*,
127).[61] The anus starts to talk independently only later on, constituting the logical conclusion of his carnival turn:

> After a while the ass started talking on its own. He would go
> in without anything prepared and his ass would ad-lib and
> toss the gags back at him every time.
>   Then it developed sort of teeth-like little raspy incurving
> hooks and started eating. He thought this was cute at first
> and built an act around it, but the asshole would eat its way
> through his pants and start talking on the street, shouting out
> it wanted equal rights. It would get drunk and have crying
> jags nobody loved it and it wanted to be kissed same as any
> other mouth. Finally it talked all the time day and night, you
> could hear him for blocks screaming at it to shut up, and
> beating it with his fist, and sticking candles up it, but noth
> ing did any good and the asshole said to him: "It's you who
> will shut up in the end. Not me. Because we don't need you
> around here anymore. I can talk and eat *and* shit." (*NL*, 127)

Like the agent who is made to believe his cover story, the carny
man's ventriloquy leaves him in a compromised situation of psychic
disintegration in which his original identity is overwhelmed by the
secondary identity he assumes. Allowing the anus to speak is fine
until it begins to talk of its own accord, shifting from ventriloquy
to independence. Interestingly, Burroughs uses the metaphor of
ventriloquy elsewhere in more explicit descriptions of his effeminophobia. In *Junkie*, Lee describes his fear and hatred of fags:

A room full of fags gives me the horrors. They jerk around like puppets on invisible strings, galvanized into hideous activity that is the negation of everything living and spontaneous. The live human being has moved out of these bodies long ago. But something has moved in when the original tenant moved out. Fags are ventriloquists' dummies who have moved in and taken over the ventriloquist. The dummy sits in a queer bar nursing his beer, and uncontrollably yapping out of a rigid doll face. (*J*, 84)

Placed side by side, these two passages are central to Burroughs' vision of homosexual identity, regulation, and schizophrenia. Both the fag and the asshole are depicted as usurping forces that overwhelm the original self. The incessant "yapping" voice (or, perhaps more accurately, verbal diarrhea) is both an attempt to assert the new self and a grotesque indication of the extent of the original subject's fragmentation.[62] The gay man who has allowed himself to follow the demands of the effeminate paradigm has given up the chance of being one of the "intact personalities" Lee mentions (*J*, 84). Thus, the fag is the asshole that has learned to talk, the anus that refuses sublimation and returns with all of the vengeance of the repressed. The end result is a subject that in Lee's eyes is non-human, indeed, a parody of humanity, a "negation of everything living and spontaneous."

The anus that learns to talk is thus clearly a metaphor for the usurpation of the masculine subject by the feminine. It is an usurpation invited by the act of mimicry, the act of *becoming woman*. The fag creates a pattern of effeminate behavior, adopting a performative identity of self-styled femininity that contradicts the "truth" of his sex. In terms of the Talking Asshole routine, this is a loss of identity, a relinquishing of sovereignty to the "feminine" anus. The passivity of the fag leads only to regulation by the dominant, a regulation that codes his body as non-autonomous.

This, then, is the zenith not simply of Burroughs' effeminophobia but, more importantly, of his vision of effeminate identity as a schizoid fragmentation of the gay male self in which masculine autonomy is lost, replaced by the state-sponsored and sanctioned identity of the fag. In effect, what the Talking Asshole routine warns against is the danger of "possession." The asshole's choice of the first person plural "we" is suggestive of an occult force at work, the babble of voices of Legion (thus, an association can be drawn between possession and schizophrenia). Similarly, the description of the fag as an empty vessel, occupied by something other-than-human is suggestive of this kind of fantastic situation. For Burroughs there is always an "outside," one from which the subject is likely to be invaded, regulated, or controlled, and also one into which the subject may be able to escape.

In the texts of the 1950s, Burroughs' use of the figure of possession is, as we have seen, a comment on the state-sponsored regulation being imposed upon the gay community by the heterosexual dominant. He never embraces the masochistic desire for psychic disintegration that Savran imagines; instead, he argues throughout his work for the end of possession, regulation, and control. He is not the masochistic white male heterosexual victim, but the white male homosexual living under the sign of McCarthyism. As will become apparent toward the end of the 1950s and throughout the rest of his following work, Burroughs begins to fantasize the total autonomy of the (queer) subject, an autonomy that is designed solely to prevent his regulation by external forces. Such a program of opposition suggests that in Burroughs' texts, at least, there is little ecstatic pleasure to be had in playing the schizophrenic or the victim. Autonomous control of the self becomes the key to Burroughs' queer project, designed to ensure that the fate of the Vigilante in *Naked Lunch,* who "copped out as a schizo possession case" after hanging several of the "fags in Lincoln Park" (*NL,* 13), is not repeated. The feminine anus needs to be regulated to avoid the disastrous collapse of the self; the story of the Arab boy "who could play a flute with his ass" that follows the Talking Asshole routine exemplifies exactly this (*NL,* 130). By maintaining control over his anus—unlike the autonomous "ventriloquy"/possession in the carny man's story—the Arab boy metaphorically phallicizes his orifice through the use of the flute, masculinizing the anus and actualizing its erotic power. As a result, he is able to dominate the "fairies," manipulating their bodies through his tunes, "hitting the most erogenously sensitive spots" and clearly delineating the difference between his active masculinity and their passive femininity (*NL*, 130).

Burroughs' paranoid vision of effeminacy and regulation suggests that if the subject (whether author or character) plays the effeminate role, he risks losing his original identity and accepts the state-regulated identity of the "fag." Immediately following the Talking Asshole routine, Burroughs has Benway draw a somewhat veiled link between the routine and state censorship:

> That's the sex that passes the censor, squeezes through between bureaus, because there's always a space *between*, in popular songs and Grade B movies, giving away the basic American rottenness, spurting out like breaking boils, throwing out globs of that un-D.T. to fall anywhere and grow into some degenerate cancerous life-form, reproducing a hideous random image. (*NL*, 128).

The asshole that talks—the regulated identity of the fag—is exactly this "sex" that the censor allows to pass uncut. The only tolerated (or even imagined) face of male homosexuality in popular culture was the effeminate gay man, as evidenced in the Hollywood films of the period.[63] That image of effeminacy is read as a "degenerate cancerous life-form" which, like the asshole, takes over its environment with disastrous consequences. Like cancer, its only purpose is annihilation of the host subject, like the carny man and like the non-effeminate gay men of the period who, in Burroughs' terms, found themselves herded by the discourses of the state towards effeminacy.

Rather than envisioning the act of mimicry as a subversive one that mocks and parodies the notion of an originary subject, Burroughs sees it as destroying the integrity or, indeed, authenticity of that original. Such a stance in the field of gender politics is in stark contrast to that taken by contemporary, postmodern theorists of identity such as Judith Butler. For Butler, the act of mimicry is politically subversive:

> The repetition of heterosexual constructs within sexual cultures both gay and straight may well be the inevitable site of the denaturalization and mobilization of gender categories. The replication of heterosexual constructs in heterosexual frames brings into relief the utterly constructed status of the so-called heterosexual original. Thus, gay is to straight *not* as copy is to original, but, rather, as copy is to copy. The parodic repetition of "the original" [. . .] reveals the original to be nothing other than a parody of the *idea* of the natural and original.[64]

Burroughs' stance is far more conservative, the antithesis of postmodern notions of gender play and the subversive possibilities of camp. His texts reject mimicry in favor of the search for an original identity that is, he argues, primary, authentic, and, most importantly, masculine. The fag's complicity with the dominant creates a state of self-revolution in which the (feminine) anus takes over the (masculine) body and mind. The fag/anus may well scream for equal rights, but the text argues that such freedom ought to be restricted and withheld for the sake of the queer body politic. In this respect, the Talking Asshole routine follows the traditional patriarchal practice of reading the phallus as a symbol of (masculine) identity and the anus as radical negation of identity, for as Hocquenghem notes, "Only the phallus dispenses identity; any social use of the anus, apart from its sublimated use, creates the risk of a loss of identity. Seen from behind we are all women."[65]

Burroughs consistently depicts the fag as passive, his body the site on which power exerts its unending control. His very personality is excised from his body, leaving him in a position of total docility like Benway's lobotomized I.N.D. ("Irreversible Neural Damage") patients—housed in the asylum wing significantly titled "Drag Alley" (*NL*, 36)—who are the result of the state's demands for "homogeneity" (*NL*, 36). Such homogeneity is brought about by the eradication of homosexuality as the site of difference, for by making the homosexual a woman homosexuality is "normalized," made to function within the gender alignments of heterosexuality and—in terms of patriarchal culture—simultaneously dispossessed of a political (i.e., masculine) voice.

The political desirability of reducing a minority group such as homosexuals to passivity is clearly underlined in Burroughs' satirical engagement with Abram Kardiner's popular psychoanalytic lay text of 1954, *Sex and Morality*. Drawing on Ford and Beach's earlier study of the sexuality of non-human primates and the Rado school's emphasis on the role of environmental forces in homosexuality, Kardiner offers a theory of homosexuality as a flight from masculinity, claiming that increased social tension during the twentieth century resulted in the emergence of homosexuality as a pathological act of self-preservation; homosexuality could thus be read as "protection against annihilation."[66] In addition, homosexuals were considered neurotic since each possessed

> a deep sense of impoverishment of resources. They cannot compete. They always surrender in the face of impending combat. This has nothing to do with their actual ability, for many of them have extraordinary talent [. . .] These are men who are overwhelmed by the increasing demands to fulfill the specifications of masculinity and who flee from competition because they fear the increased pressure on what they consider their very limited resources.[67]

The effeminate paradigm thus establishes itself as the crux of Kardiner's argument. Homosexuals are neurotic men who are female-identified; the boundaries of masculine (strong, stable and courageous) and feminine (neurotic, overwhelmed, cowardly) are strictly defined and clearly policed. Kardiner bases this thesis on the investigations into non-human primate sexuality which Ford and Beach had used in 1951, yet he focuses purely on those instances in which homosexuality in the animal community occurs as a response to violence:

> These observances were made on monkey farms. When male monkeys fight over food or a female, the defeated one indicates defeat by assuming the female sexual posture. The remarkable feature of this behavior is that the passive sexual attitude of the defeated monkey halts the assault of the stronger one.[68]

Ignoring the different strategies to which homosexuality was put to use by these animal communities, Kardiner emphasizes one specific example of monkey behavior in order to support his thesis that homosexuality equals effeminacy. Burroughs' effectively satirizes this in *Naked Lunch*. Faced with a pack of marauding students armed with switchblades, the Professor of Interzone University tries

> to disguise himself as an old woman with high black shoes and umbrella. . . ."If it wasn't for my lumbago can't rightly bend over I'd turn them offering my Sugar Bum the way baboons do it. . . . If a weaker baboon be attacked by a stronger baboon the weaker baboon will either (a) present his hrump fanny I believe is the word, gentlemen, heh heh for passive intercourse *or* (b) if he is a different type of baboon more extrovert and well-adjusted, lead an attack on an even weaker baboon if he can find one." (*NL*, 83)

In case we miss the symbolism of this Burroughs goes on to make it quite plain: "Frontier saloon: Fag Baboon dressed in little girl blue dress sings in a resigned voice to tune of *Alice Blue Gown:* 'I'm the weakest baboon of them all'" (*NL*, 83).[69] For Burroughs this is a disgraceful act, an acceptance of the *status quo* and its oppressive intentions. The shift from Kardiner's monkey to baboon is an obvious tactic—the "purple ass" of the latter underscores the importance of the anus in this situation. Like teaching the asshole to talk, offering up a Sugar Bum for passive intercourse is an act that leads to the loss of autonomy.

It is apparent, then, that these texts of the 1950s are explicitly concerned with gay themes and are obsessed with the relationship between the two meta-identities of fag and queer. Acutely aware of the relationship between the individual and the state, Burroughs effectively satirizes the medical establishment's role in the deployment of the effeminate stereotype. Such regulation is, as the texts illustrate, an assault on individual autonomy. Attempting to fulfill his role as a "strong, manly, noble type," Burroughs in his letters to Ginsberg clearly laments the dominance of the effeminate stereotype and its negation of the possibilities of a masculine-identified gay subject. In the novels that were to follow *Naked Lunch,* Burroughs would offer his readers a radical escape plan through which the regulation of the dominant could be overcome. This emphasis throughout the 1960s on notions of deconditioning, on the liberation of the individual from the chains that deny his autonomy is frequently noted by Burroughs' critics; indeed, it is exactly this kind of anti-establishment stance that has ensured the novels' cult status. However, this deconditioning has never been critically assessed from a queer position.

If, as we have seen, the novels of the 1950s are concerned with revelation, with making naked the regulation exerted upon the (gay) individual by the state, then the novels that follow, with their emphasis on deconditioning, may well have to also be read, to some degree, as suggestive of gay liberation. Burroughs' method throughout the 1950s and 1960s is one of revelation and counter-attack; the texts note the regulation of the individual in the hope that it might finally be overcome as the individual is freed from state interference and then rebuilt. However, as already noted, such utopian liberation is restricted in its intended appeal. The effeminophobia of the texts discussed so far suggests that it will be only those gay men willing to reach for a masculine identity who will be offered the chance to achieve freedom.

Burroughs' distrust of the regulation imposed upon the subject by the dominant through the medical discourse of psychoanalysis is thus quite clear. Indeed, he was always scornful of the Freudian school of analysis. In interview with J. E. Rivers in 1980, Burroughs suggested that

> the whole of western psychiatry has been sidetracked from the way that it should have gone. It should have gone along the lines of Pavlov and the conditioned reflex. Instead it was sidetracked into all this mystical nonsense of egos, superegos and ids floating around in some kind of vacuum.[70]

Such comments seem problematic; the fact that psychiatry did move toward Pavlovian response mechanisms has already been noted, particularly with reference to the attempt to "cure" homosexuality. So why would Burroughs be suggesting that analysis should have adopted a similar position? Surely that would only have increased the dominant's regulation of marginal sexualities.[71] Burroughs' advocacy of this method must be placed in the context of his interest from the 1940s onward in marginal scientific discourses that aim to deregulate the conditioned reflexes of the individual subject. The comments in the interview with Rivers point toward a utopian, alternative reality in which post-Freudian American psychoanalysis—with its emphasis upon the normality of the heterosexual position and its corresponding belief in the feminine identifications of all gay men—is replaced by a positive therapy which seeks not to dominate, regulate, and categorize the individual but instead to liberate him from the confining strictures of the social conditioning of sexuality. As Burroughs would later claim, "Only when your responses become automatic and operative without conscious volition can you perform effectively."[72]

The Pavlovian revolution that Burroughs imagines, then, is one in which the subject achieves deconditioning rather than the normalization offered by the Rado school's "cures." After having experienced such psychoanalytic attempts to "normalize" the subject, Burroughs began to search for a means of escaping state-sponsored regulation of homosexual identity. He was to find just such an alternative in the marginal scientific discourses of Count Korzybski's General Semantics and L. Ron Hubbard's Dianetics. In the texts that follow *Naked Lunch*, both of these marginal discourses are pitted in direct opposition to the dominant meta-narrative of American psychoanalysis. As will become apparent in the following chapter, Burroughs uses the work of Korzybski and Hubbard as a lens through which to conceptualize effeminate gay identity as a viral invasion of the autonomous, masculine subject. Once the effeminate paradigm has been delineated, the possibility of establishing a gay male identity that is masculine-identified becomes feasible; it is this consummation that Burroughs' following texts vigorously pursue.

Chapter Two

Imagining It Otherwise

Engrams, Effeminacy, and Masculine Identity

Freedom from Control

Although the eldest of the three authors grouped together as the principal members of the Beat Generation, Burroughs was the last to gain literary recognition. With the publication of *Naked Lunch* in 1959 and its subsequent entanglement in the literary censorship debate, Burroughs was catapulted to international fame as the novel took up a canonical position beside "Howl" and *On the Road*. In terms of Burroughs' queer project, however, *Naked Lunch* marked an end rather than a beginning; it was the final novel in which Burroughs presented the gay man as the passive victim of intractable social forces producing schizophrenia, gender confusion, and death.

Much of Burroughs' literary output of the 1950s is characterized by the frustration and confusion that the negotiation of the demands of the effeminate paradigm produced. In comparison, the post-Stonewall novels center on a vision of a new, queer social order based on all-male (and all-gay) communes in which women and effeminate gay men have no place. This fantasy of a masculine queer utopia continues throughout Burroughs' work of the 1970s, 1980s, and 1990s. In place of the dystopian images of social regulation that informed *Queer* and *Naked Lunch*, Burroughs imagines a gay community that is not only free from regulation by the heterosexual dominant but also free from the gender schizophrenia imposed by that dominant. What shift occurred during the 1960s to produce such a remarkable change in Burroughs' treatment of homosexuality?

From a historical perspective, the civil rights movement that characterized the 1960s had an unquestionable influence on the gay community. Faced with the increasingly militant stance taken by minority groups in their relationship to the dominant culture, the Mattachine Society appeared outmoded and ineffectual. As the terror of McCarthyism was increasingly forgotten by the younger generation of gay activists, many of whom had not experienced the paranoia of the previous decade, Mattachine conservatism was slowly undermined by a new radicalism. The momentous events at the end of the decade—the Stonewall riots and the emergence of the Gay Liberation Front—had a profound influence on Burroughs' literary representations of homosexuality, as it did on all gay American writers of the period. Yet this response to events back home seems to be only part of the reason for the shift of Burroughs' work from the self-loathing and confusion of the 1950s to the establishment of a masculine gay identity in the Wild Boy tetralogy.

Burroughs' literary output of the 1960s is overtly concerned with revolution and transformation. As he himself wrote to Brion Gysin in a New Year's card for 1960, the response to the coming decade should be to "Blitzkrieg the citadel of enlightenment!"[1] The guiding principle behind this search for transformation was the "cut-up" technique, an avant-garde method of prose composition with which Gysin and Burroughs had begun to play in the period following *Naked Lunch*. Burroughs started to produce art that was designed to induce sense derangement. The public availability and affordability of new technologies (film, audio recording and broadcasting systems) during the 1960s led Burroughs (and others) to create a modern, avant-garde/countercultural aesthetic of discontinuity, displacement, and derangement that intersected the experiences of recreational drug use.[2] However, the cut-up method is far more important than just a set of techniques that created new prose, film, and audio texts. Burroughs' understanding and promotion of the technique itself focused on its transformative effect, not just on the media in which it was used, but also on the individual subject.

As well as continuing the attempt to unveil the mechanisms of state regulation that he had begun in *Naked Lunch*, Burroughs began to formulate techniques of resistance and deconditioning with the hope of freeing the subject from external control. Rather than the "recording instrument" (*NL*, 212) that he had previously claimed to be, he now emerged as an aggressive editor of the recordings, cutting them up and splicing them together in an attempt to find a utopian message in the background hiss. What I want to suggest is that the theories informing Burroughs' textual experiments of the 1960s are also central to his understanding of gay sexuality.

As will become apparent, Burroughs presents the cut-up method as a metaphorical weapon with which gay men can not only defend themselves from external regulation, but can actually use to reclaim control over both their bodies and their identities. The radical, transformative potential that Burroughs sees in this technique is a direct result of its links with a collection of marginal pseudoscientific discourses (in particular Dianetics, the lay psychotherapy movement established by L. Ron Hubbard in the United States in the 1950s). Significantly, the theories informing the cut-ups' radical potential are used by Burroughs as a template through which to understand the regulation of homosexuality and to imagine a mode of queer identity that could escape the gender-schizoid position of gay male effeminacy. Rejecting psychoanalytic interpretations of homosexuality, Burroughs pursues alternative, marginal discourses in order to create his own theory of effeminacy as a conditioned response that needs to be extirpated.

After conceptualizing the effeminate paradigm as an invasive attack on the gay male subject's authentic masculinity, Burroughs

fantasizes the reconstruction of that primary identity throughout
the Wild Boy and Red Night texts of the 1970s and 1980s. The
masculine-identified Wild Boys and their counterparts emerge not
only in response to the queer radicalism of the 1960s, but also as a
result of Burroughs' delineation of effeminacy in his novels of that
decade. As a result of the thematic interrelationship between the
texts of the 1960s and those of the following two decades, it will
be necessary to juxtapose Burroughs' work of these diverse historical periods in the later sections of this chapter.

RE-PROGRAMMING THE SELF:
THE ORIGINS OF THE CUT-UPS

The "discovery" of the cut-up method and Burroughs' enthusiastic
embrace of it as a radical form of prose composition comprise a
story that has been frequently told by both the author and his critics. As Ted Morgan recounts, "while cutting a mount for a drawing, Brion Gysin sliced through a pile of newspapers with his
Stanley blade, and made a mosaic out of the strips of newspapers,
because he thought it looked visually interesting. Then when he
read it, he thought it was hilarious."[3] For Gysin, this chance occurrence was simply humorous; when Burroughs saw it, he took it
far more seriously, believing that it had important potential as a literary technique. This method of "cutting up" or "folding in" dis-
parate texts to produce a montage of words offering new meanings
and associations was hardly an original idea, with an obvious heritage that stretched back through the avant-garde to the pho-
tomontages of Dada and Tristan Tzara's own poetic cut-ups at a
Surrealist rally in the 1920s.[4]

Burroughs lauded the cut-up method's role as a literary technique, particularly with regard to its use in creating new sentence
combinations, montages, and disjunction and in producing experimental prose that sought to represent the multiplicitous nature of
reality. Increasingly, though, he also began to mythologize the
technique, suggesting that it enabled the prediction of future

events and, more importantly, that it could be used to produce a "science of words" that might "show how certain word combinations produce certain effects on the human nervous system."[5] Thus the cut-up method began to signify the search for freedom, autonomy, and liberation.

Whatever one makes of such claims, it is important to realize that the cut-up technique had a profound effect on Burroughs' literary output and status, liberating him (and his texts) from the social and formal restrictions of the 1950s. Through his near-obsessive experiments with the method in prose, film, audio, and pictorial collage, Burroughs evolved from bohemian beat writer to sixties radical. The cut-up method also gave him the opportunity to collaborate with a range of other male artists: Brion Gysin, Anthony Balch, and Ian Sommerville. No longer the heroin-addicted author of a "dirty" book called *Naked Lunch*, Burroughs became a multimedia artist working to initiate new artistic practices, forms, and techniques.

These lofty aims, though, were largely ignored, misunderstood, or flatly rejected by the majority of Burroughs' peers. When Burroughs mentioned the method to Samuel Beckett in Paris in 1959, Beckett was appalled, concluding, "That's not writing, it's plumbing," a response no doubt influenced by Burroughs' tactless explanation that he was currently engaged in producing a cut-up of the *Herald Tribune* with Beckett's own texts.[6] At the Edinburgh Writers' Conference in 1962, Burroughs met with similar disbelief and confusion as he tried to explain the method to the audience. A year later, as the ban on his work was lifted in England, a scathing attack on his novels in the *Times Literary Supplement* claimed that "if publishers had deliberately set out to discredit the cause of literary freedom and innovation they could hardly have done it more effectively."[7] The review caused a stream of correspondence both for and against (including letters from John Calder, Michael Moorcock, Eric Mottram, Edith Sitwell, and Victor Gollancz) and secured Burroughs' reputation as a controversial member of the literary counterculture of the 1960s. Despite this negative reaction to his work, Burroughs continued to pursue the cut-up method through a variety of texts. In addition, he collaborated on a series of films with Anthony Balch and experimented with tape recordings of voices and street sounds.[8] At the center of this whirl of "cutting up" lies the Nova trilogy comprising *The Soft Machine* (1961, revised 1966 and 1968), *The Ticket That Exploded* (1962, revised 1967), and *Nova Express* (1964).[9] In addition to the trilogy, the cut-up method can be seen in *Minutes to Go* (1960), *The Exterminator* (1960), and *So Who Owns Death TV?* (1967). It was finally given the status of a manifesto in the belatedly published *The Third Mind* (1978).

Although the three novels of the Nova trilogy emerged from the same thousand-page Ur-manuscript that spawned *Naked Lunch*, they differ from the earlier novel in that they create a science fiction background against which to play out their critique of all forms of social regulation. In brief, the trilogy concerns the invasion of earth by a group of intergalactic criminals known as the Nova Mob. Since they are viral beings, the Nova Mob plan to seize control of the planet by literally invading the bodies of Earth's population. Their monopoly of control is aided by the propensity of the human race to become addicted to sex, drugs, and power; indeed, they have human collaborators working for them in the form of the Board, a shadowy organization comprised of media barons, politicians and the military-industrial complex. The ultimate goal of the invaders is "nova," a condition that arises when enough "insoluble conflicts" are produced to bring about the explosion of the planet.[10]

As "conditions of total emergency" are reached, the Nova criminals prepare to escape.[11] But they have been double-crossed by one of their own members, Willy the Rat. In addition, the Nova Police have arrived on the planet in the form of Inspector J. Lee, who aims to prevent disaster with the help of Earth's partisans, headed by Hassan i Sabbah. The purpose of both Burroughs and his alter ego Inspector Lee is to put "Plan D" into effect: "Total Exposure. Wise up all the marks everywhere. Show them the rigged wheel of Life-Time-Fortune. Storm The Reality Studio. And retake the universe" (*NE*, 56). The process of demystification will, it is hoped, save both the reader and the planet itself. For the most part, the cut-ups play a central role in this resistance; they are weapons with which both Burroughs and the fictional partisans can "Shift linguals—Free doorways—Cut word lines—" (*NE*, 58). In contrast to the reactions that Burroughs met with at the Edinburgh conference, more recent critics approaching the cut-up method have been enthusiastic in reclaiming its esotericism. Tony Tanner, for instance, believes that Burroughs' use of the cut-up method is a version of "the well-established American dream of freedom from conditioning forces" and suggests that it signifies the author's belief in "the possibility of countertactics" and in developing "methods of *deconditioning* and *decontrol*."[12] Offering one of the most extended readings of the cut-ups, Robin Lydenberg follows a similar line of argument as she discusses the way in which the novels highlight "the intertextual nature of all discourse and all human experience," claiming that the cut-up method aims to promote a combination of "familiarity, dislocation, premonition."[13]

Such readings are typical of criticism of Burroughs' texts in that they consistently overlook the queer thematics of the novels. Lydenberg claims that the main goal of the cut-up method is to induce an alteration in the reader's consciousness—in other words, to form a literary trip—"if the self is sufficiently fragmented, emptied out, and dispersed, one will no longer fear its loss [. . .] the cut-up also offers the possibility of a more radical dissolution of identity."[14] Just as with Murphy's valorization of schizophrenia discussed in the last chapter, the queer status of Burroughs' texts is discounted as irrelevant. From a white, heterosexual (academic) position both schizophrenia and the dissolution of the self may seem like attractive goals, yet does this remain true for marginalized identities such as that of American homosexuals in the 1960s? If the gay man is regulated by external forces, his "self" is not his to lose. Dissolution is of little political value unless the self is free to begin with. As Burroughs himself warns in a short cut-up text from the early 1960s, it "is NOT good to lose the self before it is yours again."[15]

The purpose of the Nova trilogy is to make the self "yours again" by freeing it from external regulation. The cut-up texts do not offer

a literal means to affect the dissolution of some bourgeois, heterosexual self, but rather fantasize the transformation of the regulated
gay male self. Whatever Burroughs' hopes may have been with regard to the literal usefulness of the cut-up method as a weapon of
revolution (and at times he does sound as though he regards the
cut-up as just such a weapon), he uses it within the texts as an
image of the deconditioning and escape he wants to offer the gay
subject. The difference between dissolution and transformation is
important since it highlights the fact that the trilogy is not concerned with anarchic destruction (or even Buddhist nirvana);
rather than the "negative poetics" that Lydenberg reads in the trilogy, Burroughs is actually offering a complex fantasy of (queer)
transformation.[16]

Much of this emphasis on the transformative nature of the cut-
up technique emerges from two discourses that Burroughs adapted
to form a theoretical basis for his textual practice: Korzybski's
General Semantics and Hubbard's Dianetics. These pseudoscientific discourses ostensibly offer a plan for purification that aims to
free the subject (regardless of his or her sexuality) from what we
might loosely term social conditioning. According to the testi-
monies of Korzybski and Hubbard, the subject who pursues these
self-help "therapies" will be transformed, purified and, most importantly, liberated from old, ingrained patterns of harmful response, emotion, and behavior.

Burroughs' critics rarely acknowledge the important influence
of these marginal discourses on the texts of the 1960s and have
never discussed their possible role in shaping Burroughs' views
on sexuality and gender.[17] In many ways this is somewhat my-
opic; Burroughs was introduced to Dianetics by Gysin at about
the same time that the two artists began to collaborate on the
cut-up method. In the first cut-up publication, *Minutes to Go,*
the influence of that discourse can be clearly seen in repeated
references to Hubbard's concept of the "reactive mind."[18] Similarly, Burroughs' letters of 1959 betray an enthusiasm for Hubbard's work; writing to Ginsberg in October, Burroughs advises
his friend to "give Hubbard a run for his money," and signs the

letter with phrases from a Dianetics processing routine: "William Seward Burroughs 'Hello-Yes-Hello'" (*Letters*, 430). Much of this enthusiasm was, no doubt, a result of the similarities between Hubbard's work and Korzybski's theory of General Semantics, which had been a topic of Burroughs' letters to Ginsberg a decade earlier (*Letters*, 44–45).

Reading the texts of this period in relation to these discourses does far more than simply explicate the aims of the cut-up method; it also allows us to understand the reasons behind the shift in Burroughs' treatment of homosexuality over the course of the 1960s. The model of identity, conditioning, and liberation upon which these discourses are predicated is one that Burroughs adapts in order to negotiate the problems of gay gender identification and effeminacy that had been a central concern in the texts of the previous decade. In both General Semantics and Dianetics, the subject is always at the mercy of external, regulating forces that threaten to compromise his or her autonomous status. These forces create physiological "blocks" which trap the subject into certain patterns of behavior. Clearly, a parallel emerges here between this vision of conditioned response and Burroughs' depiction of the regulation of the gay male subject through the deployment of the effeminate paradigm.

In the absence of a mainstream psychoanalytic school that followed "Pavlov and the conditioned reflex" (as discussed at the close of the previous chapter) Burroughs adopts the techniques of Korzybski and Hubbard for his own very personal plan of queer deconditioning. Finding little solace in the bigoted, heterocentric stance of the post-Freudians and their attempts to cure homosexuality, Burroughs turns to these pseudoscientific discourses in the hope that they might provide one means of conceptualizing effeminacy not as the "natural" state of gay males (as American psychoanalysts were suggesting) but instead as a conditioned response that had been imposed upon the gay male subject by an external force.[19] Before discussing the intersection between these discourses and Burroughs' vision of queer deconditioning, though, it is necessary to outline the main points of Korzybski's and Hubbard's work.

In 1939, Burroughs attended a series of lectures held at the Institute of General Semantics in Chicago. The lecturer was Count Alfred Korzybski, a Polish nobleman whose book *Science and Sanity: An Introduction to Non-Aristotelian Systems and General Semantics* had impressed a large audience on its publication in 1933.[20] Korzybski promoted General Semantics as a discipline that "explains and trains us how to use our nervous systems most effectively."[21] His basic theory was that language and, in particular, inappropriate linguistic structures or practices could be harmful, debilitating, and restricting. Viewing language with a radical skepticism that has since become *de rigueur* in postmodern discourses, Korzybski sought to highlight the gaps between signifier and signified in an attempt to suggest that language was only a convenient means of mediating the objective truth of reality and could never actually represent that truth without distorting it:

> Our actual lives are lived entirely on the objective levels, including the un-speakable "feelings," "emotions," the verbal levels being only *auxiliary,* and effective only if they are translated back into first order un-speakable effects, such as an object, an action, a "feeling," all on the silent and un-speakable objective levels.[22]

Korzybski's most often repeated example is that of the chair. A chair, he claims, is never the object designated by the word "chair," for there is always a gap between signifier and signified, with the result that "we cannot sit on the noise we made or the name we applied to that object."[23] Thus the Aristotelian "is" of identity can be overturned; the object never *is* what we decide to say it is; in other words, "*Ceci n'est pas une pipe,*" as René Magritte had famously declared in *The Treason of Images* (1928–29).

Much of Korzybski's work seems fairly elementary by today's standards. What separated him from other thinkers in philosophical circles who were similarly questioning cherished truths about epistemology and language, was his belief that language's role as a mediator between objective reality and our consciousness could produce physiological problems. In a series of experiments, Korzybski concluded that the subject's grasp on reality could be un-raveled by relentless demands to define the language he or she used:

> We begin by asking the "meaning" of every word uttered, being satisfied for this purpose with the roughest defini-tions; then we ask the "meaning" of the words used in the definitions, and this process is continued usually for no more than ten to fifteen minutes, until the victim begins to speak in circles—as, for instance, defining "space" by "length" and "length" by "space." When this stage is reached, we have come usually to the undefined terms of a given individual. If we still press, no matter how gently, for definitions, a most interesting fact occurs. Sooner or later, signs of *affective dis-turbances* appear.
>
> Often the face reddens; there is a bodily restlessness, sweat appears. [. . .] Here we have reached the bottom and the foundation of all *non-elementalic meaning*—the meaning of *undefined terms,* which we "know" somehow, but cannot tell. In fact, we have reached the un-speakable level.[24]

Through revealing the non-significations of language Korzyb-ski hoped to promote better mental and bodily health, reprogram-ming the human nervous system by making the link between the inaccuracies of language and physical "affective disturbances" ex-plicit. The subject's belief in his objective position is shattered, of-fering the possibility of a decentered reorientation as the narcissistic belief in the primacy of the self in evaluating and guar-anteeing an external reality is lost. In the Nova trilogy, Burroughs takes Korzybski's belief in a non-verbal plane of objective reality as the motivation for his attempt to *"rub out the word forever"* (*NE,* 12). The cut-ups are an attempt to subvert the control exercised through language, literally to cut the word lines and to convince the reader that "In the beginning was the word and the word was bullshit" (*TTE,* 198). In the trilogy, silence is truly golden.

For Korzybski freedom is the direct result of transcending the limitations of language: "By making ourselves conscious of abstract-ing we prevent the animalistic *un*conscious of abstracting and so pre-vent arrested development or regression."[25] Conscious awareness is the key: "When we live in a *delusional* world, we multiply our worries, fears and discouragements, and our higher nerve centers, instead of protecting us from over-stimulation, actually multiply the semantic harmful stimuli indefinitely. Under such circumstances, 'sanity' is impossible."[26] The training that General Semantics offers aims to reveal the ineffectual ability of the Aristotelian either/or construct in signifying and explaining the world. In place of Aristotelian semantics, General Semantics will

> quiet down affective, semantic disturbances, sharpen orientation, judgment, the power of observation, and so forth; it will eliminate different psycho-logical blockages, help to overcome the very annoying and common "inferiority" feelings; it will assist the outgrowing of the adult *infantile state*, which is a nervous deficiency practically always connected with some pathological sex-reactions or lack of normal and healthy impulses.[27]

As semantic conditioning is transcended, a liberated subject, freed from internal limitation and external control is produced. Once "delusional" structures of relating self to world are overthrown, the subject can reach his full potential.

In the trilogy, Burroughs' cut-up technique is used literally to destroy the "faulty" structures of our semantic heritage. As Burroughs suggests, the cut-up challenges "the mental mechanisms of repression and selection" that work against the subject.[28] He explicitly links this with General Semantics: "You remember Count Korzybski and his idea of non-Aristotelian logic. Either-or thinking just is not accurate thinking. That's not the way things occur, and I feel the Aristotelian construct is one of the great shackles of Western civilization. Cut-ups are a movement towards breaking this down."[29] The technique's attack on the "shackles" produced by language seems obvious enough; yet what interests Burroughs most is the relation between "word-locks" and physiological disturbances. The conditioned response is considered one that robs the subject of his bodily autonomy.[30] The overriding interest in regaining this *bodily* freedom, of ending the regulation of the physical realm, is one of the central uses of the cut-ups as a tool of queer liberation.

The nature of this search for bodily autonomy becomes increasingly clear if we examine Burroughs' use of Hubbard's theories. During the 1940s, a "Korzybski fad" raged throughout the American science fiction community.[31] Among the many acolytes that Korzybski's work found was author L. Ron Hubbard, who expanded upon the key concepts of General Semantics to create a theory of mental health dubbed "Dianetics." First appearing as a lengthy essay—"Dianetics: A New Science of the Mind"—in *Astounding Stories* magazine, Hubbard's work quickly gained a wide audience, the first Dianetics book selling 55,000 copies in just three months and 5,000,000 copies by 1989.[32] In mid-August 1950, there were reported to be 500 Dianetic auditing groups across the United States.[33]

Dianetics proposes a radical rethinking of subjectivity. Hubbard suggests that the human mind is made up of three compartments: the analytical, reactive, and somatic. The analytical mind is consciousness, it "perceives and retains data to compose and resolve problems. [. . .] *It thinks in differences and similarities.*" The reactive mind is the unconscious; it "files and retains physical pain and painful emotion and seeks to direct the organism solely on a stimulus-response basis. *It thinks only in identities.*" The somatic mind is that which "directed by the analytical or reactive mind, places solutions into effect on the physical level."[34]

According to Hubbard the mind of the organism constantly records during its lifespan on various "tracks" independent of the conscious mind. Thus, when the subject is unconscious or asleep, the mind is still recording, storing away "engrams" that Hubbard defines as

a complete recording, down to the last accurate detail, of every perception present in a moment of partial or full "unconsciousness." They are just as accurate as any other recording in the body. But they have their own *force*. They are like phonograph records or motion pictures, if these contained all

perceptions of sight, sound, smell and taste, organic sensation, etc.
The difference between an engram and a memory, however, is quite distinct. *An engram can be permanently fused into any and all body circuits and behaves like an entity.* (*D*, 87–88; my emphasis)

These engrams are much like Korzybski's word-locks in that they can produce disastrous effects on the mental and physical health of the individual. Words, sounds, and sensations can be stored by the brain as an engram, to be reactivated later in a form of post-hypnotic suggestion. In the restimulation of the engrams of the reactive mind, the subject experiences inexplicable feelings of pain, loss, and impending doom. Hubbard offers the example of a woman beaten by her husband. Knocked to the floor, she is beaten and sworn at as she lies unconscious. Simultaneously, there is the sound of running water from a tap somewhere; a car outside sounds its horn. The smells, sounds, and pain are transferred into an engram that lodges itself in the reactive mind. At a later date, these sounds and smells, and the swear words she heard, could all trigger the pain stored within the engram. The sound of running water might, if combined with the sound of a car horn, "restimulate" the engram, causing it to rise out of the unconscious and manifest itself as anxiety or psychosomatic pain without her being aware of the connection between the pain and the external stimuli (*D*, 88*ff*). Depending on how many engrams/external stimuli the subject is exposed to, the response can vary between vague psychic upset and total insanity.
The purpose of Dianetic therapy, then, is to uncover and remove the engrams, to bring the unconscious back to consciousness where the pernicious influence of these stored memories can be worked through and quickly eradicated. The subject who achieves this is able "to operate on his optimum pattern" (*D*, 77) as a "Clear." The main method of locating and eradicating engrams is the practice of "auditing" and the use of a device called the "E-meter" which measures the body's electrical activity (galvanic skin response) in re-

sponse to questions and lists of words that could be contained within an engram. After placing the subject into reverie, the auditor works through experiences, emotions, and words until the E-meter gives a reading. Then this is repeated over and over until the reading shows "clear." Repetition is designed to "produce movement on the time track into areas of disturbed thought containing that word or phrase. [. . .] Repetition of such a phrase over and over, sucks the patient back down the track and into contact with an engram that contains it" (*D,* 262*n*).

Dianetic therapy—and its later incarnation as Scientology—promises the subject a liberatory release from fear and aims to re-establish the subject's physical and mental autonomy. In many ways, the therapy is an amalgamation of various ideas and practices. Commentators on the Scientology movement like Roy Wallis and Jeff Jacobsen have noted the links between Hubbard's theories and the work of Korzybski and, more importantly, Freud's early work with hypnotism and the theory of abreaction.[35] As Jeff Jacobsen has suggested, Dianetic auditing is "a virtual clone of abreactive therapy," since both therapies seek to aid the patient through bringing destructive affects into consciousness so as to re-experience them and nullify their ability to cause psychic or physical harm.[36] These scholarly responses to Dianetics consistently note the magpie appropriations that Hubbard makes, suggesting that such a method borders on plagiarism and that Dianetics is little more than a quack therapy mixing Freud with Korzybski and a good deal of hocus-pocus.

The dual discourses of General Semantics and Dianetics thread their way throughout Burroughs' texts of the 1960s, marking the extent of his obsession with regulation of the subject and the deconditioning necessary to end it. If the texts are overtly concerned with "countertactics," as Tanner claims, then it is necessary to note that such strategies are produced in reaction to the fears of regulatory control that dominated the queer thematics of Burroughs' preceding texts. But what is the relation between these fears and Burroughs' queer project, and how can the deconditioning program offered by the cut-ups aid the gay man?

LIBERATING BODY AND SOUL:
CUT-UPS AND QUEER AUTONOMY

After almost a decade spent reading Hubbard's work, Burroughs
finally signed up with the Scientologists in London in 1967 and
went on to take the "clear" course at the East Grinstead headquarters at the beginning of 1968.[37] His experience of the Scientology movement was not a happy one. Although Burroughs
claimed that "Scientology can do more in ten hours than psychoanalysis can do in ten years," he was to draw a rather terrifying
picture of his Orwellian experiences at the St. Hill headquarters
(security checks performed using the E-meter as a lie detector,
photographs of "Ron" adorning every wall, the signing of billion-
year loyalty contracts).[38]

Burroughs concluded that "the prep school nonsense" surrounding the movement was a vast hoax[39] and decried its hierarchical organization: "Scientology is a model control system, a state in fact
with its own courts, police, rewards and penalties."[40] The reactionary nature of Hubbard's ideology was also a cause of concern:
"They talk about decency, morality, the church the home the family and the evil and Godless practices of subversion. Nothing here
a Wallace folk could object to, but quite a bit that the radical left
might question rather sharply."[41] Although he remained a firm
supporter of Dianetic techniques, in particular the E-meter, Burroughs cut his ties with the church in the summer of 1968 and was
summarily placed in a "Condition of Treason" after writing dis-
paraging articles about Hubbard and the movement.[42]

Much of this ultimate dissatisfaction with Scientology is characteristic of Burroughs' appropriation of the theories of Dianetic
therapy during the preceding years. Throughout the 1960s, Burroughs had used Hubbard's work for his own purposes, employing
it as one of the theoretical foundations for his textual experimentation in the Nova trilogy.[43] Furthermore, the queer thematics of
the Nova trilogy emerge from his reading of Dianetic theory
(something that obviously ran contrary to Hubbard's homophobia). Since Burroughs believed that homosexual men were regu-

lated by the medical establishment and the psychiatric profession—both of which were intent on prescribing gay men's identities, social positions, and mental "health"—the choice of General Semantics and Dianetics as part of an oppositional queer discourse is quite appropriate. The marginal, pseudoscientific status of both of these self-help therapies offers an alternative to the dominance of psychiatry.[44]

After all, as Burroughs warns, psychiatry is a dangerous weapon of the establishment:

> I have frequently said that nine out of every ten psychiatrists should be broken down to veterinarians and shave off that goatee if you want to be popular with folks hereabouts.
>
> Yes I know about the use of psychiatric commitments as a means of political control. We have seen that happen in Russia and Germany. I am violently opposed to shock treatment or lobotomy. Most so-called mental institutions are death camps with not much pretence of being anything else. So we don't have to bat that around.
>
> Point is psychiatrists are servants of the establishment. Who is behind your Death Psychiatrist with his scythe? Who gives the orders around this shit house? The industrial giants of America, the very pivot on which it is turning. They own the place. They give the pigs and narcs, politicians, psychiatrists and newspapers their orders.[45]

Dianetics and General Semantics oppose this kind of external control, breaking down the structures that enable such regulation in order to return bodily autonomy to the subject.[46] More importantly, both discourses' understanding of autonomy prefigures Burroughs' attempts to conceive of a homosexual identity that opposes the influence of the effeminate stereotype.

In *Naked Lunch* regulation (in the guise of Benway and the like) was an external, visible force. In the trilogy, however, regulation increasingly becomes internalized. Power (like the engram, drugs, or language) begins outside the subject, but as the repeated viral image of the trilogy suggests, it then invades the subject. The Nova Mob themselves are representative of this shift away from

"solid" controllers like Benway to a more disturbing representation of power as a viral infection: "nova criminals are not three-
dimensional organisms—(though they are quite definite organisms as we shall see)—but they need three-dimensional human
agents to operate" (*TTE*, 57). The literal invasion of the subject
by power internalizes power's influence. The extent of this inter-
nalization leads to the total loss of queer bodily autonomy. The
bodies of the gay men of the Nova trilogy are repeatedly shown to
be "soft" and easily manipulated by the figures of control. In *The
Soft Machine*, for instance, the experiences of Johnny and Carl are
typical of this vision of the malleable gay male body.

Badly injured in a car accident, Johnny, the "Survival Artist"[47]
has been rebuilt by "the Big Physician" (*SM*, 54) who dubs his pro-
tégé "Pygmalion" (*SM*, 58). Johnny is yet another guinea pig in the
experiments of the heterosexual medical establishment. Not only
has he been given someone else's face, but also he is now covered
in Undifferentiated Tissue, the same substance that covered the
carny man in the story of the talking asshole in *Naked Lunch*. The
Undifferentiated Tissue is once again closely linked to issues of sex
and gender; Johnny dances for the patrons of the bar, wearing a
jockstrap of the tissue: "A penis rose out of the jock and dissolved
in pink light back to a clitoris, balls retract into cunt with a fluid
plop. Three times he did this to wild 'Holés!' from the audience"
(*SM*, 55). Finding his body transformed by the efforts of the Big
Physician, Johnny becomes confused about his sex and gender, a
confusion that is enacted in the rapid transformations of the jockstrap. He recounts the story of his "Impersonation Number where
I play this American Mate Dance in Black Widow drag" adding,
"I played both parts you unnerstand" (*SM*, 57). According to the
Big Physician, Johnny's "prick didn't synchronize at all so he cut it
off made some kinda awful cunt between the two sides of him. He
got a whole ward full of his 'fans'" (*SM*, 59). The reference to glass
blowing in the chapter's title—"The Case of the Celluloid Kali"—
becomes increasingly appropriate.

Undifferentiated Tissue plays a similar role in the episode involving Carl and the Commandante. Having survived the regula-

tion imposed upon him by Benway in *Naked Lunch*, Carl is made
to suffer yet again in a similar, although less subtle, fashion:

> The Commandante spread jelly over Carl's naked paralyzed
> body. The Commandante was molding a woman. Carl could
> feel his body draining into the woman mould. His genitals
> dissolving, tits swelling as the Commandante penetrated ap-
> plying a few touches to face and hair.
> [. . .]
> Now he is modeling a face from the picture of his novia in
> the Capital.
> "And now, how you say, 'the sound effects.' " He puts on a
> record of her voice, Carl's lips follow and the female sub-
> stance breathed in the words. (*SM*, 84–85)

There is nothing liberating about this sex/gender malleability, as
the choice of "Commandante" underscores. The slippages and re-
shapings played out here are less signs of "genderfuck" or "indeterminacy" than a nightmarish echo of concentration camp
experiments. Elaborating a Nietzschean understanding of power
and the body (years before Foucault), Burroughs suggests that
power's relationship to the flesh is always inscriptive, since, as he
expresses it: "Sex and pain *form* flesh identity" (*TTE*, 130). The
controllers are literally able to refashion the subject's physical sex
and his gender identity, reconfiguring and resignifying the status of
the individual at will.

In addition to this, the trilogy expands upon the idea of the gay
body as malleable, suggesting that it is the site of viral replication.
Throughout the texts of the 1960s, the gay body is always liable to
find itself "emptied" out, replicated or copied. The nova conspiracy
is to create a "copy" of reality that can be substituted for the "real"
thing; the role of sex in this is crucial: "Better than 'the real
thing?'—There is no real thing—Maya-Maya—It's all show business"(*TTE*, 77). The attempt to "take Johnny over" (*SM*, 96) is a
success, the plan of "Program empty body" (*TTE*, 21) enforced
with ruthless efficiency by the invaders.[48] As the talking asshole
routine and the descriptions of the fags in the early novels indicate,

the effeminate paradigm literally empties the body of the gay subject, removing his original (masculine) identity and replacing it with a regulated identity so that he loses all autonomy.

This vision of effeminacy as a loss of physical and mental autonomy is bolstered through Burroughs' appropriation of General Semantics and Dianetics. Burroughs uses the two discourses as templates on which to base his conception of effeminate gay identity as a socially conditioned response to same-sex desire. As we have seen, Hubbard suggests that the engram can be "permanently fused into any and all body circuits and behaves like an entity" (*D*, 88). Such a description is startlingly similar to Burroughs' conception of effeminate gay identity. Like the engram, effeminacy is depicted as an invasive transgression of the outside/inside dichotomy as a new identity (the asshole) usurps the original self (the carny man). The invasion produces the grotesque, puppetlike camp of the fag, which symbolizes, for Burroughs at least, a loss of bodily autonomy and the establishment of a gender-schizoid subject who is trapped in the confused space between his physical maleness and (socially required) feminine identifications. Hubbard's discussion of the two main conditions caused by engrams—"dramatizations" and "valence"—highlights the extent to which Burroughs' vision of effeminacy is dependent on Dianetic theory.

Dramatizations are the irrational actions that the subject is forced to play out when an engram is restimulated "so thoroughly that its soldered-in aspect takes over the organism." As Hubbard goes on to explain, "When it is in full parade, the engram is running off verbatim and the individual is like an actor, puppetlike, playing his dictated part" (*D*, 115–116). Such dramatization is guided by what Hubbard terms "valence"—that is, the split personality that arises when the engram-riddled subject is placed in a state of restimulation. The demands of the engram clash with the subject's original personality, leading to psychic fragmentation: "Multiple personality? Two persons? Make it fifty to a hundred. In Dianetics you can see valences turn on and off in people which would be awesome to a quick-change artist" (*D*, 118). The links between Hubbard's engram theory and Burroughs' understanding of effeminacy as outlined in his texts of the 1950s and the Nova trilogy seem readily apparent. Read as an engram, effeminacy is clearly both a dramatization that reduces the subject to the puppetlike jerking of the fag and simultaneously an example of valence as the original, masculine self undergoes schizophrenic dissolution. Effeminacy can thus be understood as an engram that is lodged in the reactive mind and constantly restimulated for as long as the male subject remains homosexual.

Similarly, effeminacy is also treated as if it were a Korzybskian word-image lock, one ratified by the medical and psychoanalytic establishments in order to convince the gay subject that he is womanly and that his gender identity must always be at odds with the reality of his sexed body. The heterosexual dominant's discourses on homosexuality are predicated on what Korzybskian semantics would consider a "delusional" relation of sign to object (gay = effeminate). The physical "affective disturbances" that this misapplication of language produces are consistently illustrated in the texts, from the "countrified sprawl" of Doctor Berger's "cured swish" (*NL*, 132) to the rapid transformations of Johnny's jockstrap (*SM*, 55). By demanding the equation of homosexuality and effeminacy, the heterosexual dominant has denied gay men their (masculine) bodily autonomy.[49]

The understanding of effeminacy that Burroughs produces through his queer appropriation of the work of Korzybski and Hubbard is one that conceives of the gender-schizoid gay male subject as a destructive amalgamation of Self and Other. He is in effect "cut-up" like the narrator at the beginning of *The Ticket That Exploded*, who describes his long journey with an enemy whose "voice has been spliced in 24 times per second with the sound of my breathing and the beating of my heart so that my body is convinced that my breathing and heart will stop if his voice stops" (*TTE*, 2–3). This is the essence of "nova," an insoluble conflict. The subject is cut-up and spliced together with his diametric opposite (a mortal enemy, a harmful engram, effeminacy). Significantly, the narrator is locked in a deadly battle with his companion/tormentor: "In fact, murder is never out of my eyes when I look at him. And murder is never out of his eyes when he looks at me" (*TTE*, 1).

Later in the novel such cut-ups are produced in the amusement park, where the unwary male, enticed by promises of earthly delights, is robbed of his autonomy as his identity is reformulated through photographic cut-ups, his self merged with that of other males. One half of the subject is literally cut up and pasted onto the half of a different subject to create a single copy of the two originals; the negative results of this are made quite clear: "'Whee' the sex act soften you up to buy death in orgasm of copy planet" (*TTE*, 77). Such cutting up and splicing together of two identities becomes problematic since it can lead to a loss of the original self, as exemplified in the "non-identity" of the photographic cut-up of Burroughs and Gysin produced by Ian Sommerville in the early 1960s.[50] In this picture the "self" of both is lost, replaced instead by a person who is simultaneously no one and "no *one*," neither Burroughs nor Gysin nor a new person, simply a "blank," a person who doesn't exist.

The model of alternation suggested in these fragmented cut-up identities can clearly be linked with the gender politics of the conditioned gay subject. In *Naked Lunch*, Benway's theory of schizophrenia was that "the backbrain is alternatively stimulated and depressed" (*NL*, 31). Control, according to Burroughs, always operates through this structure of binary opposition, conflicting commands, the impasse of "nova." In *The Job*, for instance, Burroughs discusses certain types of viral invasion as using "an old method of entry, namely the tough cop and the con cop" (*Job*, 187) and goes on to relate this to Hubbardian theories about "ally" engrams (comprised of reassuring material) and "hostile" engrams (*Job*, 191). This concept of alternation is, of course, also related to Burroughs' sympathy for Korzybski's attack on either/or logic. Such thinking is, he claims, the virus mechanism's attempt at "locking you in THE virus universe" (*Job*, 202). The locked, confused subject produced can be easily managed by power, since he is unable to resist or revolt. This theory of "contradictory commands" is illustrated by the example of the soldier conditioned through drill practice:

"TENSHUN!" The soldier automatically stiffens to the command. "AT EASE!" The soldier automatically relaxes. Now imagine a captain who strides into the barracks snapping "TENSHUN" from one side of his face and "AT EASE" from the other. (Quite possible to do this with dubbing techniques.) The attempt to obey two flatly contradictory commands at once both of which have a degree of command value at the automatic level disorients the subject. He may react with rage, apathy, anxiety, even collapse. [. . .] The result may well be complete collapse as Pavlov's dogs collapsed when given contradictory signals at such short intervals that their nervous systems could not adjust. The aim of these commands from the viewpoint of a control system is to limit and confine. All control units employ such commands. (*Job*, 41)

Burroughs explicitly links these control systems with the Mayan system[51] and the more contemporary mass media in the following pages (*Job*, 43–45) before offering a suggestion of some of the typical contradictory demands used in the "modern industrial environment," among which are: "Stop. Go. Wait here. Go there. Come in. Stay out. Be a man. Be a woman" (*Job*, 45).[52]

This is clearly yet another example of the schizophrenia that the gay subject is forced into by power. His experience of social regulation is like that of a soldier who is simultaneously commanded to "Be Male" and "Be Feminine" (the dual demands of sex and gender here are important). The attempt to be both at once can only produce a psychic and physical collapse. Importantly, such fragmentation is explicitly linked with the sexual male/female binary: "The war between the sexes split the planet into armed camps right down the middle line divides one thing from the other" (*SM*, 145). Sex war becomes a result of the invaders' plans for "nova." Yet it is also a result of the gender differences inherent within the viral project of "Other Half" discussed in *The Ticket That Exploded:* "The Venusian invasion was known as 'Operation Other Half,' that is, a parasitic invasion of the sexual area taking advantage as all invasion plans must, of an already fucked-up situation" (*TTE*, 51).

The viral contagion of the Other Half is an amalgamation of Burroughs' combined fears about language, bodily autonomy, and gender. He conceives of it as a separate entity that lives within the self, threatening to take over the original subject, to alter him from what *he* is to what *it* is:

> Like a Siamese twin ten thousand years in show business en-
> gaged by a silver cord to all erogenous zones—lives along the
> divide line—is an amphibious two-sexed actor half-man
> half-woman-double-gated either sex can breathe air or the
> underwater medium up your mother's snatch—"the Other
> Half" is "You" next time around—born when you die—that
> is when "the Other Half" kills you and takes over—(*TTE*,
> 159–160)

Reading Burroughs' image of the Other Half as the effeminate paradigm hardly requires an imaginative leap. Existing as some hermaphroditic entity on the "divide line" of the binaries of both sex and gender, the Other Half seems ready to impose itself aggressively upon the original subject through murderous usurpation. This is closely tied to the violent revolution undertaken by the talking asshole. The "nova" that the trilogy so fears, then, can be seen as directly linked with this idea of "the Other Half." If nova represents an impasse caused by alternation of forces, orders, or desires, then what clearer impasse is there in Burroughs' work than the opposition of masculine/feminine, queer/fag, man/woman? Nova becomes the point at which the gay subject, caught within the either/or (heterosexual), binary logic of Western civilization is rendered schizoid and powerless since he is consistently made to experience both positions simultaneously.

For heterosexual society, these binary oppositions demarcate the limits of both sex and gender. The man is always masculine, the woman always feminine; slippage is impossible unless one is prepared to dissolve the stability of sex/gender alignments. The experience of the gay male, as the texts illustrate, is far less stable. For the gay subject, the binary structure of gender and sex identification is not reassuringly rigid but rather the very focus of his misery since he is caught in a perpetual oscillation between the reality of his sexed body and the demands that he identify himself as feminine. Buffeted between the two sides of the binary, he is caught in the space between male and female, masculine and feminine, left uncertain as to which half of the binary structure he ought to identify with.

This image of the gay subject as a schizoid cut-up is clearly influenced by Burroughs' appropriation of the two marginal discourses. But what hope does he draw from these discourses about the possibility of reconfiguring gay identity? I have no wish to suggest that the Nova trilogy ought to be read as a literal deconditioning program for gay men. The experience of reading the trilogy is certainly a unique one, having little similarity to the more conventional flows of linear narrative. Yet the primary importance of the trilogy is the way in which it presents the cut-up technique as a metaphorical image of subversion and revolution. If gay identity is made to conform to a cut-up relation of sex and gender, as the trilogy suggests, then Burroughs' own gay-male-authorial appropriation of the cut-up strategy can be seen as a reclamatory challenge to the heterosexual dominant's discourses. Outlining gender-schizoid gay identity as cut-up, Burroughs goes on to use the cut-up technique for his own purposes.

In many respects, the cut-up method transformed Burroughs as an author. The shift away from the confused gender registers that characterized the routine form was a direct result of the relentless pursuit of the cut-up throughout the 1960s. By following the descent into chaotic chance that the cut-up offered, Burroughs was actually establishing an authorial stability, an assertion of his own autonomous standing as a writer. In this respect his use of the cut-up intersects his overt concerns with queer autonomy. Rather than making the cut-up a tool of automatic writing/production, Burroughs consistently takes pains to emphasize conscious intention over the automatic. As the cut-ups are created, an element of chance or spontaneity is thrown into the textual equation, for although the author provides the material to be cut up, he can never predict the outcome of the process. Such a practice seems to indicate the end of conscious intent and the end of autonomy as the authorial subject gives himself up to forces outside his control.

However, Burroughs is keen to underscore his role in choosing which cut-up sentences to use. In *The Job*, he claims: "The selection and arrangement of materials is quite conscious but there is a random factor by which I obtain the material which I use then, select and work over into an acceptable form" (*Job*, 30). The cut-ups strengthen, rather than disperse, the artist's own autonomy as he becomes increasingly conscious of his choice of materials (as a result of his alienation from them through the transformative cut-up process). The cut-up technique can thus be read as ensuring that the finished text is the author's *own* words, syntax, and structure, rather than the effect of some predefined discourse, by continuously making the author aware of the choices available to him. Autonomy replaces automatism.

By repeating words and phrases, and by literally cutting them up, pasting them to each other, jumbling them together, Burroughs creates a textual parallel to the therapies' attempts to purify the individual. Thus the cut-up method produces not Lydenberg's dissolution of the reading subject, but rather a textual metaphor of the kind of liberation-through-purification that Burroughs was seeking in each of these therapies. Allen Ginsberg's comments on the cut-up method are important; he suggests that the technique was designed less for the sake of readers and more for the author's own benefit, literature as self-help therapy:

> the cut-ups were originally designed to rehearse and repeat [Burroughs'] obsession with sexual images over and over again, like a movie repeating over and over again, and then re-combined and mixed in; so that finally the obsessive detachment, compulsion and preoccupation empty out and drain from the image [. . .] And that's the purpose of the cut-ups: to cut out of habit reactions, to cut through rehearsed habit, to cut through conditioned reflex, to cut out in the open space . . . [53]

From this perspective, the repetitive "pornographic" style of passages such as "The Streets of Chance" (*SM*, 108–138) makes much more sense, their purpose being similar to the self-purification enacted by the auditing process. The repetition of the audit seeks to remove the engrams stored in the reactive mind, bringing them to consciousness; Burroughs' repetitions seek to bring the mechanisms of control into consciousness, allowing the subject to recover his original identity—that is, the one that existed prior to regulation.

The queer intent of the Nova trilogy is never made explicit, but it is readily apparent once we recognize the importance of the effeminate paradigm in Burroughs' conception of gay subjectivity. The main goal of the trilogy is the delineation of methods of deconditioning designed to create an autonomous subject. As an author, Burroughs pursues his own autonomy through the textual experimentation of the cut-up, literally cutting his writing free from previous forms of textual production. Yet even more interesting than this personal transformation is the manner in which the obsession with themes of control and autonomy, regulation, and freedom in the Nova trilogy intersects with Burroughs' queer politics. Drawing on Hubbardian and Korzybskian models of the relation between the subject and "the outside," Burroughs produces a theoretical template of gay male regulation. Effeminacy becomes yet another means of denying individual autonomy—an invasive construct that, like the virus, the word-lock, and the engram, usurps the primacy of the subject.

However, Burroughs' vision of this does not involve the kind of Dianetic auditing one might expect. Rather than having to rehearse the feminine over and over again in order to purify themselves, the queer heroes are led into a violent confrontation with it as they cut all ties with both femininity and heterosexuality. In an attempt to overcome the schizophrenic oscillation between the poles of the gender binary that characterizes gay experience, Burroughs' queer heroes begin a radical appropriation of the masculine realm, vehemently upholding the half of the binary opposition that they have been consistently denied—the masculine.

It is clear, then, that the cut-up technique is more a metaphorical process of deconditioning the gay male subject than an actual "therapy." Contextualizing the cut-up practice and theory with reference to the work of Korzybski and Hubbard, it becomes apparent that Burroughs appropriates these marginal discourses for his own queer ends in order to offer a very personal challenge to the American psychoanalytic establishment. Rejecting the American post-Freudians' belief that the male homosexual always identifies with the feminine, Burroughs uses General Semantics and Dianetics to illustrate his belief that effeminacy is not a natural gay identity, but rather a deliberately conditioned position that the heterosexual dominant demands the gay man adopt.

If effeminacy is not an authentic mode of being, then clearly there must be an original gay identity waiting to be reclaimed once the engrams and locks of effeminacy are swept aside. Burroughs suggests that if the asshole can be made to stop talking, then perhaps the carny man can be rediscovered, the body put back in order, the psyche purged of the traits of effeminacy that power had inflicted on the subject. With such hopes in mind, Burroughs' following novels of the 1970s, 1980s, and 1990s consistently attempt to outline the creation of a gay male subject who is no longer schizophrenic, confused, or disempowered.

MAINTAINING AUTONOMY:
BURROUGHS' MASCULINE UTOPIAS

The Nova trilogy's dominant concern with the regulation of the individual subject by external forces was a theme typical of the decade in which it appeared. Burroughs' increasingly radical textual and sexual politics drew upon the anti-establishment discourses of the 1960s. The Nova trilogy facilitated an understanding of effeminacy as an ersatz subjectivity imposed upon the gay man by an aggressive heterosexual dominant. Significantly, the texts of the 1970s and 1980s—in particular the Wild Boy tetralogy and Red Night trilogy—build upon this template of queer regulation in order to fantasize a violent re-establishment of queer autonomy. Throwing off the shackles of the effeminate paradigm, Burroughs' queer heroes contrive the spectacular destruction of the heterosexual dominant, a fantastic cutting up that involves bloodletting, guns, and ammunition as opposed to the scissors and paste of the Nova trilogy.

In this manner, Burroughs' post-Nova trilogy texts consistently re-create the radical politics of the 1960s, building upon the increasing militancy of the gay community both before and after Stonewall. It is this thematic continuity between the Wild Boy and Red Night texts that necessitates their discussion together. The establishment of a "Wild Boy," masculine gay identity is always presented in direct relation to the issues of autonomy and the invasive nature of the effeminate paradigm that the Nova trilogy initiated. For this reason, the following two sections of this chapter will deal with a historically diverse range of texts in order to demonstrate the way in which Burroughs' post-Nova trilogy texts outline a deconditioned gay identity with the Wild Boys and Johnsons as "clears." The extent to which this is dependent not only on Burroughs' literary output of the 1960s but also on the historical events of that decade will quickly become apparent.

As we have seen, Burroughs believed that the combined discourses of the heterosexual dominant had consistently attempted to excise all traces of the masculine model of gay identity, replacing it with the effeminate paradigm's emphasis on the incompatibility of the gay male's anatomical sex and gender identifications. Historically, the masculine model had enjoyed just one brief moment of cultural dissemination in the modern period, at the end of the nineteenth century during the height of the sexologists' research. Adolf Brand and Benedict Friedländer's aggressive vision of the masculine gay man imagined a future social order in which the homosexual was not merely offered equality but was recognized as *superior* to the heterosexual male. The *Gemeinschaft der Eigenen* ("Community of Free Spirits") had been a radical counterpoint to Hirschfeld's *Wissenschaftlich-humanitäres Komitee* (*WhK* or "Scientific-Humanitarian Committee"), the first gay movement. As James Steakley has pointed out, the German gay masculinists

argued that the family was the institutionalization of heterosexual desires, while the political state arose from equally natural male homosexual relations. The true *typus inversus*, as distinct from the effeminate homosexual, was seen as the founder of patriarchal society, and ranked above the heterosexual in terms of his capacity for leadership and heroism.[54]

Such a revision of the social and political order was quickly stamped out by the heterosexual dominant (hardly surprising given Friedländer's rabid heterophobia). By the 1930s, the Nazis had banned both the *WhK* and the *Gemeinschaft der Eigenen*. Yet the vision of a gay "utopia" in which homosexuality became the superior form of sexual interaction finds expression decades later in Burroughs' creation of the "Wild Boys" and their counterparts. However, the liberation symbolized by the Wild Boys was not just a reworking of pro-masculinist sympathies that had emerged much earlier, but, more importantly, also a response to the increasing radicalism of the gay scene.

In America, at least, the masculine model of gay identity had been slowly gathering strength throughout the postwar period in response to the extensive social regulation of homosexuality that characterized the 1950s. Yet historical documentation of the emergence of a masculine gay style in the early postwar period has largely been passed over by queer historians, leaving only scattered references to this subculture within the larger gay subculture. The majority of these sparse references center on the popularity of motorcycle clubs in the 1950s. The motorcyclist became an image of butch masculinity; Allen Ginsberg, for instance, praised those who "let themselves be fucked in the ass by saintly motorcyclists, and / screamed with joy."[55] In Los Angeles, one of the first of these gay motorcycle clubs—the Satyrs—was formed in 1954–1955 by a group of enthusiasts, among whom were two former Mattachine Society members.[56]

The dissatisfaction with the effeminate style that we have noticed in Burroughs' texts was reflected in other parts of the gay scene. The protagonists of Vidal's *The City and the Pillar* (1948) and Baldwin's *Giovanni's Room* (1956) distance themselves from the "fag" in the same way as Burroughs' texts of the period do.

Baldwin's narrator says of effeminate gay men, "I always found it difficult to believe that they ever went to bed with anybody for a man who wanted a woman would certainly have rather had a real one and a man who wanted a man would certainly not want one of *them*."[57] In a similar fashion, Vidal's protagonist tries desperately to separate himself from the "league of dressmakers and decorators."[58] Such diversity of gender identification on the gay scene was, of course, far from new. What was occurring in America in the 1950s was the beginning of homosexual dissent and a vocal opposition to the effeminate paradigm that the discourses of the American medical and psychoanalytic establishments had made into a stereotype. Yet the creation of visible modes of gay macho would not become an issue until the 1970s.

However, there is also another important context against which to set Burroughs' desire to delineate a masculine identity. Timothy S. Murphy notes that the publication of *The Wild Boys* in 1971 occurs in the aftermath of a "period of cultural unrest"; he suggests that the Wild Boy novels were "self-consciously written in the shadow of the Paris student riots of May 1968, the occupation of Columbia University (the alma mater of Burroughs's friends Ginsberg and Jack Kerouac), and what Norman Mailer called 'the siege of Chicago'."[59] However, by linking Burroughs' Wild Boys with the leaders and members of the student movements it is possible to overlook the boys' status as *homosexual* revolutionaries. The fact that *The Wild Boys* was published in the wake of the Stonewall riots—which Murphy inexplicably ignores—seems of immense importance both to an understanding of the text and the climate in which it was produced. While Burroughs is clearly drawing parallels between the Wild Boys and the youth movements of the 1960s, it seems disingenuous to ignore the fact that one of the central civil rights movements after 1969 was the Gay Liberation Front and that for Burroughs, the emergence of a gay macho style throughout the 1950s and into the 1960s leads directly into the beginnings of radical gay politics.

In the early 1960s, as John D'Emilio notes, there was a marked shift in the gay community away from the Mattachine Society's

conservatism toward a more radical, aggressive demand for liberation. The old guard of the Mattachine was largely left behind as a
new, youth-oriented movement began to emerge. The direct action
techniques of the civil rights activists and the violent readiness of
countercultural groups such as the Black Panthers and the Weath-
ermen suggested the possibility of marginalized groups launching
an armed struggle against the American establishment.

Throughout the 1960s, the homophile movements of the previous decade were becoming increasingly out of step with the
younger generation of gay men and women who had not had firsthand experience of the fear and paranoia of the McCarthy years.
The dissolution of the Mattachine Society's national structure was
followed by the emergence of a new, East Coast militancy.
Franklin Kameny is credited with providing much of the impetus
that caused the transformation of the American gay movement
from Mattachine Society to Gay Liberation Front. His dedicated,
militant campaigning throughout the 1960s flew in the face of the
old-guard Mattachine leadership's conservatism and its fears that
confrontational politics might lead to a return to the witch hunts
and harassment of the 1950s.

Rejecting the cheek-turning passivity of the accommodationist
position advocated by Donald Webster Cory, the militants campaigned under the equal rights for minorities banner, attacking the
medical model of homosexuality as sickness and perversion, and
fighting social injustice and prejudice. The gay movement slowly
transformed itself, broadening its appeal as it lost its Mattachine
stuffiness, finally reaching out to grassroots levels and attracting
interest and support from the gay club and bar circuit.[60] The turning point came at the end of the 1960s, with the Stonewall riots.

The raid on the Stonewall Inn on Greenwich Village's Christopher Street, on Friday, 27 June 1969, led to the first moment of
mass gay civil disobedience and the creation of the Gay Liberation
Front a few weeks later. The riots that occurred as police officers
raided the club and tried to arrest some of the patrons (who were
mostly young, non-white drag queens) came to symbolize a moment of triumphant reversal. No longer were gay men easy targets

for harassment by the police and judicial system; suddenly they had become an oppressed minority group that was willing to fight back, and demand its freedom. Interviewed by a reporter from *The Village Voice,* Allen Ginsberg was one of the first people to articulate just how significant the battle with the police was for gay identity: "You know, the guys there were so beautiful. They've lost that wounded look that fags had ten years ago."[61]

In the months following the Stonewall riots, the gay community increasingly adopted a radical, aggressive attitude. Taking up the political stance of the New Left, the Gay Liberation Front (GLF) was established to channel this energy toward social reform. The GLF's "Statement of Purpose" was adamantly utopian:

> We reject society's attempt to impose sexual roles and definitions of our nature. We are stepping outside these roles and simplistic myths. We are going to be who we are. At the same time, we are creating new social forms and relations, that is, relations based upon brotherhood, cooperation, human love and uninhibited sexuality. Babylon has forced us to commit ourselves to one thing—revolution![62]

In their attempt to achieve such goals, the GLF followed a policy of direct action, organizing marches, occupying publishing houses that printed hostile articles, even invading medical and psychiatric conventions and demanding that homosexuality be removed from the list of pathologies. The aim was to secure acceptance of homosexuality and bring about the end of the heterosexual dominant's legal and medical regulation of the gay subculture.[63]

Read against this background of social unrest and gay radicalism, Burroughs' novels of the period seem to be a fantastic expression of the kind of utopianism that fueled the GLF's "Statement of Purpose." Having explained effeminacy as the mark of power's influence over the gay subject and conceptualized its operation as an invasive force robbing the gay male of both his masculine gender and his physical autonomy, Burroughs valorizes the establishment of a self-accepting, revolutionary gay subjectivity in terms of the appropriation of the masculine. While gender identification was rarely a matter of interest for the radical gay activists (whose style throughout the 1970s was increasingly androgynous), Burroughs' reading of radical gay politics is one in which masculinity is the defining trait. His queer radicalism centers on overturning three restrictions: the effeminate paradigm, the notion of homosexuality as sickness/perversion, and the passive accommodationist position of the Mattachine Society.

The main focus of Burroughs' Wild Boy tetralogy is an apocalyptic world in which the social order is disrupted enough to allow gay men the possibility of forming separate communities. The eponymous characters of *The Wild Boys* band together in the deserts of North Africa to create an alternative to heterosexual society and simultaneously wage war on an intolerant, heterosexual social order that refuses them independence. The American military tries to wipe them out but fails, overcome by their Viet Cong–like guerrilla tactics. The boys are the central focus of *Port of Saints* and, to a lesser extent, *Ah Pook is Here*, in which their stylization as countercultural adolescent radicals of the 1960s is continued. In *Exterminator!*—a collection of thematically linked short stories—they are largely absent, but their violent, revolutionary ethos is mirrored in the terrorists, pest exterminators, and animalistic adolescents on which the stories focus.

Burroughs repeatedly links the boys with the youth movements of the late 1960s. He cites Genet's belief that "It is time for writers to support the rebellion of youth not only with their words but with their presence as well" (*EX*, 96) and suggests that "the emergent Yippie uniform is crash helmet, shoulderpads and aluminum jockstrap" (*EX*, 96). This expression of political commitment was put into action by both writers as they attended the Chicago demonstrations (and subsequent rioting) of August 1968.[64] The Wild Boys can thus be read as a progression from the riots of Chicago and Stonewall in that they are a radical group of youthful, queer, multiracial revolutionaries who echo Burroughs' own belief that non-violent action is not enough.[65]

The all-male communes that become the focal point of Burroughs' fiction from this point onwards into the 1970s and 1980s are environments in which the effeminate paradigm has no place. The schizophrenic oscillation of the gender binary has been completely overturned. The queer heroes that Burroughs imagines are wild (rather than Wilde) boys, whose claim to masculinity resides in their adherence to the dual values of extreme violence and misogyny. As Strobe in *Cities of the Red Night* illustrates, the decision to adopt a policy of violent confrontation is one that alters the straight world's perception of the gay man. The mutinous crew of the pirate ship disregards Strobe "as an effeminate dandy," but is quickly made to realize that homosexuality no longer signifies passivity: "After he had killed five of the ringleaders they were forced to revise this opinion."[66] Instead of offering their Sugar Bums in an act of passive placation, Burroughs' post-Stonewall gay characters are always prepared to defend their sexuality and prove their status as men through violence.

Such violence is consistently styled as liberatory in its role as a defense against the homophobia of the dominant, a form of queer self-determination as exemplified in Kim's barroom shoot-out with two men who "don't like drinkin' in the same room with a fairy."[67] Rather than accept homophobia and work through the accommodationist Mattachine ethos of the 1950s, Burroughs' new heroes are prepared to use violence as part of a program of self-reliance, copying the willingness of some of the more radical minority groups, like the Black Panthers, to fight for their rights. Indeed, Burroughs makes clear the link between the fight for racial equality and gay rights in the story "Davy Jones" (*EX*, 17–19), which concerns the sentencing of a young black man for armed robbery. Audrey sits in the dock watching the spectacle, excited by the cool insolence of the young Davy Jones and the unflinching authority of his father. Audrey's own passivity—he is shouted at by the court officials (*EX*, 17)—attracts him to the pair's nonchalance, and their ability to unsettle the court. It is this air of thinly veiled violent confrontation that attracts Audrey, and the implicit suggestion is that he must put aside his feminine passivity and follow the example of these black men who are able to strike fear into their opponents: "Why did they take it from him? Because they were afraid of him. Davy Jones father and son and Clutch destroy the whole white world" (*EX*, 19).

This rejection of effeminacy in favor of a radical masculinity results in misogyny, the logical extension of Burroughs' effeminophobia. Reacting against the view of the gay male as passive, feminine, and weak, the texts argue for the total separation of the masculine and feminine spheres, even going so far as to characterize American society as matriarchal in order to suggest that the all-male communes are a subversive attack on a "feminine" civilization. The misogyny and fear of the feminine that Burroughs' texts display is infamous. From Mary in *Naked Lunch*, who bites off and eats her partner's cock (*NL*, 93) to the B-movie scorpion-women who attack an English country village in *Exterminator!* (*EX*, 39), Burroughs presents us with a fantastic universe to which the Sex War mentioned at the end of *The Soft Machine* (*SM*, 145) is the backdrop. In the attempt to overturn the effeminate paradigm, the texts envisage a world within which the gay male subject can achieve autonomy only through destroying the feminine Other that threatens to contaminate him.

This emasculating, contaminating feminine influence is exemplified in a brief episode that replays the logic of the Talking Asshole routine in the 1980s' text *The Place of Dead Roads*. Kim's band of gay gunslingers—The Wild Fruits—rush into a gunfight dressed in drag (*PDR*, 98–100). Dressing as women—complying with the dominant stereotype of the "fag"—gives the gang a brief advantage, for their opponents are tricked into underestimating these supposed queens. The Trojan Horse tactic succeeds, but during the shoot-out the dangers of gender impersonation are made apparent. One of Kim's gang is a youthful innocent whose sense of self-identity is apparently not yet strong enough to cope with the rigors of impersonation and the loss of self that such an act brings about:

> Twelve of those lousy macho shits died in the shoot-out. We lost one boy—a sad quiet kid named Joe had got himself up as a whore in a purple dress with a slit down the sides. Had

his gun in a shoulder holster and it got caught in his strap-on tits. Hit five times. (*PDR*, 100)

The passage is clearly bathetic, yet there is also a serious edge to it. Performative identities, Burroughs suggests, are acceptable only as long as the subject is able to retain a sense of his essential self, and to protect that essential self from the contaminating influences one gives oneself over to in the act of impersonation. Allowing the host to be exposed to the parasitic influences of the feminine can easily lead to disaster. Since Burroughs' understanding of masculinity is always informed by the subject's ability to deal with violent situations, Joe's failure even to unholster his gun properly suggests his total emasculation.

Throughout the Wild Boy and Red Night texts, Burroughs consistently styles American society as a matriarchy, arguing that masculinity can be maintained only outside of the feminine sphere of influence. In *The Wild Boys*, for instance, the Green Nun is styled as one of the principal controllers, her dormitory/asylum a microcosmic image of society in which adult men are reduced to children, their sexuality restrained and repressed: "The patients sleep on their backs under a thin blanket. Erections are sanctioned with a sharp ruler tap from the night sister."[68] While the middle-aged inmates are thus emasculated, the Green Nun indulges her penis envy by dressing as "Christ with a strap-on" and paying nocturnal visits to one of the younger nuns (*WB*, 27). *Pace* Catherine Stimpson, who claims that lesbians in Burroughs' fiction "lift male fears, because they at once eschew raids on the phallus that is so desirable to other men and so vulnerable to women," the texts characterize lesbianism as a grotesque perversion on a par with that of the effeminate gay man.[69] Lesbians in Burroughs' novels are always described in terms of *penisneid*, like those in *Nova Express* with their "glazed faces of grafted penis flesh" (*NE*, 57). When a crack squad of lesbian commandos, the Darlings, are sent out to tame the Wild Boys, their presumptuous usurpation of the violence belonging to the masculine realm is quickly punished as the boys tear them to "screaming ribbons."[70]

The gender-separatist logic informing the vision of the Wild Boys is one that argues that masculinity and homosexuality are the natural state of all human males. The purification of the male subject that occurs in the absence of the feminine is exemplified in the texts' creation of several variants of the prelapsarian utopia. In *The Wild Boys*, the Dead Child and Xolotl escape from a Mayan village. Not wanting to "stay where the women were" (*WB*, 112) they create a home in the jungle and embark on a utopian, masculine life of self-reliance: "There was a clear blue stream with deep pools and plenty of fish" (*WB*, 112). Their idyllic routine of sex and hunting is ultimately doomed, though, as Xolotl is killed by a jaguar and heterosexual society invades the jungle. In a similar vein, *Port of Saints* offers two revisions of creation myth:

> According to the legend an evil old doctor, who called himself God and us dogs, created the first boy in his adolescent image. The boy peopled the garden with male phantoms that rose from his ejaculations. This angered God, who was getting on in years. He decided it endangered his position as CREATOR. So he crept upon the boy and anaesthetized him and made Eve from his rib. Henceforth all creation of beings would process through female channels. But some of Adam's phantoms refused to let God near them under any pretext. After millennia these cool remote spirits breathe in the wild boy who will never again submit to the yoke of female flesh. And anyone who joins them must leave women behind forever. (*PoS*, 97)

A few pages later:

> In this Eden the first man landed in a crippled spacecraft. He lived there with the animals waiting for a pickup. But the Fifth Colonists arrived. One day when the first man was having intercourse with a shy young lemur he was slapped from behind by a fat cop. The police doctor cut out a rib. The whisky priest muttered over it and it turned into a Lesbian policewoman who screamed at the dazed Adam . . .
> "WHAT ARE YOU DOING IN FRONT OF DECENT PEOPLE?" (*PoS*, 105)

Gay masculine sexuality is thus transformed from sickness and perversion into the natural and authentic state of all human males, a condition that has been contaminated by the moralistic discourses of a feminine, heterosexual dominant. The texts' antipathy to this leads to the misogyny and effeminophobia of their absolute rejection of the feminine in the queer communes of the 1970s and 1980s: "Look at these faces that have never seen a woman's face nor heard a woman's voice" (*PoS*, 92). This separatist tactic produces a vision of gay masculinity in which the masculine is everything that is *not feminine*. The fantasy of adolescent boys attacking a matriarchal social order becomes a telling comment on Oedipal understandings of homosexuality as excessive mother-love. Burroughs' queer heroes kill off their metaphorical mothers in an ironic critique of Freudian theory.

The Wild Boys are admittedly styled as "masculine" in their love of violence; yet they seem most assured of their gender status when attacking all that the text designates as feminine: women, the matriarchal social order, anyone who lacks a real penis, or any male who is unworthy of possessing such an organ (the coward, the physically inept). General Greenfield's troops sent out to exterminate the Wild Boys are an emasculated group—overweight, over-the-hill, and a danger to themselves:

A guard officer has had one too many. He approaches a portly guest . . . "Bovard, I could kill you in twenty seconds . . . ten as a matter of fact . . . like this . . . I put my elbow against your Adam's apple throw a knee into your left kidney and bring the heel of my hand up sharp under your chin."

"Hey, what do you think you're doing?" The two men reel, lose balance and fall overturning the table of food. They roll flailing at each other in a welter of lobster Newburgh, chicken salad, punch and baked Alaska. (*WB*, 122)

This attack on the "feminine" reaches a crescendo with the Wild Boys' trump card: they possess technology that can allow their separatist communities to remain autonomous and self-procreating. Reproduction is no longer a biological function that requires both male and female. With genetics, artificial wombs, and cloning skills at their disposal, the boys can create independent masculine communities: "Wild boy not born now. First he made from little piece one boy's ass grow new boy. Piece cut from boy after he get fucked" (*PoS*, 72). The benefit of this usurpation of bio-power by the separatist communities is obvious; it allows Burroughs' characters to create a new version of the mythical society that haunted him and Gysin: the Muslim leader Hassan i Sabbah's all-male commune at Alamout.[71] Burroughs makes Hassan i Sabbah and his legendary assassins mythic precursors of the queer Wild Boys: "The phallic gods of Greece, the assassins of Alamout and the Old Man himself, dispossessed by generations of female conquest, still linger in the hills of Morocco" (*PoS*, 93).

The texts' representations of homosexuality thus overturn the Christian fundamentalist accusation that it is sinful because it is not procreative. As the boys produce new beings through gay sex, they empower both themselves and the site of their desire, the anus. The heterosexual fear of the anus as "a grave," as death, and as nothingness, is challenged and transformed into a queer celebration of its role as a site of desire and alternative reproduction. Burroughs deliberately and repeatedly underscores this transformation of gay sex into a more natural and reproductive sexuality than heterosexuality. In *Ah Pook is Here*, almost every emission offered by the boys is outrageously procreative. Since "Any sex act can now create life,"[72] boys are depicted "ejaculating roses, cherries, opals, bird eggs and gold fish" and "jack off spurting robins and blue birds" (*APH*, 59). In *The Wild Boys*, gay sex produces "Zimbus," phantomlike creatures who are made solid through the boys' sexual acts (*WB*, 155–161).

Following the kind of radical claims for the superiority of masculine-identified homosexuality previously made by Friedländer and Blüher at the beginning of the century, Burroughs employs a strategy of queer resistance that reverses the dominant/subordinate binary, so that the marginalized can claim an authentic, natural position, which is then simultaneously denied to the members of the dominant. Homosexuality thus becomes more natural, authentic, and pure than heterosexuality. The texts explicitly style themselves as a manifesto for all males, calling on every man to relinquish heterosexual conformity, to unleash the "perverse" desires that society is sublimating for homosocial purposes. Furthermore, it is a call to all men to embrace their masculinity. If taken at face value, the texts' vision of society condemns heterosexual life and brands all males who are not masculine-identified homosexuals as effeminate since they are contaminated by the influence of the feminine.[73]

As part of the texts' reverse discourse on homosexuality, Burroughs repeatedly emphasizes the adolescence of his heroes. *The Wild Boys* in particular establishes its theme of queer revolution and social transformation within a very childish world of amusement parks, funfairs, candy, and adolescent sex, producing a kind of gay male version of J. M. Barrie's *Peter Pan*. The *mise en scène* is one of jockstraps, dormitories, showers, and toilet cubicles, the childhood dressing rooms revisited. No longer does the gay child feel alienated from the other children, for here his desires and fantasies are reciprocated and can be played out. The gay adolescent is still young enough to be able to overcome the conditioning imposed upon him by the homophobic, prohibitory discourses of the dominant.[74] In addition, by marshalling the adolescent forces of the Wild Boys against the middle-aged world of Greenfield, the Countesses, Hart and Bickford, Burroughs is also able to suggest that homosexuality is far more vibrant and free than heterosexuality.

Much of the importance of the communities of boys and young men thus becomes their ability to undermine the social order. Increasingly, the family is styled as an outmoded concept in need of radical reassessment. In *Port of Saints,* Burroughs outlines his belief in the transformative possibilities offered by the creation of an all-male family in terms of a rejection of moralistic attitudes toward sexual behavior. In addition, the shared masculinity of such families allows uninhibited self-development. As John Guzlowski suggests, the heterosexual family in Burroughs' fiction represents a prohibitive, repressive force, one that denies its offspring "their experiences, their inner selves, their unconscious worlds of dreams,

desires and wishes."[75] The all-male families allow individuality—
in particular, masculine identity—to be explored, as the story of
Jerry in *Port of Saints* demonstrates. Caught masturbating by his
father and brother, Jerry passes out in a combination of ecstasy and
shame. On awakening he is surprised to find that he is treated with
love and respect rather than censure (indeed, the passage even
hints at incest): "When he came to, his father was rubbing his face
with a cold towel and his brother was smiling and unbuttoning his
shirt" (*PoS*, 122). This "sexual rapport" between the family's men
enables Jerry to discover his masculine identity: "He took lessons
in Jiu Jitsu and began to get over his physical cowardice" (*PoS*,
122). In the absence of women, shame and decency disappear, allowing the male subject the freedom to find his essential self.

At the same time, though, Burroughs seems to be self-conscious
about the way in which his interest in extreme forms of fiction
could be read as "adolescent." His skit about the attempts of the reviewers at *ONE* to justify his texts is symptomatic of this self-
consciousness; the reviewers explain away his work's extreme imaginary as "boyishness," "gangrened innocence," and "schoolboy
smut."[76] Burroughs' use of genres normally read by adolescent boys
(science fiction, horror, fantasy, and the British tradition of "Boys
Own" adventure) seems to be part of this deliberate use of adolescence; he also refers to the pulp magazines of his own childhood,
such as *Amazing Stories* and *Adventure Stories* (*PoS*, 60). The extent
to which this is a deliberate policy is suggested in *The Wild Boys*, in
which such genres are simultaneously alluded to and affectionately
mocked by the text: Audrey reads adventure stories and imagines
himself as "a gentleman adventurer like the 'Major' . . . sun helmet,
khakis, Webley at the belt a faithful Zulu servant at his side. A dim
sad child breathing old pulp magazines" (*WB*, 32). In *Port of Saints*,
Audrey is described again in similar terms: "These dreams were
banal and childish even for his years, consisting mostly of gun
fights at which he excelled. Since adventure was a virtual impossi-
bility in a midwestern matriarchy, these were paper thin dreams,
19th century nostalgia" (*PoS*, 60).

Burroughs self-consciously creates a boyish fiction; indeed, the original subtitle of *Cities of the Red Night* was to have been "a boy's book."[77] This underlines his fantasy of capturing the adolescent male at a moment prior to his Oedipal socialization into compulsory heterosexuality (and homophobia) in order to transport him along a different path toward a queer adulthood. Burroughs thus becomes the queer pied piper leading the children of the world "astray," offering them an alternative to the family, the mother, heterosexuality: "Dear Mom and Dad: I am going to join the wild boys. When you read this I will be far away. Johnny" (*WB*, 123). This theme is underlined in the ending of *Port of Saints:* "The Dussenberg disappears over the hills and far away" (*PoS*, 174).[78] Such childhood fantasies of rebellion are a part of the "teentakeover" sub genre epitomized by Dave Wallis's *Only Lovers Left Alive* (1964) in which the adults commit suicide, leaving social reconstruction in the hands of their children. This kind of fantasy/fear reached its zenith in J. G. Ballard's appropriately titled *Running Wild* (1988), which imagines the violent rebellion of a group of teenagers against their liberal, middle-class parents.[79] Burroughs' version of the genre is, naturally, a queer extrapolation of its main themes.

Since America has failed its children, Burroughs fantasizes a revolution that not only indicts the heterosexual system, but also challenges those discourses suggesting that homosexuality can never be natural, pure, or authentic. But this reliance on adolescence as the site of a sexual revolution is problematic. As we will see in the following chapter, it is inclined to let "boyishness" degenerate into excess, violence, and fascism. As Burroughs later warns, "You want adolescent sex, you have to pay for it in adolescent fear, shame, confusion."[80] However, before turning to the problematic nature of Burroughs' vision of a youth rebellion, it is important to note that the play of adolescence in his novels seems to emerge from a very American literary tradition, a tradition of the boy's book, the frontier, and the homosocial bond between men fleeing from a restrictive, heterosexual—and feminine—society.

QUEERING THE AMERICAN MASCULINE:
FIEDLER, HOMOSEXUALITY, AND THE FRONTIER

According to Geoff Ward, "William Burroughs writes, and has always written, as if the nineteenth-century novel had never happened."[81] This suggestion transforms the texts into a bizarre revision of the eighteenth-century novel, a mixture of Fielding's bawdy, Defoe's picaresque, and Swift's misanthropy. However, what such an Anglocentric comment overlooks is the relationship between Burroughs' texts and the nineteenth-century American novel. Burroughs' queer appropriation of the mythic space of the American frontier throughout the Wild Boy and Red Night texts establishes a dialogue between himself and the American masculine tradition.

What is so interesting about this dialogue is the manner in which it engages with one of the seminal texts of 1960s literary criticism, Leslie Fiedler's *Love and Death in the American Novel.* The revision of the American canon that Fiedler undertook illuminates Burroughs' own radical project of appropriation and rewriting in the texts of the 1970s and 1980s. Growing out of Fiedler's Freudian reading of the canon, Burroughs' Wild Boys and Johnsons can be seen as a parodic response to Fiedler's sex/gender politics. What this section aims to illustrate is the manner in which Burroughs' appropriation of the masculine sphere is a transgressive appropriation of a heterosexual tradition of American masculinity. Using Fiedler's work to mediate his revision of the canon, Burroughs continues his previous strategies of queer resistance to effeminacy, marginalization, and regulation as outlined in the Nova trilogy. Yet his attempt to imagine a masculine queer subject wiped free of the engrams of effeminacy initiates a problematic relation between his texts and the heterosexual masculine mainstream to which Fiedler ultimately belongs. The play of transgression and conformism upon which Burroughs/Fiedler exchange is based is one that is characteristic of gay appropriations of the masculine, as we will see in the next chapter.

In 1948, Leslie Fiedler published his article "Come Back to the Raft Ag'in, Huck Honey!" in which he argued that one of the central tropes of American literature was the flight of the white male protagonist into the wilderness in order to escape from social responsibility, civilization, and the influence of the feminine.[82] Rejecting the "petticoat government" of the Widow Douglas of American culture, the white hero establishes a homoerotic relationship with a non-white male companion in the ruggedly masculine forest, wilderness, sea, or frontier landscape. On its publication in *Partisan Review*, Fiedler's essay caused a storm of controversy, with many readers outraged at its (supposed) suggestion that the central characters of nineteenth-century American fiction were homosexuals. Philip Rahv, the editor of *Partisan Review*, panicked at the response to the essay and claimed that he had published it only because he thought it was an elaborate hoax.[83] Fiedler's reaction was one of bemusement. While relishing the attention that such a controversy produced, he claimed that his essential point had been misinterpreted. He was not arguing that characters such as Huck and Jim or Ishmael and Queequeg were, in his words, "queer as three-dollar bills,"[84] but rather that their relationship was illustrative of what he dubbed "the peculiar American form of innocent homosexuality."[85]

In 1960 Fiedler expanded upon the essay to create a vast survey of the American literary canon in *Love and Death in the American Novel*. Further clarifying his thesis, Fiedler continued to counter the accusations that he had queered American literature. Negating the *façade* of sexual radicalism that the original essay had cultivated, Fiedler argued that American literature was characterized not by homosexuality but rather by homoeroticism—a subtle distinction that he assigned increasing importance. Reading the key texts of the American canon such as *Moby Dick*, *Huckleberry Finn*, and the Leatherstocking tales through the lens of Freudian theory, Fiedler suggested that the American literary trope of interracial male-male couplings against the background of the wilderness were part of an idyllic masculinist fantasy from which women were excluded.

While remaining conscious of the potency of this fantasy, Fiedler suggested that it was indicative of American literature's failure to deal with mature (heterosexual) desire. The male-male relationships of American fiction—with their focus on chaste, adolescent desire—were, Fiedler argued, regressive fantasies that threatened to subvert the heterosexual social order. By bonding with the non-white male Other, the hero of the nineteenth-century American novel failed to engage with the real demands of heterosexual society and thereby risked losing himself to the non-procreative sterility of homosexuality:

> The typical male protagonist of our fiction has been a man on the run, harried into the forest and out to sea, down the river or into combat—anywhere to avoid "civilization," which is to say, the confrontation of a man and a woman which leads to the fall to sex, marriage, and responsibility.[86]

There is, he argues

> no heterosexual solution which the American psyche finds completely satisfactory, no imagined or real consummation between man and woman found worthy of standing in our fiction for the healing of the breach between consciousness and unconsciousness, reason and impulse, society and nature [. . .] Is there not, our writers ask over and over, a sentimental relationship at once erotic and immaculate, a union which commits its participants neither to society nor sin—and yet one which is able to symbolize the union of the ego with the id, the thinking self with its rejected impulses?[87]

Fiedler argues that the search for such unity in the wilderness is doomed to failure since it rejects the demands of heterosexual society. By replacing heterosexuality with "chaste male love" the nineteenth-century American novel must always be, in Fiedler's own terms, a "boys' book" which refuses to move towards social responsibility, heterosexuality, and procreation.[88]

What is so interesting about Fiedler's revision of the American canon in this respect is his treatment of homosexuality. By repeatedly emphasizing his reading of the male-male relationships in Cooper, Melville, Twain, and others as homoerotic rather than homosexual, Fiedler suggests that it is the "innocence" and chastity of the love between the interracial characters that is the fantasy's predominant attraction.[89] As opposed to the biological realities of heterosexual love (with its procreative potential) and the fearful specter of homosexual consummation, the homoerotic relationship becomes—in Fiedler's reading—a refuge from the feminine. That the homoerotic should be situated between the engagement with the feminine that heterosexuality demands on one side and homosexuality on the other side is indicative of Fiedler's implicit understanding of homosexuality as a feminization of the male subject.

Fiedler's pseudo-psychoanalytic reading of homosexuality reiterates many of the gender prejudices that we noted in the discourses of the American psychoanalytic establishment in the previous chapter. His understanding of homosexuality as a neurotic flight from masculine heterosexual responsibility is clearly influenced by the work of post-Freudians such as Sandor Rado. The implicit assumption of Fiedler's discussion of the homoerotic is that if Huck and Jim were ever to consummate their relationship they would no longer be part of a masculine tradition, since the confirmed gay man must always be effeminate (unlike the ostensibly heterosexual man, who can retain his masculinity as long as he merely plays with the idea of homosexuality, rather than playing with his male companion).[90]

In this respect, Fiedler's discussion of American literature simultaneously displays a sympathy toward the male-male innocence of the boys' book, but also fears that its homoeroticism might lead to a more dangerous manifestation of homosexual desire:

> The existence of overt homosexuality threatens to compromise an essential aspect of American sentimental life: the camaraderie of the locker room and ball park, the good fellowship of the poker game and fishing trip, a kind of passionless passion at once gross and delicate, homoerotic in the boy's sense, possessing an innocence above suspicion.[91]

This eventuality is coded as threatening because it promises to feminize at least one of the two men. Fiedler's reading is so intertwined with postwar discourses on homosexuality as effeminacy that he is unable to conceive of any sexual male-male relationship that might exist outside of the active/passive, masculine/feminine

binaries of the heterosexual matrix. The implicit misogyny of
Fiedler's position thus informs his reaction to homosexuality—an
effeminophobic terror of the confrontation with the feminine. Rejecting homosexuality on this basis, Fiedler argues for a cautious
compromise, the negotiation of the feminine through heterosexuality. Whereas homosexuality (in Fiedler's spurious vision) can
only ever lead to the terrifying sight of a man becoming a woman,
heterosexuality allows a strict demarcation of sex/gender roles.[92]

The extent of Fiedler's sex/gender conservatism is even more
apparent in his essays on postwar youth culture. In "The Un-
Angry Young Men" (1958) and "The New Mutants" (1965), for
instance, Fiedler's attack on the beat and hippie movements of the
1950s and 1960s illustrates the extent of his distrust of the feminine.[93] Playing the American masculinist, lamenting the popularity of LSD (a drug of feminine insanity, he claims) and bemoaning
the student radicals' use of passive demonstration, Fiedler reveals
himself to be terrified of the potential feminization of a whole generation of American men as they become "more seduced than seducing, more passive than active."[94] He accuses both the beats and
the hippies of having feminized the American male through their
renunciation of masculine heterosexuality:

> Few of us, however, have really understood how the Beatle
> hairdo is part of a syndrome, of which high heels, jeans
> tight over the buttocks, etc., are other aspects, symptomatic
> of a larger retreat from masculine aggressiveness to female
> allure—in literature and the arts to the style called "camp."
> And fewer still have realized how that style, though the in-
> vention of homosexuals, is now the possession of basically
> heterosexual males as well, a strategy in their campaign to
> establish a new relationship not only with women but with
> their own masculinity. In the course of that campaign they
> have embraced certain kinds of gesture and garb, certain ac-
> cents and tones traditionally associated with females or fe-
> male impersonators.[95]

Fiedler's distrust of the "rejection of the ideal of marriage and
the family and of men who are men (i.e., Gary Cooper)" is star-

tlingly clear.[96] Women, Fiedler suggests, have been given the upper hand as the white males of English and American culture attempt to "assimilate into themselves (or even to assimilate themselves into) that otherness, that sum total of rejected psychic elements which the middle-class heirs of the Renaissance have identified with 'woman'."[97] Horrified by this, Fiedler notes the social repercussions of such a strategy: "the invention of the condom had at least left the decision to inhabit fatherhood in the power of males, its replacement by the 'loop' and the 'pill' has placed paternity at the mercy of the whims of women."[98]

Setting Burroughs' texts of the 1970s and 1980s against this reading of American literature and postwar youth culture, it is possible to trace the influence of Fiedler's work. The frontier landscape is frequently used by Burroughs as the backdrop to his attempts to establish a masculine queer identity, from Lee's gun-toting arguments with the Latin American populace in *Queer*, to the jungle and deserts of *The Wild Boys* and *Port of Saints*, the sea voyages of *Cities of the Red Night*, and, of course, the explicit use of the Western genre in *The Place of Dead Roads*. At moments such as the river journey of Farnsworth and Ali at the opening of *Cities of the Red Night*, Burroughs' appropriation of the frontier relationship trope seems particularly self-conscious (here the older black man, younger white boy motif of *Huckleberry Finn* is reversed).

Similarly, the flight of the male protagonist into the wilderness is one of the repeated motifs of Burroughs' Wild Boy and Red Night texts. His use of adolescent queer heroes inevitably subverts Fiedler's understanding of male sexuality. The exodus of American youth into the deserts of North Africa to join the Wild Boys is at once an update of the American literary trope and also a radical queering of its Fiedlerian exposition. While Fiedler remains unable to conceive of homosexuality as anything other than the feminization of the male subject, Burroughs reverses the hierarchy of subject positions that Fiedler's texts establish, in order to suggest that the real threat to the male-male relationships of the American canon is the heterosexual dominant.

In Burroughs' texts, the abandonment of the masculine idyll of the frontier does not initiate a journey towards experience, adulthood, and masculinity, but rather precedes the castration, conditioning, and feminization of the male subject as he is forced into the heterosexual order and made to confront the feminine Other. Burroughs' reworking of Fiedler's sex/gender politics suggests that masculine homosexuality is more pure, authentic, and natural than its heterosexual counterpart because it has excised all links with the feminine. If homosexuality does not have to signify the loss of masculine identity (but rather the validation of its uncorrupted, uncontaminated state), then Burroughs' vision of male communes is the next logical step for the tradition of American literature that Fiedler validates to take (promasculine, effeminophobic, misogynist). From this perspective, Burroughs emerges as Fiedler's homosexual, non-academic double: misogynist (in his fear of "feminine" passivity), homophobic (in his similar hatred of effeminacy and camp), and overtly concerned with remaining masculine. Burroughs' texts simply shift the balance of sexuality—a leap that Fiedler is unable and unwilling to take himself.

The doubleness of Burroughs and Fiedler emerges from the fact that Burroughs' vision of the masculine is always mediated through heterosexual understandings of sex and gender. Although he effectively queers Fiedler's reading of the male-male relationship, Burroughs never subverts the masculine identity that Fiedler champions. Aping Fiedler's effeminophobia and misogyny, Burroughs' discourse on masculinity could almost be described as an attempted "passing," for it occupies the same paradoxical position of similarity and difference that all acts of passing assume. Burroughs' texts thus oscillate between transgression and conformism; their pro-masculinist sentiments mirror Fiedler's own, but their queerness must always be opposed to the latter's heterosexuality.[99]

Significantly, Fiedler's reaction to Burroughs was frequently antagonistic and dismissive. In "The New Mutants," for instance, Fiedler ignores the effeminophobia of the novels and proclaims Burroughs "the chief prophet of the post-male, post-heroic world; [*Naked Lunch* is] no mere essay in heroin-hallucinated homosexual pornography—but a nightmare anticipation (in Science Fiction form) of post-Humanist sexuality."[100] So ingrained is Fiedler's understanding of homosexuality and effeminacy that he is blind to the fact that Burroughs is equally as terrified of the feminization of the male subject: "What is at stake from Burroughs to Bellow, Ginsberg to Albee, Salinger to Gregory Corso is a more personal transformation of the Western male."[101] As we have seen, Burroughs' texts consistently battle against any such transformation of the male subject.

Denied its position in the masculinist tradition of American literature, Burroughs' work of the 1970s and 1980s seems increasingly anxious to refute Fiedler's claims.[102] Drawing on the wider interest in American literary tropes of the frontier which Fiedler's work was just one instance of, Burroughs' texts play with themes of masculine identity, homosexuality, the savage/civilized binary, and interracial sex (which might even be considered miscegenation since so much of the gay sex in Burroughs' later work—the Wild Boy and Red Night texts in particular—is *reproductive*). As Eric Mottram suggests, the goal is a misogynist vision of masculine autonomy, with the Wild Boys as "a male revenge on women as dividers, a manic myth of singleness which is the foundation of the ultimate totalitarian unity and a state which at last fulfils the American dream of 'self-reliance.' The Wild Boys succeed in achieving male undivided confidence at last."[103]

Working through the cultural archetypes of the outlaw, gunfighter, and Native American—whether in an Old West setting or not—the texts resignify notions of the outlaw-hero, transforming him from masculine heterosexual to masculine homosexual. Sexuality is altered without affecting gender identification. The Wild Boys, streaming out of the wilderness like a Native American war party, and the Johnsons, represented in *The Place of Dead Roads* by the gun-toting gang "The Wild Fruits" (*PDR*, 94), are two examples of the outlaw turned queer. Inhabiting the border, the frontier, the wilderness, Burroughs' queer heroes offer an alternative to "petticoat government" in a manner that makes them the *gay* male heirs of Natty Bumppo/Chingachgook, Ishmael/Queequeg, and Huck/Jim.

Able to survive in a harsh environment that almost kills Green-field's troops, the gay outlaws are a reinscription not only of the nineteenth-century motif of the "bad boy"—the fear that American youth was backsliding into savagery—but also the Edenic qualities of the frontier myth.[104] Living outside of civilization, away from women and surrounded only by other boys/men, Burroughs' queer heroes are able to establish an idyllic life, a "retroactive Utopia" (*CRN*, xiv) in which the heterosexual dominant is ignored out of existence. See, for instance, the detailed acts of domestication that some of Burroughs' queer heroes go through with their lovers, moving through a pattern of consumer fantasy, self-reliance, and liberation as they purchase tools, make a home, and have sex (*CRN*, 255–265 and *PDR*, 46–57).

The Wild Boys and Johnsons can thus be read as an attempt to imagine an alternative male American experience of the frontier. The mores of puritan civilization are rejected in favor of an anti-Christian, anti-matriarchal, pro-homosexual historical revision in which the spiritual heritage of the Native Americans is preserved as part of a wider interaction between the two races. Kim's hatred of churches (and his general antipathy to all ideas of "decency" and "morality") in *The Place of Dead Roads* (*PDR*, 12) is symptomatic of this belief that America's spiritual potential has been fore-stalled.[105] The conflict between savage and civilized becomes apparent in the words that summon new Wild Boy recruits:

> Calling all boys of the earth we will teach you the secrets of magic control of wind and rain. Giver of winds is our name. We will teach you to ride the hurricanes [. . .] We will teach you control of animals and birds and reptiles [. . .] We will show you the sex magic that turns flesh to light. We will free you forever from the womb. (*PoS*, 94)

Increasingly, the subversion that Burroughs offers is not only of literature, but also of cultural history. Resignifying the cowboy as queer, Burroughs unleashes the repressed imagery of the frontier that heterosexual cultural history has held in check. The frontier becomes a place where men escape from women, not into some "innocent homosexual" relationship based on unconsummated homoerotic love, but rather into an all-male community based on explicit sexual desire and masculinity. Burroughs transforms the frontier into the site of queer pornography in a queering of America's mythic self-identity.[106] At the same time, he resignifies the frontier's role as part of the American promise of liberty, self-sufficiency, and independence, using it to offer freedom for marginalized social groups, both gay men and ethnic minorities. The frontier becomes truly utopian only through a radical revision of its concerns with gender and sexuality, and it is this revision that in turn illustrates just how corrupt the social promise of the American Dream has become; Burroughs' radicalism indicts the intolerance that masquerades as "democracy" (the contradictory nature of this, given his exclusion of women, effeminate gay men, and heterosexuals is never broached).[107]

In *The Place of Dead Roads*, Burroughs' most sustained use of the Western genre, he offers us the Wild Boy/Johnson hero Kim Carsons as a simultaneous resignification of American adolescence, the gunfighter, and the frontiersman. As David Glover notes, the novel is a combination of the Western with "elements of a modern *Bildungsroman*, a reprise of boyhood alienation from school and community."[108] Kim's fantasies replay the heterosexual relationships of classic pulp genres as queer—" 'No danger to body or soul can keep me from *her.*' (Kim will change her sex of course)" (*PDR*, 37)—and signal the transgressive resignification of the Western genre that Burroughs himself is undertaking. Kim, the lonely child excluded because of his sexuality, takes his revenge on a heterosexual society, challenging anyone who mocks his sexuality with violence (the fact that Kim Carsons is said to be the pen name of the writer "William Seward Hall" suggests the level of autobiographical involvement occurring here). As he kills two homophobic aggressors he feels "good—safer. Two enemies will never bother him again" (*PDR*, 74). This moment of violent self-determination marks the epitome of Burroughs' queer project; the sad, shy, gay child is transformed into a self-fulfilled, self-reliant (and thus masculine) individual.

What this clearly suggests, then, is the extent to which Burroughs' vision of the queer masculine is informed by—but also transforms—a discourse of masculinity that is explicitly American and heterosexual. By stealing the thunder of heterosexual masculinity within the "freedom" symbolized by the frontier, Burroughs suggests a radical revision of the definition of the American masculine, naturalizing homosexuality by adopting a position that styles the queer masculine as more natural than its heterosexual counterpart. As such, Burroughs' strategy is a transgressive appropriation that challenges the heterosexual monopoly on the masculine sphere by engaging with one of its most vocal postwar supporters.

It is this radical appropriation toward which the texts of the 1960s slowly build. Burroughs' attempt to "imagine it otherwise" is possible only after the extent of homosexual regulation has been outlined in the Nova trilogy. Searching for an alternative identity to that of effeminacy, Burroughs appropriates the heterosexual masculine in order to ensure that the gay subject will never again be forced into a gender-schizoid position. In this respect, the 1960s prove to be the formative period of Burroughs' queer politics; using the marginal discourses of Korzybski and Hubbard to oppose the American psychoanalytic establishment's understanding of homosexuality, Burroughs creates a deconditioned, "clear" gay identity that intersects the radical gay politics of Stonewall. Arguing for the authenticity and purity of this new identity, Burroughs engages with the 1960s' revision of the American canon undertaken by Fiedler in order to complete this process of naturalization. The delineation of this new queer identity stretches out of the 1960s into Burroughs' subsequent texts.

While Burroughs' queer appropriation never challenges the definition of the masculine per se (it is rather a subversion of heterosexual discourses on homosexuality), it always remains oppositional in its empowerment of the marginalized. Even as Burroughs' texts play out a reactionary masculinity based upon violence, misogyny, and effeminacy, heterosexual masculinists such as Fiedler are unable to accept their vision.[109] This paradoxical position of transgression and conformism is, as we will see in the following chapter, one of the central problems haunting any gay male appropriation of the masculine sphere.

CHAPTER THREE

POWERS OF PLEASURE

HYPERMASCULINITY, HEDONISM, AND SELF-MASTERY

"WHY NOT?"

In 1978 a young, relatively inexperienced filmmaker named Howard Brookner began to shoot a documentary film centered on Burroughs. Initially destined to be little more than a twenty-minute short film for his course at New York University's film school, Brookner's project slowly grew into a full-length documentary that was released in 1983. It remains the most complete cinematic testament to the Burroughs legend, perfectly capturing the artist's mythological persona with shots of him playing out scenes from his novels (as Doctor Benway, with a drag queen as his nurse) interspersed with a series of celebrity interviews and meetings (everyone from Allen Ginsberg to Francis Bacon to Tennessee Williams).

The Brookner film supposedly offers access to a very privileged realm, the man behind the myth. Filming Burroughs at home, with friends, with his son, and being interviewed, the film tries to present an image of the "real" Burroughs, a fly-on-the-wall documentary insight into the artist. Yet the subject himself consistently frustrates this desire. There is a strange ambivalence to Burroughs' character as it appears on-screen, an ambivalence that seems directly to challenge the viewer's response, a mercurial refusal to show us his "real" self. Seemingly bemused by the attention he is receiving, Burroughs appears nervous, shy, and reticent. Simultaneously, he provocatively taunts the camera, offering an image of himself as not only eccentric but also dangerous. Playing the poker-faced ironist he seems at times so impassive that he leaves himself open to the charge of not being ironic at all, but deadly serious.

One of the most startling and yet hysterically comic moments in the film emerges as Burroughs displays his arsenal to the filmmakers. Brandishing knives, blackjacks, and blowguns, he acts out bloodthirsty scenarios of attempted muggings and arbitrary acts of violence. If you don't like what someone is saying, he advises, you simply slit his throat with a hideously large machete, cutting him off in mid-sentence. But as Burroughs replaces his weapons in their bedside drawer, he offers the coup de grace, with his confession that, of course, he abhors violence. The juxtaposition of frail, aging writer and reactionary weapon-fetishist is unsettling, leaving the viewer uncertain how to interpret Burroughs' unusual brand of play.

This ambivalence informs a later moment in the film. Sitting in an armchair drinking, Burroughs turns his attention to the subject of gay rights:

> The gay state, that's what I'm aiming for and I want us to be as tough as the Israelis. Anybody fucks around with a gay any place in the world we're gonna be there. [*Cut*] Well we're a minority, why the hell don't we have the right to protect ourselves? [*Cut*] We have to build up an international organization with false passports, guns on arrival, the whole lot, the whole terrorist lot. We are a precarious minority, we gotta fight for our lives. Do you understand? If they oppose the gay state we're going to find them, track them down and kill them. [*Pauses to finish drink*] Why not?[1]

This is, without doubt, his most outspoken moment in the whole film. Overcoming his shyness—through a combination, one suspects, of being drunk and, more probably, stoned—Burroughs is obviously ad-libbing his speech. Yet at the same time, he sounds deadly serious in his partisan bias. Addressing the camera straight-on, Burroughs is deadpan as he outlines his belief that gay men should copy the political extremism being played out in the Middle East of the 1980s (the site of so many Reaganite anxieties).[2] Can this really be read as ironic?

In many respects, the hyperbolic-yet-deadpan extremism demonstrated in the "gay state" monologue is to be found throughout the Wild Boy and Red Night texts.[3] Burroughs' vision of the queer masculine revolution is always so effeminophobic, misogynist and heterophobic that it borders on undermining itself as an ironic parody of extremism (yet never quite does collapse in this manner). Potential seriousness and ironic play co-exist together to create ambivalent and problematic images of the queer masculine. While the violence against the feminine that the texts imagine is worryingly reactionary, the hyperbolic, fantasmatic play of such violence is frequently styled in a comic-book fashion. The issue is never resolved, leaving the texts to oscillate between utopian and dystopian positions.[4] This ambivalence is perhaps most vividly illustrated in Thomi Wroblewski's painting Wild Boys. In the painting, seven naked youths lie sprawled in what could be either sleep or death. Daubed across their bodies are symbols, predominantly those of oppression: swastikas, fighter planes, and dollar signs. Are these dead boys tattooed with the marks of their nemesis, or do the symbols represent their dreams, waiting to be actualized once they wake?[5]

Similarly, is Burroughs merely "imagining it otherwise" in an attempt to delineate what might occur if gay politics were to embrace the violent, extreme partisanship of other minority groups? Or is he expressing a very personal fantasy that is not intended to have any bearing on the sociopolitical reality to which it is a response? Throughout the 1960s, Ginsberg had tirelessly promoted Burroughs' potential role as a theorist of gay liberation (a typically magnanimous gesture given that it was actually Ginsberg himself who was at the forefront of the intersection between the Beats and sixties' gay politics): "Somebody has got to sit in the

British Museum again like Marx and figure out a new system; a new blueprint. Another century has gone, technology has changed everything so it's time for a new utopian system. Burroughs is almost working on it."[6]

"*Almost* working on it" is a particularly suggestive phrase, since it prefigures the dystopian elements of Burroughs' ultimate vision of queer revolution outlined in the Wild Boy and Red Night texts and, in addition, indicates the problematic relation between Burroughs' unique brand of queer fantasy and the sociopolitical reality it presumably opposes. Burroughs never quite offered a blueprint for queer social reorganization as Ginsberg had hoped. Rather than "theory," the texts offer a fantastic vision of revolution that mixes marginal pseudoscientific discourses with various popular genres to create a literature more adolescent than revolutionary— the queer boys' book.

In contrast to Ginsberg's hopes, Burroughs' own comments have occasionally indicated the possibility of excusing the texts' vision of the queer masculine as private, very personal fantasies, thereby absolving them of any sociopolitical responsibility. In an interview with *Rolling Stone* in the early 1970s, Burroughs was asked whether or not he considered the Wild Boys a projection or a prediction: "Is the book a projection? Yes. It's all simply a personal projection. A prediction? I hope so. Would I consider events similar to 'The Wild Boys' scenario desirable? Yes, desirable to me."[7] When asked to explain the exclusion of women from the Wild Boy groups, Burroughs refers to his interest in sex separatism, claiming "I certainly have no objections if lesbians would like to do the same."[8] The idea of a female commune, though, clearly holds little interest for him; as the interviewer enquires about the possibilities offered by lesbian communes, Burroughs sarcastically replies: "I don't know. They could mutate into birds, perhaps."[9]

Reading the texts in this manner allows us to consider the reactionary extremism of their fantasy as part of Burroughs' attempts to experiment with revolutionary desire. As he himself has often stated, "My work is a series of exploratory universes."[10] His use of the "Book of the Dead" format in *The Wild Boys* and in much of his post–1969 work seems in keeping with this deliberate use of fantasy.[11] Where better to pursue a blend of chaos/social critique/fantasy/reactionary politics than in a fiction which underlines its own fictional status? The fact that critics such as Skerl have seized upon the idea of "freedom through fantasy" in Burroughs' work (particularly the Red Night trilogy) is suggestive of the extent to which this kind of reading negates the more problematic elements of the texts.[12]

Indeed, Murphy has suggested that Burroughs' use of fantasy could be considered as a political strategy in itself. Discussing Deleuze and Guattari's distinction between radical and reactionary desire, Murphy argues that

> the investment of desire in and through fantasy can remain enmeshed in institutionalized, serialized ideology, but it can also itself produce group formations that are hostile (though not necessarily opposed, in the strict dialectical sense) to the given relations of production, class, and subjectivity, without necessarily presenting themselves as permanent replacements for those relations.[13]

This distinction between groups that are hostile (but not an alternative) to the dominant is particularly useful with regard to Burroughs' texts: "The construction of viable subject-group fantasies and the consequent fantasmatic production of revolutionary groups, is the burden of Burroughs' writing in *The Wild Boys* and later works."[14] However, the issue of ambivalence returns; Murphy suggests that the Wild Boys are always characterized by "their paradoxical conservatism, their preservation of the opposing world order in the specular structure of their own negation of it."[15] As such, the revolutionary gesture of the boys becomes trapped in a familiar postmodern impasse.

In order for the texts to be "amodern" as Murphy claims they have to overcome the characteristic double bind of the postmodern position. Murphy argues that their experimental play with the revolutionary gesture is an attempt to work through the problematic desires that inform all opposition to the dominant culture. Burroughs' texts do not offer "representative desires, samples of revolutionary desire to be copied" but instead reveal "the unconscious conflicts within the very form of the subject that can undo whatever revolutionary potential that subject may hold in its preconscious libidinal investments."[16] Murphy goes on to suggest that in the Red Night trilogy, Burroughs (like Deleuze and Guattari) attempts to counter these conflicts by producing "topographies of deterritorialization, anatomies of desire, taxonomies of fragmented part-subjects that can serve as touchstones for an affirmative reconstitution of desiring-production."[17] Negotiating the *aporia* created by the texts' radical/reactionary ambivalence, Murphy radicalizes Burroughs in terms of schizophrenia, "deterritorialization," and becoming.

In this chapter I want to consider Burroughs' ambivalent fantasies of revolution in terms of the heroes' queer status. Since critics have predominantly passed over the sexuality of the heroes, the possible role of fantasy as a mode of queer self-fashioning and resistance has not been broached.[18] In approaching the texts from a queer/gender perspective, it will become apparent that their ambivalent interplay between radical and reactionary positions is always intimately tied to their appropriation of the masculine sphere. Contextualizing the Wild Boy and Red Night novels against the sociohistorical reality of the appropriations of masculinity that were occurring in the gay community during the 1970s and early 1980s—in particular the clone scene—it will be seen that the texts' vision of masculine communities in which women and effeminate men have no place has a historical context. Furthermore, the juxtaposition with the clone scene will highlight the extent to which the double bind of masculine appropriation played out in the texts is one that has been frequently addressed in both queer theory and practice.

Significantly, this queer/gender perspective will suggest that if the texts do manage to overcome the radical/reactionary paradox that their heroes play out, it is not in favor of the radical—as Murphy argues—but rather the reactionary. Like many commentators on the clone scene Burroughs is wary of valorizing the hedonistic pleasure that the queer appropriation of the masculine encourages. As we will see, the texts repeatedly style such pleasure as feminizing. Thus the negative representation of the queer heroes is not an ironic undercutting of their violent masculinity, but rather a result of their *not being masculine enough*. The gay subject who allows himself to be overwhelmed by his desires is re-feminized, thereby losing his hard-won autonomy. In an attempt to salvage the political potential of their heroes, the texts outline an extension of the Nova trilogy's deconditioning program in order to inoculate them against the dangers of hedonism.

This demonization of pleasure is in stark contrast to the aims of queer theory in the post-AIDS period. Using Foucault's model of modern queer "ascesis" as a comparison, it will become clear that Burroughs' vision of training and deconditioning is antithetical to queer theory's understanding of the political possibilities of pleasure in transforming the subject. While queer theory moved toward undermining the masculine model of identity during the 1980s (through employing "feminizing" strategies of pleasure), Burroughs' texts fall increasingly out of step with the times, still searching for stability even when queer politics begins to demand the destabilization of the male subject. It is this continuing quest for the masculine—as opposed to the "deterritorializations" pursued by Foucault and others—that indicates that at best we must read the texts as trapped in a double bind (centered on gender), and at worst as reactionary expressions of a very problematic form of masculinity.

QUEER APPROPRIATIONS:
MASCULINITY IN THEORY AND PRACTICE

The appropriation of the masculine sphere by gay men was, as we have seen, part of a sociological trend that began during the 1950s in response to the heterosexual dominant's discourses on effeminacy. Burroughs' novels are illustrative of this rejection of the effeminate paradigm and the search for new, masculine models of identification that followed it. Indeed, in *The Wild Boys* he establishes one of the first American literary images of the explicitly gay and masculine man. The freedom to imagine new forms of gay identity was a direct result of the gay liberation movement's commitment to a vocal, direct, and uncompromising political discourse in the post-Stonewall period.

Rejecting the secrecy and reticence that the McCarthy years had stamped on the movement when it first emerged during the 1950s, gay liberation adopted a radical program that sought to end the social regulation of homosexuality and encourage gay self-acceptance (in contrast to the predominant confusion and self-loathing of the 1950s). As the 1970s drew to a close, the benefits of such political outspokenness were being enjoyed by the gay community and resulted in the emergence of a new model of masculine-identified homosexuality, the "clone." As Martin P. Levine suggests, the clone scene of the late 1970s and early 1980s represented a historical shift in gay subjectivity that had been gradually developing since the Mattachine years: "When the dust of gay liberation had settled, the doors to the closet were opened, and out popped the clone. Taking a cue from movement ideology, clones modeled themselves upon traditional masculinity and the self-fulfillment ethic [. . .] Accepting me-generation values, they searched for fulfillment in anonymous sex, recreational drugs, and hard partying."[19]

Pleasure and self-acceptance were the main forces behind the rejection of camp (which was considered, as Levine remarks, "more about self-hatred than self-acceptance").[20] Gender deviance was frowned upon and replaced by rigid conformity to a well-defined set of signifiers such as "manly" physical attributes and adherence to a fashion style modeled on "the male icon of the Marlboro cowboy/body-builder." The clones sought "a hard, muscular 'butch' image and wore flannel check shirts, button-up Levis, work boots, short haircuts and moustaches."[21] At the center of this strictly defined, physical identity were the sadomasochistic (S/M) practices that characterized much of the clones' sex. Masculine fashions and appearance required new forms of sexual pleasure, as Levine suggests: "Hot sex. Rough sex. Gay sex. But decidedly *masculine* sex.

The clone 'took it like a man' and he also 'gave' it like a man. It was in their sexual conduct—both the cruise and the contact itself—that gay men demonstrated most convincingly that they were 'real men' after all."[22] S/M—of various degrees of intensity—gendered this sexual contact through a "masculine erotic script" that included bondage, urophilia, anal fisting, humiliation, light spanking, role playing, and erotic fantasies staged around hypermasculine themes (including the gym, the military, and the police).[23]

The links between the clones and Burroughs' queer heroes seem readily apparent, although it is important to note that the Wild Boys diverge from the clones in two respects: their physical attributes (which are stereotypically adolescent, as opposed to the hard, gym-pumped bodies of the clones), and their lack of interest in S/M (Burroughs consistently refused to style S/M as a subversive mode of gay sex).[24] These differences aside, the overriding link between the clones and the Wild Boys/Johnsons is their united desire to overthrow an oppressive dominant through the appropriation of that dominant's most carefully guarded prize: the masculine. Burroughs' heroes are cousins of the clone, since both are born out of the rejection of the effeminate paradigm during the 1950s and 1960s and the sociopolitical liberation symbolized by Stonewall. Like the clones, the boys are obsessed with the subcultural markers that indicate masculine status. Wild Boy identity is based upon adherence to a new fashion of muscles, weapons, and jockstraps. In addition, they are, of course, all "clones" themselves, making them a fitting symbol of the clone scene's demand for homogeneity (a demand that, as in Burroughs' texts, rested on the exclusion of women and effeminate gay men).[25]

The communities that were established by this desire for homogeneity brought about a radical reorganization of the gay social sphere. The clones created wide-ranging social networks, new interactions of groups and individuals that transformed the social order of the urban gay communities of the 1970s. Levine notes the way in which clone culture centered on alternative, same-sex families, entry into which was regulated through a process of initiation or "socialization" and through "mentoring and role modeling." The clones' creation of a veritable queer family—replete with "Kid Brothers," "Big Brothers," "Best Friends," and "Gay Mothers"—is remarkably similar to the queer communities that Burroughs' texts in part establish.[26]

The radical social reorganization undertaken by the clones was, however, not enough to convince many on the gay scene that they were a progressive force. The clones have always occupied a problematic position in queer theory and history because of their appropriation of the masculine. As Jamie Gough notes, responses to gay masculinization have generally focused on either moralistic condemnation or bland acceptance.[27] Whether condemned because of their supposed "hedonism," lack of political commitment, and replication of negative, aggressive modes of (heterosexual) masculinity, or marginalized as little more than a playful joke, the clones have consistently been denied a radical position.

Dennis Altman's reading of the clone scene and its participants in his essay "What Changed in the Seventies?" is the seminal critique of the emerging macho style. For Altman, the clone represents not only the gay apotheosis of the consumerist impetus that was becoming increasingly widespread throughout the 1970s, but also the end of gay radicalism. He suggests that gay macho is an obvious product of "the developing ideology of consumerism, hedonism and spectacle that derives from modern capitalism."[28] Such a vision explicitly contrasts the "hedonism that seems the hallmark of the new male homosexual" with the post-Stonewall era of political activism:

> Homosexuality is now signified by theatrically "macho" clothing (denim, leather, and the ubiquitous key rings) rather than by feminine style drag; the new "masculine" homosexual is likely to be non-apologetic about his sexuality, self-assertive, highly consumerist and not at all revolutionary, though prepared to demonstrate for gay rights. This one might note, is far removed from the hopes of the early seventies liberationists who believed in a style that was androgynous, non-consumerist and revolutionary.[29]

The guilty pleasures of the clones—their political apathy, consumerism, hedonism, and narcissism—are repudiated by Altman as a regressive set of desires that are complicit with the larger (heterosexual) patriarchal culture. Clearly influenced by the intersection of gay culture and the feminist movement (he cites both Millett and de Beauvoir), Altman argues that the main political goal of the 1980s ought to be the "breakdown of the dichotomy homo/hetero in both discourse and practice."[30] Such an aim requires the rejection of the carefully proscribed homosexual identity of the clones in favor of embracing the "greater fluidity of sexual desire among many women" that resists the temptation to transform specific sexual behavior into a rigid identity.[31]

This attack on the clones has continued in different guises ever since. Consider, for instance, Colin Spencer's recent discussion of the clone scene. Adopting a distinctly moral tone, Spencer suggests that the clones' aggressive, "rough" sex was "surely only another form of self-punishment. It was the gay aping the very worst excesses of the chauvinistic sexist male, treating his sexual partner with insensitivity and cruelty."[32] The phrase "worst excesses" is typical of such warnings about the dangers of the hypermasculine style. Seymour Kleinberg focuses on the main point of contention as he suggests that the central message of the macho bar world is that "manliness is the only real virtue; other values are contemptible. And manliness is not some philosophical notion or psychological state; it is not even morally related to behavior. It lies exclusively in the glamorization of physical strength."[33]

In many respects, the main suspicion about the clone scene has been the fact that it is based upon an appropriation of a mode of male identity that has always been a heterosexual preserve. Commentators on the clone scene frequently note the clear links between the masculine styles that the clones adopted and those of the heterosexual dominant. The intersection of feminism and gay liberation (particularly during the late 1970s) meant that all modes of masculinity (whether gay or straight) were problematized because of the association between "the masculine" and patriarchal forms of oppression. Unsympathetic commentators on the clones strengthened this connection by suggesting (as Spencer does) that gay macho was merely an attempt to imitate the heterosexual masculine realm.

Interestingly, some commentators have attempted to reclaim the masculine appropriations of the clone scene by employing one of feminist theory's discursive templates. Drawing on gender theory's post-structuralist understandings of parody and play, some male queer theorists have discussed the gay masculine style as a parodic subversion of heterosexual masculinity. From this perspective, the masculinity of the clones becomes yet another kind of drag; the clone, the leatherman, and the macho man highlight the *lack* of an essential masculinity. In this manner, the appropriation of the masculine becomes a subversive strategy that ironically undermines that mode of gender identity through hyperbolic parody. By appropriating the symbols of masculinity, the gay man works towards exposing the masculine position as a mere mask. As Richard Dyer argues:

> By taking the signs of masculinity and eroticizing them in a blatantly homosexual context, much mischief is done to the security with which "men" are defined in society, and by which their power is secured. If that bearded, muscular beer-drinker turns out to be a pansy, how ever are you going to know the "real" men anymore?[34]

In the words of Healy, writing on gay skinheads, "What gay masculinity reveals is the masquerade of *all* maleness."[35] Significantly, however, much feminist gender theory—such as Judith Butler's work—has remained notably silent on gay male macho identities, basing its discussions of performativity on the drag queen, camp, and butch/femme lesbian identities. This is suggestive of the extent to which masculine identities are considered too closely tied to the dominant to be truly subversive.

Leo Bersani has voiced many doubts about the possibility of reading masculine appropriation as a political strategy of gender subversion. While agreeing that such subversive intentions are commendable, Bersani suggests that their effect is largely negligible, since their play is performed outside of the (heterosexual) mainstream: "It is difficult to know how 'much mischief' can be done by a style that straight men see—if indeed they see at all—from a car window as they drive down Folsom Street."[36] Even when gay macho style receives heterosexual recognition, Bersani believes that it does little to upset the heterosexual man's own unconscious masculine "performance" since gay macho is always excluded from heterosexual understandings of "masculinity." The straight man "recognizes in the gay-macho style a *yearning* toward machismo that, very conveniently for the heterosexual, makes the leather queen's forbidding armor and warlike manners a *per*version rather than *sub*version of real maleness."[37]

Since homosexuality is always defined in terms of effeminacy, the concept of a masculine homosexual is, in the discourses of straight society, an oxymoron. The appropriation of the masculine by the gay community serves to underline the extent of gay exclusion from the dominant. The gay man who claims to be "masculine" instantly violates that masculine identification when he expresses (gay) sexual desire. Masculinity and gay sex can never be equated, trapping the gay man in a paradoxical position: possessing the anatomical sex of a man and identifying with the masculine gender, the macho gay man is at once a part of the masculine dominant and forever excluded from it because of his sexual desires. Every attempt he makes to include himself within the discourses of masculinity leads to his violation of the whole concept of "masculinity" as he becomes a perversion of its very (heterosexual) definition. As such, masculine-identified male homosexuality, as Bersani suggests, "has always manifested itself as a highly specific blend of conformism and transgression."[38] Elsewhere, Bersani claims that this is because gay men "are an oppressed group not only sexually drawn to the power-holding sex, but also belonging to it themselves."[39] This, without doubt, is the reason for Butler's reluctance to engage with gay macho. Its "specific blend of conformity and transgression" is not to be found in either lesbian butch or gay male drag.

The unique position of the masculine-identified gay man is one that Earl Jackson Jr. has theorized in terms of what he calls "double articulation" and "negating affirmation." Jackson suggests that

"Gay men as men live dually within the systems of meaning of the dominant order and within their own constitutive transgressions and betrayals of that order."[40] Falling somewhere between "phallic citizenship and sodomitical forfeiture," the gay man's affirmation of the masculine is always negated by the nature of his sexuality.[41] This double bind is ultimately the paradox that underlines Burroughs' queer vision, leaving the texts to oscillate between radical and reactionary positions. In the Wild Boy and Red Night texts Burroughs offers a vision of the masculine that is similar to Jackson's understanding of negating affirmation. In pursuing the masculine, the queer heroes reach toward increasingly extreme forms of that gender, yet they are constantly denied a masculine position. However, this denial does not signify Burroughs' own dissatisfaction with the masculine model *per se*. Rather, it marks the return of his problematic fears about "feminization" through pleasure, co-option, and possession.

QUEERING THE NEGATIVE: HEDONISM, CO-OPTION, AND FEMINIZATION

The appropriation of the masculine by Burroughs' heroes always centers on two factors: (revolutionary) violence and the exclusion of all those who are considered feminine. The Wild Boy and Red Night texts present the revolution as the first step toward the creation of a mythical frontier culture, a monosexual environment in which masculine self-reliance and homosexuality predominate. The novels repeatedly style this as utopian. The Wild Boy communes are futuristic social groupings that seek to undermine a post-apocalyptic heterosexual dominant through Viet Cong–like guerrilla warfare. The Johnson networks and pirate communes of the Red Night trilogy are even more fantastic challenges to the primacy of the heterosexual dominant as a result of their status as retroactive utopias.

Captain Mission's pirate community in *Cities of the Red Night* is established in the eighteenth century, in the historical moment before the liberal principles it supports are subverted by the "windy lies in the mouths of politicians" in the aftermath of the French and American revolutions (*CRN*, xiv). In *The Place of Dead Roads* and *The Western Lands*, the Johnson family are similarly pledged to support a frontier ethic of self-reliance, independence and liberty.[42] Their good offices are challenged by the evil Venusians and their human confederates, who seek to extend the capitalist order and line their own pockets by doing away with deregulated frontier culture. The Johnsons represent "Potential America" (*PDR*, 154), a country that could have existed had capitalism been halted, and swear to "fight any extension of federal authority and support States' Rights. We will resist any attempt to penalize or legislate against the so-called victimless crimes . . . gambling, sexual behavior, drinking, drugs" (*PDR*, 98).

This presentation of queer self-determination as utopian is, however, consistently challenged by the texts themselves. Co-existing alongside the positive images of the heroes is an ironic awareness of the extent to which their brand of revolutionary violence is problematic, unappealing, and ultimately complicit with the dominant heterosexual culture. The guiding principle behind the texts is the implicit assumption that "It is a familiar pattern: *the oppressed love the oppressors and cannot wait to follow their example.*"[43] This deliberate undermining of the revolution is of particular importance since it marks the problematization of one of the two qualities that define the queer heroes as men. Burroughs' vision of the masculine is always centered on violence and the exclusion of the feminine. By undermining the revolutionary violence employed by his heroes, Burroughs seems to be critiquing the masculine identity they so desperately want to appropriate by erecting a strangely moral discourse on the intersection of violence, masculinity, and pleasure.

Significantly, this distrust of the queer heroes had one important precursor in a brief passage in *Naked Lunch*. Not long after the effeminophobic strictures of the Talking Asshole routine, Burroughs presents us with Captain Everhard and his Huntsmen. Knowingly based on the small, internal subsection of the gay community of the

1950s (a forerunner of the 1970s clone scene) that was overtly concerned with leather fetishes and macho identities, the Huntsmen
make only a fleeting appearance in the novel, taking up just three
paragraphs (*NL*, 130). They prepare for the evening's entertain-
ment—"a purple-assed baboon stick from motorcycles"—by in-
stalling themselves in the Swarm Bar, "a hang-out for elegant
pansies," where they "strut about with imbecile narcissism in black
leather jackets and studded belts, flexing their muscles for the fags
to feel. They all wear enormous falsie baskets. Every now and then
one of them throws a fag to the floor and pisses on him" (*NL*, 130).

The repetition of the novel's characteristic conflation of the fag
and the baboon is clear enough; both are victims of the Huntsmen's virile, aggressive masculinity. Yet at the same time, the text
seems intent on mocking these macho men, clearly styling their
"imbecile narcissism" and "bestial laughter" as unattractive. This is
perplexing, since Burroughs' effeminophobia would suggest that
Captain Everhard and his Huntsmen are logically heroes, proto-
types of the later Wild Boys, rather than villains.[44] Are we to take
this criticism of the macho Huntsmen as a comment on their
replication of a heterosexual-based social organization (which occurs as they become the site of their effeminate hosts' desire,
thereby repeating the masculine/feminine hierarchies of gay relationships that we saw in *Queer*), or is it to be read as a commen-
tary on their seemingly mindless violence? By the time of the
post-Stonewall texts, of course, such violence on the part of Burroughs' gay men has become a consistent theme of the novels (although it is important to note the shift of emphasis from
effeminophobic violence to militant direct action against the heterosexual dominant) and is consistently styled as problematic at
the same time as it is fetishized. Violence becomes a guilty desire,
a dangerous pleasure.

The violence that characterizes the hypermasculine is frequently
presented as problematic as it becomes more than just a means to
an end. In *The Place of Dead Roads*, Kim's use of violence threatens
his autonomous status as he becomes hooked on its supposed pleasures: "Killing can become an addiction. Kim wakes up thin. He's

gotta have it one way or another" (*PDR*, 80). Eventually forcing one of the locals into a gunfight, Kim receives the fix he needs; the link between violence and sexual gratification is made clear: "YESSSSSSSS, Kim's 44 Russian leaps into his hand. He can feel his way into the kid's stomach with the slug and the kid grunts, doubling forward, a grunt you can feel. Is it gooooood. Now the kid slumps to the floor in a *delicious* heap" (*PDR*, 80).[45] Such a lack of self-control is explicitly styled by Burroughs as a result of his hero's adolescence—"One is not serious at seventeen" (*PDR*, 277)—underscoring the fact that the pursuit of pleasure for its own sake is a result of inadequate training, preparation, education.

In the second book of the Wild Boy tetralogy, *Exterminator!*, the link between violence and self-gratification is made clear. Revolution is the driving impetus behind most of the novel's narratives. This is succinctly illustrated in the story "Twilight's Last Gleamings" (*EX*, 85–92) which concerns "a conspiracy to blow up a train carrying nerve gas" (*EX*, 85) dreamt up by a host of America's malcontents, among them the gay Audrey, the lesbian Miss Longridge, the Chinese Mr. Lee, and the black Jones. The terrorists plan to exterminate the majority of the population of the United States; however, it is soon revealed that the motivating factor in this act of violence is predominantly self-gratification rather than political ends. Ignoring their leader's warning that there is "[s]uch a thing as too much fun" (*EX*, 90), the revolutionaries indulge their murderous desires with results that alternate between disturbing and comic:

> In a deserted roadhouse Audrey rapes a young sailor at gunpoint while Lee impassively films the action [. . .] Miss Longridge rapes two female hitchhikers. And then, stark naked, she kills them with a baseball bat. (*EX*, 89)
> Audrey is restrained at gun point from mass rape of a Boy Scout troop. (*EX*, 90)

The revolutionaries fail to complete their terrorist project; since they have so many rapes and murders to their credit—"leaving a trail like a herd of elephants" (*EX*, 90)—the FBI effortlessly catches them. The moral of the story is clear: the search for self-gratification seduces the revolutionary subject away from his political goals, as the act of revolution becomes more important than the goals themselves. The train carrying the nerve gas does explode, but by accident, killing off Audrey and friends along with everyone else.

This moral reading of violence and pleasure is characteristic of Burroughs' post-Stonewall novels. It is as if Burroughs is arguing that the increased social freedom of gay men must be properly theorized and policed if it is to produce a new social order. If the Wild Boys remain wild once the revolutionary moment has passed and upheaval has become social transformation, then the utopian potential they possess may well be squandered. The difficulty of the boys effecting this change in themselves is, of course, underlined by the fact that their wildness is part of their identity. In keeping with his frequent use of the tropes of the frontier, Burroughs styles this renunciation of the political in favor of pleasure in terms of degeneration—one that sees the Wild Boys and Johnsons transformed into both beasts and fascists.

As James Grauerholz has suggested, "It is not the unchained sexuality of the wild boys that is most distinctive, but their animal freedom."[46] The Wild Boys are repeatedly styled as animals, and bestial imagery is frequently used in the descriptions of them and their sexual acts. In *Port of Saints* this use of animal imagery reaches its zenith as the Wild Boys descend into battle against the lesbian commandos, the Darlings: "[The Wild Boys] throw back their heads and howl and the howl blurs into a snarl that snaps the head forward, flashing teeth and burning eyes, and all around dogs stir and bristle and run in packs" (*PoS*, 104).[47] The mutation of the boys into dogs, then later, leopards, cats, iguanas, bats, and all manner of other creatures seems on one level to be a negative representation of their desires and violence: "The boys are coming now teeth bare eyes burning hair bristling . . . red animal hair sprouts all over their bodies canines tear through bleeding gums a boy shivers and kick asshole vibrating as a tail sprouts out his spine . . ." (*EX*, 16). Such scenes frequently recur throughout the Wild Boy and Red Night texts.

The stylization of the heroes as fascists is similarly disturbing. In *Cities of the Red Night,* Krup's "Hitler *Jungen* boys, one looking just like another, all with rosy cheeks and yellow hair" (*CRN,* 213), are reminiscent of Burroughs' Wild Boys.[48] In *The Place of Dead Roads,* allusions to fascism are taken even further; Kim Carsons' hatred of "civilization"—that is, the religious, prohibitive, feminine "law" of the frontier towns he inhabits—leads him to fantasize a program of "Shit Slaughter," a mass purgation of all who oppose his brand of queer self-reliance. In the story he writes—entitled "The Baron Says These Things" (*PDR,* 29–37)—the "theory and practice of Shiticide" is outlined: "Boys will be organized into Shit Slaughter troops . . . the S.S., with two phosphorescent spitting cobras at their lapels" (*PDR,* 33). Kim then goes on to compose a marching song for these combat troops: "*Wenn scheissen Blut von Messer spritz / Dehn geht schon alles gut /* (When shit blood spurts from the knife / Then everything is good)" (*PDR,* 34).[49] The rest of the novel charts Kim's use of a variety of weapons and tactics—from smallpox viruses to more virulent plagues and cloning—to effect this purge. Notably, he describes his pistol as a "Sperm Gun," since "Spitting death seed, it would father the Super Race" (*PDR,* 106).

Such negative images are consolidated in the presentation of Kim Carsons himself, whose lack of appeal assumes epic-comic proportions: "Kim is a slimy, morbid youth of unwholesome proclivities with an insatiable appetite for the extreme and the sensational. [. . .] He wallows in abominations, unspeakable rites, diseased demon lovers [. . .] In short, Kim is everything a normal American boy is taught to *detest.* He is evil and slimy and *insidious*" (*PDR,* 16). Explicitly linked with contagion—"He loved to read about diseases, rolling and savoring the names on his tongue" (*PDR,* 18)—Kim is intent on embracing all that the dominant culture styles as negative, using the dominant's discourse on homosexuality as filthy and diseased for his own ironic purposes.[50] That the novel appeared during the height of the AIDS crisis is particularly relevant.

Are we supposed to read these negative stylizations as part of an ironic strategy of reversal, a critique of the masculine, or as something else? Kendra Langetieg has suggested that Kim represents a very deliberate (queer) strategy: "affirming society's negative construction of homosexuality as disorder, rather than being victimized or overpowered by it, turns the cultural bias against the 'outlaw' on its head—a fatal strategy that transforms the homosexual's mythic toxicity and problematic exile into a paradoxical means of empowerment and resistance."[51] Such ironic employment of the negative is, of course, characteristic of a long-established queer strategy of the "reverse discourse" in which, as Foucault famously remarked, homosexuality begins "to speak in its own behalf, to demand that its legitimacy or 'naturality' be acknowledged, often in the same vocabulary, using the same categories by which it was medically disqualified."[52]

As such, the negativity of Burroughs' heroes could be read as a challenge to the dominant's own construction of homosexuality as negative. For instance, in *The Place of Dead Roads*, Burroughs quotes the opinion of Reverend Braswell writing in the *Denver Post*: "Homosexuality is an abomination to God and should never be recognized as a legal human right any more than robbery or murder" (*PDR*, 155). The text challenges these sentiments by explicitly exaggerating the extent to which its queer heroes are outlaws. In *Cities of the Red Night*, Burroughs parodies H. P. Lovecraft as he dedicates the novel to "the Ancient Ones, to the Lord of Abominations, *Humwawa*, whose face is a mass of entrails, whose breath is the stench of dung and the perfume of death [. . .]" (*CRN*, xvii). Similarly, in *The Place of Dead Roads*, Kim performs sex magic and black magic rituals in defiance of the small-town community that he inhabits (*PDR*, 19). Glamorizing homosexuality's negative construction as abomination and crime, Burroughs reveals just how homophobic the comments of religious men like Braswell are and enacts an ironic undermining of their power.

However, the understanding of the relation between negativity and empowerment that Langetieg develops with regard to the use of "toxicity" in the Red Night trilogy is not a sufficient template for an understanding of Burroughs' negative stylization of the queer heroes throughout the Wild Boy and Red Night texts. What I want to suggest is that the representation of the heroes as fascists and beasts is actually best understood in relation to the gender dynamics of the texts. Burroughs' ironic undermining of his heroes does not indicate a critique of the masculine but is instead a gender-based view of their failure as men. By allowing themselves to be overwhelmed by pleasure and thus controlled by their desires, the queer heroes repeatedly fall short of Burroughs' masculine ideal. The supreme Burroughsian male is the subject who is autonomous and self-possessed. The Wild Boy and Johnson heroes are rarely able to sustain this position.

As such, this queer/gender perspective on the texts offers a possible reorientation of the established critical view of Burroughs as a countercultural sixties radical. While heterosexual readings of the texts have consistently emphasized their anti-establishment thematics, a queer/gender reading must challenge the extent to which Burroughs can be read as a radical author. In this respect, what emerges is a vision of Burroughs' queer politics that has to negotiate the fact that the texts refuse to repudiate or undermine the fantasy of masculine appropriation. As a result, any queer reading must either explain the texts' undiluted misogyny, effeminophobia, and heterophobia as ironic or consider them indicative of the texts' reactionary desires. This is undoubtedly why Burroughs has been excluded from discussions of gay literature for so long. It is not that his texts are too extreme, "pornographic," or adolescent in their fantasies; rather, their exclusion is a result of their support for an un-ironic, masculine model of gay identity that (despite the texts' comedy) is too problematic and reactionary to be easily negotiated.

During the 1980s, some queer theorists sought to radicalize gay appropriations of the masculine by charting the manner in which certain sexual practices characteristic of the gay macho scene (S/M in particular) actually brought about a feminization of the participants. Such arguments suggested that gay macho could be read as a subversion of the masculine that aimed to create a new masculine/feminine subjectivity distinct from the heterosexual model. In comparison Burroughs' texts of the 1970s and 1980s remained committed to a very narrow conception of the masculine that denied its transformation by excluding women, and effeminate gay men. What is so characteristic of the Burroughsian paradigm is the paranoia that accompanies masculine appropriation. The queer heroes of Burroughs' texts are always threatened by the return of the feminine, a fatal event against which they have constantly to guard.

In the Wild Boy and Red Night texts this re-feminization and subsequent loss of autonomy is a result of the heroes' pursuit of pleasure. The Huntsmen of *Naked Lunch* are illustrative of this; although their hypermasculine bodies ought to denote stable gender identification, the episode actually sees their masculine forms subverted into femininity. The Huntsmen are implicitly undermined by the text's description of them. Everhard and his followers are coded as masculine pretenders because they wear "enormous falsie baskets" (*NL*, 130). Comparisons with the "sex-changed Liz athlete" (*NL*, 63) of an earlier passage—who wears a "leopard skin jockstrap with enormous falsie basket" and stands about "smiling stupidly and flexing her huge muscles" (*NL*, 64)—are quite obviously meant to be drawn.

Like the lesbian, the Huntsmen are merely pretending to be "men," adopting signifiers (the leather jackets, belts, motorcycles, and codpieces) of virile masculinity but not actually achieving such status. Interestingly, the baboon hunt that they are gathered for ends in a bloodbath as the baboons—so frequently a caricature of the fag, as we have seen—surprise the hunters by fighting back. Captain Everhard's dubious reputation as a masculine pretender is obviously based upon more than just the rumor about his "palming a jockstrap in a game of strip poker" while in the Queen's 69th regiment (*NL*, 130).[53] Burroughs' heroes diverge from the hypermasculinity of the huntsmen's bodies, approaching a more subtle, adolescent masculine paradigm: firm, youthful bodies with stomachs of "flexible marble" and a graceful boyishness (*PDR*, 42). However, this does not rescue the boy heroes from feminization in pleasure.

Kim's addiction to violence, the Wild Boys' thirst for "wild" destruction, and the Johnsons' plans for "Shit Slaughter" all signify the beginnings of a hedonistic excess that threatens to overwhelm the male subject. Eventually, even the queer revolution itself is jeopardized. As Joe the Dead complains with reference to Kim, unregulated pleasure can be disastrous and feminizing: "Sooner or later he would have precipitated a senseless disaster with his histrionic faggotries."[54] Thus pleasure becomes an external force that, like the effeminate paradigm, threatens to rob the subject of his autonomy. As the queer revolution proceeds untrammeled, violent excess leads to the end of the utopian possibilities of the conflict as the participants become beasts and fascists. Such loss of autonomy marks the re-feminization of the boys as they compromise their hard-won masculine status.

Such an understanding of pleasure's relation to gender is part of a long-established discourse on pleasure, desire, and masculinity. As Theo van der Meer suggests, in the early modern period, masculinity was idealized in terms of restraint and self-control:

> By giving in to hedonism and in particular to sodomy, a man violated his body over which he was not sovereign but only reigned as God's steward, and which he was ordained to keep clean; he also violated the natural hierarchy between male and female that ordained him to sobriety. In short, he would become like a woman, insatiable, that is, unmanly. In that sense we can understand a seventeenth-century observation that men who engaged in same-sex behavior suffered from an "effeminate disease."[55]

A parallel exists between this concept of an "effeminate *disease*" and Burroughs' presentation of gender and viral invasion. If the queer subject is not properly inoculated, then his masculine identification may be quickly usurped by the effeminate infection to which his love of pleasure exposes him. Such infection—or "possession"—is, as ever, the mark of the subject's feminization. In *The Wild Boys*, the link between pleasurable excess and invasion is made quite plain as Audrey races through an Eastern market on a wagon, tipping over the stalls: "He was possessed by an ugly spirit of destroying speed." Such recklessness can be disastrous: "He caught sight of a large cobra by the side of the ramp and swerved to run over it. Writhing fragments flew up in his face. He screamed" (*WB*, 169). Possession marks not only the point at which the subject loses his right to masculinity but also (the two are intimately connected) the moment when he relinquishes his autonomous status.

Burroughs' fears about the intersection of masculinity and pleasure even leads him to employ a discourse that is a disturbing echo of right-wing responses to AIDS. The Hanging Fever episode in *Cities of the Red Night* conflates libertinism, *fin de siècle* Wildean decadence, and the clone scene. The revels of Tamaghis are a self-conscious parody of the clone scene's hedonism. S/M scenes—both real and imagined—are endlessly played out, drugs are freely available, and the revelers are offered a choice of "massage parlors, Turkish baths, sex rooms, hanging studios, cubicle restaurants, booths selling incense, aphrodisiacs and aromatic herbs" (*CRN*, 175). Such pleasures, though, lead to viral contagion: "The virus is like a vast octopus through the bodies of the city, mutating in protean forms: the Killing Fever, the Flying Fever, the Black Hate Fever" (*CRN*, 176).

The intersection of hedonism and viral infection parallels the kind of discourse being employed by commentators on AIDS and the gay community in the early 1980s, in which reactionary religious and political figures condemned the "immoral" activity of the post-liberation years and suggested that AIDS was a fitting, divine punishment. Burroughs' distrust of the hedonism of Tamaghis is most notably indicated by the sexual chaos that prevails as "Idiot males" rush into the arms of transvestite "Sirens" who hang them and collect their sperm (*CRN*, 177). Using AIDS as a touchstone for his gender-biased reading of pleasure, Burroughs places his fantasy of queer masculine revolution in a problematic relation to both queer theory and the heterosexual dominant. The oscillation between radical and reactionary positions thus remains constant.

The nature of the "inoculations" that will save the subject from the danger of pleasure is, as we will see, an extension of the kinds of queer training proposed in the Nova trilogy. The aim is the reestablishment of masculine autonomy in the face of viral invasion by the feminine. Yet there is a marked difference between this strategy of self-empowerment and the emphasis on the transformative intersection of pleasure and the masculine that was being outlined in post-AIDS queer discourses. The extent to which Burroughs' texts of the 1970s and 1980s are in direct opposition to the vision of transformation expressed throughout American and European queer theory during the 1980s is illustrative of the way in which the texts' narrow vision of the masculine is ultimately their main limitation.

REGULATING PLEASURE:
FOUCAULT AND ASCESIS

The overriding problem with which Burroughs' masculine queer fantasy presents the reader is its unfaltering reliance on a definition of the masculine based upon heterosexual models. In the previous chapter we saw how this vision derives from the masculine tradition of American letters, placing Burroughs in a curious relation to misogynist (and often effeminophobic) heterosexual discourses. Many of the desires voiced in Burroughs' texts replicate the exclusion, denial, or rejection of the feminine that some male American literature has repeatedly put forward, although the presentation of this in Burroughs' texts is always queer.

The total denial of the feminine that the texts enact is one that centers on a denial of *difference*. The monosexed, monogendered communes of the novels are designed to create homogeneity. The main characteristic of the queer heroes is always their masculine-identified homosexuality; individual characterization of the Wild Boys and Johnsons (with the exception of the central protagonist of each novel) is sparse. The boys' diversity, if it can even be called that, relies solely on their particular skills: roller skate boys, glider boys, shaman boys and so on (*WB*, 147). Such diversity does little to hide their essential "sameness."[56]

The queer political efficacy of such a strategy is that the "sameness" created in gay relationships must always transgress the heterosexual dominant's organization of the sexual sphere in terms of binary hierarchies: male/female, active/passive. Queer theorists have suggested that male-male, masculine-focused gay relationships resist assimilation into the heterosexual binary. For instance, Earl Jackson Jr. discusses an imaginary meeting of two men in a bathhouse, claiming that their sexual relationship instantly transcends (or cannot be contained within) heterosexual arrangements of desire: "Each man asserts his masculine privilege to act as subject of desire in order to elicit the desire of the other; each claims his gendered right to look in order to give his embodied self up to the 'annihilation' of the other's gaze."[57]

Such understandings of homosexuality are possible only in the post-Stonewall era of masculine-identified homosexuality. The two gay men, both "masculine" in their own and each other's eyes, are able to create new paradigms of subject interrelationship through the absence of the feminine and hence overcome the heterosexual binaries of male/female. "Masculine" sex offers an alternative to active/passive readings of the fag/"real" man paradigm. In such a situation, it is no longer clear who will occupy a passive or active role. Indeed, the terms are emptied of value; gendered readings of sexuality are exploded as each partner adopts both positions.

However, while queer theory champions such momentary *absences* of the feminine as potentially subversive, Burroughs uses them as justification for his disturbing vision of separatism and the total *exclusion* of the feminine (often by violent means). In many respects the texts seem self-conscious in their attempt to replace the Other with the Same. In *Exterminator!* the revolutionary impetus is exemplified in Audrey's words: "Other people are different from me and I don't like them" (*EX*, 88). The end result of this paranoid narcissism is often presented in a characteristically ambivalent manner, as in the story "Johnny 23." The "beautiful disease" virus developed by Doctor John Lee (the use of Burroughs' *nom de plume* is significant) is "an image concentrate of himself that would spread waves of tranquility in all directions until the world was a fit place for him to live" (*EX*, 53). On being released it results in the mass extermination of the world's population, with the only survivor being the virus' creator, finally happy at last. In *Naked Lunch*, such paranoid totalitarianism was the motivating factor behind the Divisionist Party, a group of "latent or overt homosexuals" (*NL*, 159) dedicated to populating the planet with replicas of themselves. The Divisionist plan is explicitly fascistic in that it marks an attempt to recreate the world according to a single vision: "Every replica but your own is eventually an 'Undesirable.'" Such a situation leads to the all-out wars of the "'Schluppit' (wholesale massacre of all identifiable replicas)" (*NL*, 158).

At other moments, though, the texts seem far less ambivalent in their presentation of masculine-identified gay sex as a transgressive challenge to heterosexual binaries. The following passage from *The Place of Dead Roads* (written against the background of 1980s queer theory) is indicative of much of the gay sex in Burroughs' novels. The blurring of active/passive binaries becomes so complete that it is unclear who is penetrating whom:

> Standing by the ruined railway on the sandy bank of a deep pool Carl wraps his hips around Kim with his right arm around Kim's waist holding him up the flute in his left hand playing right into Kim's left ear phantom train whistles from lonely sidings boy cries from trestles and pools thin ghostly fading into the inky blackness of space Kim hooks his hands around Carl's buttocks pumping him in his blank face turned to the sky the hot meaty rush of a nosebleed down his chest spatters his spurting cock with blood. (*PDR*, 70).

The repeated references to "left" and "right" emphasizes the merging of the two bodies, an occurrence paralleled in the similar merging of train whistles, flutes and human cries, nosebleeds, and ejaculations. The boys' sex transgresses the binary structures governing heterosexual couplings. Neither of these boys can claim a masculinity that is denied the other; their relationship is such that gender roles are no longer applicable. As *Port of Saints* makes clear, gay sex between Burroughs' queer heroes is always represented as a challenge to the hierarchies of the heterosexual matrix: "I pulled off my clothes. He looked at me with unsmiling appraisal. 'You fuck me this time,' he decided." (*PoS*, 69).

Such sex produces a situation in which similarity replaces difference. The exclusion of all forms of the feminine means that the boys begin to merge into one another. Not only do they become identical clones, but their sexual enjoyment is also based upon the texts' representation of their similarity to one another, a similarity that allows closeness and intimacy (and therefore produces the "telepathic" relationship that Lee had searched for throughout *Queer*). This "similarity" is, of course, part of the etymological origin of "homosexuality," in which "homo" derives not from the Latin "man," but from the Greek "same." The following passage is indicative of this: "We dropped our pants and shorts and stepped out of them facing each other both hard and I saw that his was just like mine and felt a drop of pearl squeeze out of the tip and at the same time a drop squeezed out the tip of his" (*PoS*, 52).

Instances of this kind of "recognition" recur throughout Burroughs' texts and he claims that they are one of the main privileges of the queer position:

> To what extent do you think sex consists of wanting to be someone else, to be in their body? It's a crucial factor in homosexual relationships, to be the other person. [. . .] In homosexual sex you know what the other person is feeling, so you are identifying with the other person completely. In heterosexual sex you have no idea what the other person is feeling.[58]

This denial of difference—no matter how self-conscious it might be—is the central problem that any queer reading of Burroughs' texts must negotiate. This is not simply because of the reactionary politics of which such denial is indicative, but also because it creates a stunted vision of the queer masculine that, in comparison to queer theory discourses of the 1970s and 1980s, is always based upon the desire to imitate the heterosexual masculine. By slavishly chasing the dominant's images of the masculine, Burroughs' texts consistently fail to produce an independent vision of the queer masculine. It is this that marks the political failure of the texts. While explicitly claiming to pursue a supposed "new" vision of gay identity, the texts actually produce a masculine identity that is indebted to heterosexual definitions of that gender. This, of course, is what links Burroughs' vision of the masculine and the clone scene. As Murray Healy writes:

> It is no accident that the masculinized subculture came to be christened the "clone" scene, with everyone expected to wield the same phallic symbols, and uniformity still rules in its subsequent permutations. Difference—signifiers of femininity—is often forcibly disallowed, with door policies at these clubs barring women and drag queens, and ensuring that uniform codes are strictly adhered to by clubbers.[59]

Citing Irigaray, Healy suggests that if it is "only difference that will re-empower the phallus, then this hyperaccumulation is doomed to failure as it leads only to a uniform, extreme masculinity."[60]

In the 1980s, however, some queer theorists attempted to reclaim the masculine appropriations of the clones, replacing readings of hedonism with a politically charged embrace of pleasure as transformative. This shift marks the clear break between Burroughs' fantasies and queer theory; while Burroughs demonizes pleasure as a feminizing influence that can only ever (with regard to the gay male subject) be negative, queer theory reclaims pleasure as a transformative force, suggesting that the intersection of pleasure and the masculine leads to an undermining of phallocentricism that creates radical, progressive forms of masculinity. The unique position of the gay man as both part of and excluded from the heterosexual masculine sphere is what allows him to subvert that masculinity from within. Not surprisingly, this is a strategy of which Burroughs' texts want no part.

Jackson's concept of negating affirmation suggests that "Between phallic citizenship and sodomitical forfeiture, there can occur a ruptural shift between the homosexual's 'imitation' of men and the gay male's iconoclastic accession to sexual subjectivity by at once claiming his masculine prerogative and contravening its conditions of possibility."[61] The subversion of the masculine that gay appropriations can produce becomes one means of reclaiming the clones (and their later followers) from charges of apolitical hedonism. Jackson, for instance, argues that the main goal of masculine-identified homosexual relationships is not a stable, phallic identity, but rather the subversive pleasure to be found in the renunciation of such an identity through *jouissance*. He suggests that the heterosexual body is primarily "monocentric (phallic) and apotropaic, sexually actualized as a weapon in defense of its own paranoiac integrity: it cannot—must not—be penetrated" while, in comparison, the gay male body is "polycentric and ludic, sexually actualized as a playground."[62] In this manner pleasure (as long as it is between two or more masculine-identified gay men) becomes a point of resistance, subversion, and transgression. Building on the paradoxical nature of negating affirmation, Jackson argues that the gay male body can be read as both belonging to and subverting the patriarchal order in its very pleasures:

> Gay male lovemaking is a pulsation of inter-ruptions of subjectivity, of inter-irruptions into the subject's somatic extension of his imaginary selfhood by the subject whose object he has ec-statically become. Subjectivity within male coupling is episodic, cognized and re-cognized as stroboscopic fluctuations of intense (yet dislocated, asymmetrical, decentred) awareness of self-as-other, self-for-other, via interlunations of psychic and sexual exuberance. If the heterosexual male imaginary includes a defense against ejaculation as loss of self, risk of nonmeaning, or abyss of meaning, gay male sexuality (with the anal drives restored) is a circulatory system of expenditure and absorption, taking/giving and giving/taking.[63]

Jackson's erudite, clearly partisan argument is tellingly significant of the extent to which queer studies have merged with poststructuralist discourses to present a challenge to conventional, heterosexual understandings of sexuality and subjectivity. In addition, it also marks the point at which the gay male body is mobilized as a revolutionary force through its use of pleasure and its paradoxical social position as both a part of and a negation of the (heterosexual) male order.

This transformation of (queer) pleasure from the antithesis of political engagement to a radically subversive act has much to do with Michel Foucault, who suggests that the S/M activities of the clones created oppositional subjectivities and social reorganizations. For Foucault, sadomasochistic practices can help

> make one's body into the site of production of extraordinary polymorphous pleasures, pleasures that at the same time are detached from the valorization of the genitals and especially of the male genitals. After all, the point is to detach oneself from this virile form of obligatory pleasure—namely orgasm, orgasm in the ejaculatory sense, in the masculine sense of the term.[64]

This degenitalization of the body, the subversion of its phallic monocentricism in favor of the polycentric is central to his interest in both the clones and their sexual practices. Much of Foucault's discussion of contemporary gay identities is to be found in a series of articles published in the French gay press during the 1980s. In *Saint Foucault,* David Halperin produces an interesting overview of these scattered pieces to present a reevaluation of Foucault's importance to the gay and lesbian community's negotiation of sexual identities, politics, and resistances. According to Halperin, Foucault's interest in queer identities is greatly preoccupied with the role of S/M in clone culture as a transformative sexual practice; more importantly, it is the only practice that Foucault chose to outline as a possible site of resistance (for fear, no doubt, of prescribing the limits of such resistances).[65]

The radical potential of S/M resides in the desexualization of the phallic body (and therefore the simultaneous demasculinization of it) through the creation of new erogenous zones across the surface of that body. The end of phallic monocentricism creates— as Jackson argued—the destabilization of the participating subject. Halperin writes:

> S/M therefore represents a remapping of the body's erotic sites, a redistribution of its so-called erogenous zones, a breakup of the erotic monopoly traditionally held by the genitals, and even a re-eroticisation of the male genitals as sites of vulnerability instead of as objects of veneration. In all of those

respects, S/M represents an encounter between the modern subject of sexuality and the otherness of his or her body.[66]

This "degenitalization" of the body is coupled with Foucault's philosophy of pleasure. In an attempt to separate his own stance from that taken by philosophers of desire (such as Lyotard, and Deleuze and Guattari), Foucault highlights pleasure as a transformative power that is free from "the medical and naturalistic connotations inherent in the notion of desire."[67] Whereas desire has been categorized effectively through the various agencies of religion, the law, and Freudian psychoanalysis, pleasure is a term that Foucault claims is

> virgin territory, unused, almost devoid of meaning. There is no "pathology" of pleasure, no "abnormal" pleasure. It is an event "outside the subject," or at the limit of the subject, taking place in that something which is neither of the body nor of the soul, which is neither inside nor outside—in short, a notion neither assigned nor assignable.[68]

The idea that pleasure is "neither assigned nor assignable" constitutes the beginning of the destabilization of the subject. Foucault advocates the use of "*good* drugs" and anonymous, bathhouse sex as two possible ways of continuing this rupture in subjectivity.[69] Pleasure, he claims, has "no passport, no identification papers," and as such can create a decentered subject freed (however briefly) from the matrix of power.[70] While other commentators brand the clone scene "hedonistic"—in its drug use, anonymous sex, sadomasochism, and unbridled pursuit of self-fulfillment—Foucault suggests that it is these very characteristics that produce the clones' oppositional potential. Heterosexual society is completely unable to assimilate such (queer) hedonism because it produces a problematic, "fluid" play of power. The S/M of the clones disperses power by highlighting its potential for producing "effects of pleasure instead of effects of domination."[71]

According to Foucault, clone culture's masculinity "does not at all coincide with a revalorization of the male *as* male" since S/M power games and their accompanying degenitalization of the body rob the phallus of its power. Thus the clone scene can be read as a masculine environment in which "masculinity" is humiliated, degenitalized, penetrated, made "fluid" (and thus "feminized"). Simultaneously treasured and violated, masculinity is transformed into something Other, then reinstated again only to be violated once more. This gloriously perverse circularity is a becoming without end. S/M practices play with masculinity in a manner that highlights the negating affirmation inherent within the gay appropriation of the masculine itself.

In addition, such oppositional practices can create social transformation. The clones' reorganization of the social sphere through the creation of an alternative community (rigidly policed and defined) and the establishment of alternative familial structures within that community offer an indication of the extent to which sexual pleasure can be used to effect real social, political, and ethical change. As Halperin explains: "what may have intrigued Foucault most about fist-fucking was the way a specific non-normative sexual practice could come to provide the origin for such seemingly remote and unrelated events as bake sales, community fund-raisers and block parties."[72]

In this way, the appropriation of the masculine by gay men can be read as a spectacular transformation of its heterosexual definition. Since gay men are forever caught within the double bind of negating affirmation, all queer appropriations of the masculine offer the possibility of a subversive transformation of its phallocentric stability. S/M practices and social regroupings are two very definite examples of the rupture of heterosexual masculinity as it is appropriated by gay men.[73] The political value of such appropriations lies not only in undermining heterosexual understandings of the masculine, but also in creating a new identity, one that is neither masculine nor feminine, but a transformed combination of the two. Whereas Burroughs' texts argue for the exclusion of the contaminating influences of the feminine, Foucault valorizes the simultaneous masculinization and feminization of the clones, their bodies and subjectivities. From this perspective, the clones create a new mode of being that cannot be assimilated back into the heterosexual binary, since it occupies both masculine and feminine positions.

Unlike more recent queer theorists—such as Jackson—Foucault does not suggest that *jouissance* should be read as transformative in itself. Rather, pleasure has to be *utilized* for political ends, and it is only through a specific set of sexual "ethics" that this can be consistently possible. At this point, two different strands of Foucault's work intersect as he uses his historical analysis of Greek and Roman philosophers on sexual pleasure to inform his vision of modern queer identities. Throughout the second volume of *The History of Sexuality,* Foucault repeatedly comments on the ways in which these texts and philosophers create a body of thought and knowledge concerned with guiding and regulating pleasure through the dual structures of *askesis* and *epimelesthai sautou.*

According to Foucault, *askesis* (or, ascesis) signifies "training, meditation, tests of thinking, examination of conscience, control of representations" and was essential in the formation of an ethical paradigm that "constituted one of the basic instruments used in the direction of souls."[74] Coupled with this ascesis were the discourses that informed *epimelesthai sautou,* which translates as "to take care of yourself."[75] The importance of these classical techniques for orientating and regulating the self resided in their role in helping the subject cope with his desires, thereby transforming him into an ethical subject. Both ascesis and the care of the self were intended to save the male subject from "what constituted ethical negativity *par excellence* [. . .] being passive with regard to the pleasures."[76] The moral man, the ethical subject, was one able to "endure" pleasure without letting it overwhelm him. As Foucault notes, much of this thinking was explicitly tied to ideas about sex and gender: "Self-mastery was a way of being a man with respect to oneself [. . .] in short it was a way of being active in relation to what was by nature passive."[77]

These techniques of the self were designed in order to ensure that the man remained masculine, for the "man who was not sufficiently in control of his pleasures—whatever his choice of object—

was regarded as 'feminine'."[78] Self-mastery, for the Greeks, became the key to masculinity; the man who lost control of himself in pleasure relinquished his right to claim masculine status, regardless of the social relation between himself and others. One's relation to oneself was of vital importance, for masculinity depended on attaining a balance between control and enjoyment. Virility and effeminacy were a result not of one's sexual choices but rather the subject's attitudes towards the pleasures:

> the traditional signs of effeminacy—idleness, indolence, refusal to engage in the somewhat rough activities of sports, a fondness for perfumes and adornments, softness (*malakia*)—were not necessarily associated with the individual who in the nineteenth century would be called an "invert," but with the one who yielded to the pleasures that enticed him: he was under the power of his own appetites and those of others.[79]

The importance of ascesis to Foucault extended far beyond its origins as a historical concept in Socratic discourses. In his work on modern queer identities, Foucault repeatedly referred to it as a technique for managing pleasure.

In the modern context, Foucault suggests that ascesis could be considered "an exercise of self upon self by which one tries to work out, to transform one's self and to attain a certain mode of being."[80] This political and ethical self-fashioning produces a queer (that is, sexually marginalized) subject who constitutes a resistance to power. While sexuality (or at least the classification of sexualities in order to define them as acceptable or deviant) is part of the network of power, the use of ascesis attempts to create a subject and a community that reaches toward the establishment of new possibilities. If, as Foucault claims, gay men and women have to "invent A to Z a relationship without form," then it is exactly this need for self-creation which can be read as politically transformative. As Foucault remarks, "It's up to us to advance into a homosexual ascesis that would make us work on ourselves and invent (I don't say discover) a manner of being that is still improbable."[81]

What is most intriguing in the relation between Foucault's historical analysis of classical systems of self-fashioning and his adaptation of these discourses for the modern gay community is the extent to which he undermines the problematic gender politics of the classical texts. While many of the classical discourses on ascesis emphasize the gender dynamics of regulating pleasure (the effeminate man as the passive hedonist), Foucault's vision of modern queer ascesis ignores this problematic gender bias, emphasizing the extent to which classical ascesis signified a mode of *self*-fashioning that was not a part of the drive towards conformity but rather part of an attempt to make the self exemplary. Thus Foucault emphasizes the transformative play of ascesis, bringing it into line with his understanding of pleasure as a force that can rupture the (heterosexual) masculine sphere. Modern ascesis aims at guiding the self toward a becoming that radically alters the fixed gender categories employed by the classical authors and their modern counterparts.

As Halperin suggests, what interested Foucault about ascesis was that it operated "not to enable those who conformed to ethical norms to become more normal, more average, more capable of losing themselves in the crowd, but, on the contrary, to enable a few moral athletes to stand out, appear special, and become conspicuous."[82] The important difference thus becomes that between "self-fashioning or ascesis, on the one hand, and mass obedience or conformity to laws of conduct, on the other."[83] As Halperin notes, this is the overriding point of Foucault's comparison of ancient and modern treatments of sex; whereas sex in the modern arena is defined by a set of discourses, rules, and laws prescribed from without, in the ancient arena it was the individual who took care of his own pleasures and his relation to them. As Foucault argues, in the ancient world

> reflection on sexual behavior as a moral domain was not a means of internalizing, or formalizing general interdictions imposed on everyone; rather, it was a means of developing— for the smallest minority of the population, made up of free, adult males—an aesthetics of existence, the purposeful art of a freedom perceived as a power game.[84]

Foucault's rejection of the conservative gender dynamics of the classical authors is indicative of the attempt to imagine new forms of self-transformative queer masculinity. Refusing to valorize the male as male, Foucault—and other queer theorists, such as Jackson—have attempted to imagine a reconfiguration of the masculine that challenges the gay gender stereotypes supported by the heterosexual dominant. Rejecting both the effeminate paradigm and the slavish imitation of heterosexual modes of masculinity, the Foucauldian ideal seeks the creation of a new gender identity.

The comparison between this project and Burroughs' texts is important in terms of both gender identity and self-fashioning. Burroughs, as we have seen, is almost as wary as the classical authors in his fears about the vulnerability of the male body and subject with regard to excessive pleasure. His paranoid fears about "possession" and the loss of masculine sovereignty through being "invaded" by the feminine seem similar to Greek concerns about penetration and social inferiority/disgrace. Furthermore, Burroughs' texts also present self-mastery as the principal means of maintaining (masculine) political and social autonomy; feminization is a constant fear. As he remarks in *The Wild Boys*, what distinguishes his heroes is the fact that "You need special training to contact those boys" (*WB*, 166).

Initially we might be tempted to draw a comparison between Burroughs' Wild Boys and Foucault's vision of modern queer identities. Both are centered on a radical restructuring of social relationships in order to create utopian communities of shared knowledge and resources. In *Port of Saints*, the Wild Boys organize an annual festival at which they "meet in one spot to compare weapons and fighting techniques and to indulge in communal orgies" (*PoS*, 72). In *Cities of the Red Night*, the relationship between Dink and Noah illustrates the way in which the Wild Boy communes are organized around this kind of transfer of knowledge (*CRN*, 126–128). Dink, who has mastered the Burroughsian holy grail of absolute body control, teaches his friend the secret; the relationship parallels Halperin's suggestion that modern ascesis can create "new forms of relationship, new modes of knowledge, new means of creativity and new possibilities of love."[85] As Burroughs' vision of the academy suggests, such social reorganization is as much a part of his queer utopia as Foucault's:

> I would suggest that academies be established where young people will learn to get really high . . . high as the Zen master is high when his arrow hits a target in the dark . . . high as the karate master is high when he smashes a brick with his fist . . . high . . . weightless . . . in space. This is the space age. Time to look beyond this rundown radioactive cop-rotten planet. Time to look beyond this animal body.
>   [. . .]
> The students would receive a basic course of training in the non-chemical disciplines of Yoga, karate, prolonged sense withdrawal, stroboscopic lights, the constant use of tape recorders to break down verbal association links. Techniques now being used for control of thought could be used instead for liberation. (*Job*, 137)[86]

The emphasis on physicality in this passage is important since the academies offer their students the chance to regain their physical autonomy (or masculinity). Such training, for Burroughs, is the key to the survival of the human race (or at least its male constituents) through the production of an environment and a subjectivity without fear, control, or repression; indeed, the academies even facilitate a fantastic re-write of history as World War II is averted and the atom bomb remains undeveloped (*Job*, 217–224).

However, what is important to note is the manner in which Burroughs' texts always present training as a means of regulating the masculinity of the subject in order to prevent usurpation by the feminine. Such training does not seek the political *jouissance* that Foucault's vision of modern queer sex reaches toward (the transformation and dissolution of a masculine identity), but instead a consolidation of masculinity through overcoming the threat of feminization in pleasure. The aim is to give oneself up to pleasure while remaining in control of it. In an attempt to negate the dissolution of the Wild Boy uprising into gratuitous violence and self-gratification, Burroughs suggests a training program that will ensure that excess never overwhelms the boys. Thus self-mastery in Burroughs' texts is not concerned with the Foucauldian transformation of fixed gender categories. Like the classical authors, Burroughs suggests self-mastery as a means of regulating masculinity in order to *prevent* its transformation. The comparison of Burroughs, Foucault, and classical discourses on ascesis illustrates the extent of Burroughs' divergence from modern queer theory.

The extent to which ascesis—in the post-Stonewall novels—operates as an extension of the earlier deconditioning tactics of the Nova trilogy is important. The Dink and Noah relationship is illustrative in this respect. Noah's training centers on sexual abstinence (which is, incidentally, a typical technique of classical ascesis). Being in complete control of his sexual energy, Noah finds the "key to body control. Errors, fumbles, and ineptitudes are caused by uncontrolled sexual energy which then lays one open to any sort of psychic or physical attack" (*CRN*, 128). Such an emphasis on errors and fumbles is reminiscent of the Korzybskian/Hubbardian discourses on self-transformation through bodily autonomy. As in the cut-up process, the ascesis that follows it is focused on ensuring that the liberated subject maintains and consolidates his new freedoms. In *Exterminator!*, Burroughs makes his commitment to such programs of training clear in the section "The Discipline of DE" (*EX*, 55–67), which offers a fairly deadpan piece of self-help therapy. DE, or "Do Easy," is a system that aims to instruct the pupil how to do "whatever you do in the *easiest* most relaxed way you can manage which is also the quickest and most efficient way" (*EX*, 58). DE teaches complete body control: "You will discover clumsy things you've been doing for years until you think that is just the way things are" (*EX*, 62).

DE offers to liberate the subject from old and crippling methods of thought and behavior through a process of replaying mistakes and fumbles: "It's just like retaking a movie shot until you get it right. And you will begin to feel yourself in a film moving with ease and speed. [. . .] Repeat sequence until objects are brought to order" (*EX*, 60). Repetition becomes the key to overcoming one's physical ineptitude and thus preserving one's autonomy. DE allows

one to attack the negative forces of the unconscious, expose oneself to them, and obliterate them. Such a practice allows the subject to gain complete physical autonomy: "DE applies to ALL
operations carried out inside the body . . . brain waves, digestion,
blood pressure and rate of heart beats" (*EX*, 66–67).

This desire for complete autonomy is closely related to the issue
of pleasure. In *Port of Saints*, Burroughs highlights the way in
which the repetitions of the orgy can be used to train the subject,
allowing him to retain control over his desires even at the moment
of highest pleasure. Thus the orgy is not a total surrender to the
lusts of the flesh, but rather a detached, almost scientific attempt
to overcome those lusts. A swastika rug—on which the swastika is
comprised of a picture of boys linked together in various kinds of
sexual acts—is brought out, precipitating an explosion of sexual
desire among those present:

> At the sight of the rug the boys begin to prowl around each
> other like tomcats smelling feeling with purrs and grunts and
> whines faces swollen with blood rapt inhuman showing their
> teeth like wild dogs the boys are all around the swastika lick-
> ing feeling squatting here and there jacking off they form a
> fuck line and in this exercise the trick is to keep your face
> from moving just be there the rapt pilot faces steering
> through this hydraulic tunnel of squirming quivering flesh
> faces bursting from the pressure riding the bucking loins.
> *This is the exercise of purposeful abandonment.* (*PoS*, 167–168;
> my emphasis)

The use of the swastika, that twentieth-century symbol of fascist terror and mass murder, represents a radical reappropriation of
what was once a symbol of sexual, phallic virility. In many ways, the
passage highlights Grauerholz's remark about the bestial nature of
the Wild Boys, yet something else is occurring here. The "rapt pilot
faces" steering the bodies through this scene of lust and sex are part
of the event's status as an "exercise of purposeful abandonment."
The Wild Boy participants, well-trained in body control, are not
indulging in an orgy but rather in some kind of test of the indi-

vidual, a scientific investigation of the vagaries of the flesh. Thus the scene becomes a perfect illustration of the transformation of an act of hedonistic pleasure (the orgy) into a political tool ("purposeful abandonment").

The detached status of the participants allows them to transcend their position as subjects, "riding the waves of lust while maintaining a cool remote pilot's hand on the controls [. . .] and then you get the blue light explosion which blows the YOU and ME right out of your head" (*PoS*, 128–129). As in the Scientology program, the engrams of sexuality are replayed again and again until they lose their hold over the individual. The orgy becomes the eponymous "port of saints," the space port that will allow transcendence, leading the subject out of the body: "The program proposed is essentially a disintoxication from inner fear and inner control, a liberation of thought and energy to prepare a new generation for the adventure of space" (*Job*, 138). In this manner, every one of Burroughs' queer heroes is a "cowboy in the seven-days-a-week fight" (*CRN*, 175), as they are all locked in a continuous battle to preserve their autonomy and freedom.

"Purposeful abandonment" thus becomes the texts' guiding principle in defining the relation of the self to pleasure. Hedonistic excess (such as that enjoyed by Audrey and Kim) can be accepted only if it is used for social or personal transformation. Ascesis ensures that pleasure is always more than just self-gratification, that it is also self-liberation. This forms the basis of the transgressive reinscription that the texts offer. Reworking notions of homosexuality as effeminate hedonism—which, as Sinfield argues, was the characteristic model of gay identity from Wilde onwards—the texts reinscribe the dominant's negative conception of homosexuality. Rather than using all that is styled as "negative" in order to empower the subject, as Langeteig suggests, the texts warn against the dangers inherent within transgression and attempt to regulate transgression and pleasure so that the subject can maintain his masculine status.

Foucault's vision of masculine-identified gay men using S/M practices to rupture the phallocentric stability of the gay male body leads to a reconfiguration of gay subjectivity as it becomes other-than-masculine. Burroughs' fear of the feminine leads to a narrow focus on the purely masculine that precludes the possibility of its transformation. The sheer physicality of Burroughs' imagined program of training seems important in this respect, since it is a response to this fear of feminization.[87] The yoga, martial arts, and bodily training that the texts reference are all designed to create an impenetrable body; unlike the gay male body imagined by Foucault and Jackson, the supreme Burroughsian body is not susceptible to rupture. This (paradoxically) impenetrable gay male body is designed to withstand the feminizing effects of pleasure and is thus comparable (on one level) to a fascistic conception of the body as machine.

Interestingly, Klaus Theweleit's work on the discourses and ethics of the self in Nazism foregrounds the attempted creation of a stable, self-regulating masculine subject whose primary goal was maintaining "ego-stability." The fascist soldier male, in Theweleit's account, was taught to use a number of activities to ensure this stability, including "his imposition of commands upon himself, 'pulling himself together,' the whole range of forms of deliberate self-control available to him; his alertness, his constant watchfulness; 'keeping fit' to drill his own body; his 'masculine' posture and demonstratively upright bearing."[88] Such a rigorous attempt to make the body rigid is, for Jackson, "the logical extreme of the male heterosexual subject produced under the regime of misogynist compulsory heterosexuality."[89] As Theweleit suggests, for the fascist male, "Pleasure, with its hybridizing qualities, has the dissolving effect of a chemical enzyme upon the armored body. Attitudes of asceticism, renunciation and self-control are effective defenses."[90]

In a similar fashion, Burroughs is so terrified of a return of the effeminate paradigm and its recoding of the gay male body as a jerking, puppetlike grotesque that he is unable to imagine the masculine as anything other than a physical rigidity. Having rejected the schizophrenia, instability, and confusion into which gay identity was thrust in the 1950s, Burroughs' quest for masculine stability continues into the 1980s and 1990s at a time when such a quest had become an anachronism. Dissatisfied with all available masculine forms, and constantly afraid of impending re-feminization, Burroughs' vision of the gay masculine seems trapped within its own narrow scope.

Throughout the later novels of the 1980s and 1990s, particularly the final book of the Red Night trilogy and the handful of shorter pieces that Burroughs published just prior to his death, the injunction that "we are here to go" becomes increasingly important. Ascesis, for Burroughs, leads directly to a longing for the transcendence of the body. After the texts' complicated attempts to effect the masculinization of the gay male, this desire to escape the flesh seems confusing. It is a change of strategy that reached its zenith during the period in which Burroughs becomes increasingly aware of his own mortality (foregrounding himself in the texts as an aging writer preparing for death) and in which the gay community found itself having to confront death with daily regularity. This transcendence of the body also plays an important role in Burroughs' attempt finally to solve the impasse of masculine gay identity. Taking his Wild Boys and Johnsons past the body, Burroughs reaches for a transgendered world beyond this one, a queer afterlife that attempts to undo the binaries of male/female, masculine/feminine, dominant/marginal, and body/soul once and for all.

CHAPTER FOUR

THE FLIGHT OF THE SOUL FROM THE BODY

"LEFT THE FLESH BEHIND"

When Burroughs died on 2 August 1997, word of his death spread quickly across the Internet. The proliferation of sites devoted to his life and work expanded overnight as tribute homepages were established in response to the news, while the existing Burroughs-related sites relaunched themselves with suitably somber text and graphics. The web memorial at "The William S. Burroughs Files Inter*Web*zone" carried comments from fans and academics across the world indicating just how influential and important his work had been.[1] What was so interesting about these responses was the manner in which they drew on the mythology of death and afterlife which Burroughs' texts of the 1980s and 1990s had created. Many fans took comfort from the fact that much of this work had been explicitly concerned with death, the transcendence of the body, and the afterlife (and had frequently discussed these issues with regard to the aging author's own mortality).

Throughout the Red Night trilogy and the late texts—*Ghost of Chance* (1991), *The Cat Inside* (1992), and *My Education: A Book of Dreams* (1995)—Burroughs had shared his ruminations on death

with his readership, developing a fantasy of a non-Christian afterlife based in Egyptian mythology.[2] Such material offered fans the
chance to envisage Burroughs in "The Land of the Dead," thus allowing his death to be viewed in more positive terms. Indeed, in a
curious instance of death imitating art, Burroughs' friends held a
Tibetan-Buddhist/Egyptian "Bardo" in Lawrence, Kansas after his
death to ensure that his souls successfully completed their journey
across the Duad to the Western Lands.[3]

The "end of the body" had been a staple concern of Burroughs'
fiction since *Naked Lunch,* as critics have frequently noted. Lydenberg, for instance, has linked the longing for the transcendence of
the flesh with contemporary literary theory in her suggestion that
in the Nova trilogy, "The direct experience of the 'Algebra of Need'
[is] of life trapped within the body, manipulated by its needs and
fears."[4] Drawing on Roland Barthes' *The Pleasure of the Text,* she
argues that the narrative technique of the trilogy indicates that
"The body, time, and ultimately the word must be not only released
from the predetermined patterns set by habit and routine, but more
thoroughly obliterated."[5]

Gregory Stephenson offers an interesting counterpoint to Lydenberg's reading of the texts as sites of self-initiated deconstruc-
tion by associating them with the Gnostic tradition. The
intersection between this twentieth-century writer and the spiritual ideas that "flourished in the Middle East and the Roman
World from approximately 80 to 200 AD" occurs, according to
Stephenson, because "Both view the material world as illusory, the
body as the primary impediment to true being and identity, and escape from the body and the world of the senses as man's paramount concern."[6] Thus Burroughs' writing, like the mythological
systems of the Gnostics, serves "to effect self-knowledge, internal
transformation, and transcendence."[7]

This desire to transcend the physical body in order to reach
some alternative, utopian, non-corporeal realm is one of the most
important factors in Burroughs' work of the 1980s and 1990s.
However, in terms of the queer project that we have been following throughout the texts, this evacuation of the physical realm by

Burroughs' heroes is distinctly problematic. As we have seen, the texts' identity politics moves from the effeminophobia of the 1950s to the deconditioning and ascesis of the 1960s and 1970s. Central to this movement is the desire for bodily autonomy. It is only through such autonomy that the gay subject can reclaim his bodily identity from the regulation imposed by the effeminate paradigm and thus re-signify himself as male and masculine. This liberation of gay subjectivity relies upon a separatist policy to sustain itself, one that demands the exclusion of the feminine from its world. That the texts should conclude this by envisaging the end of the physical realm seems a somewhat self-defeating strategy. After spending so much time fantasizing bodily autonomy, freedom from regulation, and a masculine identity, why should queer heroes want to leave their phallic, male bodies behind?

Although the motif of the transcendence of the body in Burroughs' fiction of the 1980s and 1990s must necessarily be read in connection with the AIDS crisis, it is primarily an extension of the "purposeful abandonment" achieved through ascesis. Burroughs believes that the orgy is the moment that "blows the YOU and ME right out of your head" (*PoS*, 165) simply because—when used correctly—it can bring about the end of the body through destroying the binary logic of Western thought that Burroughs (via Korzybski) detests so much. The binaries of male/female, masculine/feminine, and soul/body are supposedly rendered obsolete by the texts' creation of a monocentric universe in which the concepts of the "female," the "feminine," and ultimately the "body" are erased through exclusion. The schizophrenic position of the effeminate homosexual, caught in the alternations of the binary opposition as his male body clashes with his feminine identifications, is finally obliterated through a dedicated policy of "oneness," a refusal to accept anything but "half" of the binary, rejecting "the Other Half" once and for all.

Gay sex (but only that between two masculine-identified men) leads to the transfiguration of the gay male subject as he enters a post-corporeal world of "space" in which he is no longer encumbered by the physical body. Referencing Aleister Crowley,

Burroughs suggests that this evolutionary jump is one that is both physical and spiritual:

> Our research is directed towards effecting biological alterations in the human artifact. The human body is much too dense for space conditions. However, we have a model to hand that is much less dense in fact almost weightless: the astral or dream body. This lighter body, "a body of light," as Crowley called it, is much more suited to space conditions.[8]

Crowley had outlined this theory of the "body of light" in his 1929 text *Magick in Theory and Practice*, in which he claimed that the "essential magical work, apart from any particular operation, is the formation of the Magical Being or Body of Light."[9] This body was variously known as "the Astral double, body of Light, body of fire, body of desire, fine body, scin-laeca and numberless other names."[10] It was to be found "within the human body" and formed "another body of approximately the same size and shape; but made of a subtler and less illusory material."[11]

Burroughs frequently appropriates this gnostic image in order to suggest the transcendent possibilities of an alternative mode of existence that transgresses the (sexual, social, environmental, and material) uniformity of contemporary Western culture. The (gay) subject who refuses to conform is transfigured as he becomes a body of light, a radiant being who outshines the dull mass of heterosexual uniformity. The creation of this new mode of being is a direct result of the "sex magic that turns flesh to light" (*PoS*, 94).[12] As the title of Burroughs' painting "Silver Boys" suggests, it is a transfiguration that is available only to the male sex (and even then only to those who are gay and masculine-identified).[13]

In his attempt to create a queer mythology of life, death, and the afterlife, Burroughs mixes heterogeneous discourses: occult texts, evolutionary theory, Egyptian mythology, Mailer's *Ancient Evenings*,[14] pseudoscientific theories about ESP, and ufology.[15] By employing these marginal discourses Burroughs attempts to sidestep the conventional (heterosexual-dominated) visions of the Judeo-Christian order. His queer afterlife places itself in direct opposition to the dominant and can be read as an extension of the queer thematics of the earlier texts. The mythology of death and transcendence that Burroughs plays with throughout the texts of the 1980s and 1990s is one that fantasizes the total autonomy of the gay man. Burroughs' understanding of the social regulation of the gay male body is so paranoid that it ultimately demands the total evacuation of the material sphere. Autonomy becomes possible only once the body has been cast aside. Furthermore, the texts' vision of sex separatism eventually renders the body an unnecessary encumbrance. In a world without women—that supposedly utopian vision that the communes seek to create—the body's role in signifying sexual difference is no longer useful. The entry into a post-corporeal world of light is Burroughs' final fantasy of masculine queer autonomy.

What this chapter will demonstrate is that the negation of the physical realm in the texts of the 1980s and 1990s is a deliberate strategy that marks a final attempt to reject the social regulation of the gay male body. In addition, the transcendence of the body represents a metaphorical celebration of a utopian world in which the need for a sexed body to signify gender is finally overcome. The main focus of this chapter will be the final novel of the Red Night trilogy, *The Western Lands*. What will become apparent is the extent to which Burroughs' fantasy of the afterlife is not simply a somewhat bizarre response to the AIDS crisis, but the culmination of his attempts to imagine a world without sexual difference and (more problematically) the feminine.

RESIGNIFICATIONS: AIDS AND THE GAY MALE BODY

Throughout the three novels of the Red Night trilogy and the later texts of the 1990s, Burroughs is overtly concerned with producing a personal mythology of death and afterlife. Drawing on a range of sources (including the Egyptian Book of the Dead), Burroughs constructs his own fantasy of what Murphy aptly terms a "plan of afterliving."[16] Interestingly, this vision of the Western Lands is one directly opposed to both Judeo-Christian and, more importantly, heterosexual constructions of the next world, for it is not only predicated on a "pagan" belief in multiple gods, but is also available only as a queer fantasy.

The Western Lands, as Burroughs repeatedly tells us, can be reached only by the masculine-identified gay man. The rest of humanity is left to wallow for eternity within the vastly overpopulated Land of the Dead, the purgatorial halfway point between the real world and the queer afterlife. Since the journey through the next world is a spiritual pilgrimage, the body is repeatedly styled as obsolete: "Your body is a boat to lay aside when you reach the far shore, or sell it if you can find a fool . . . it's full of holes . . . it's full of holes" (*WL*, 162). The fiction of the 1980s and 1990s is consistent in its rejection of the body and the physical realm as the site of power's influence. The body of light—symbolizing purity, freedom and transfiguration—becomes a liberatory image of noncorporeal radiance. Rejecting the heterosexual sociological signification of gay sex that occurred during the AIDS crisis (sex + gay men = death), Burroughs rewrites the discourses of the American media and health authorities. Rather than gay sex leading to the eternal flames of hell (as many right-wing commentators were keen to suggest during the AIDS crisis), the gay subject enters the mythological Western Lands.

The resignification of death, afterlife, and the body in Burroughs' gay texts during the 1980s and 1990s initially seems to be a response to the centrality of death in the gay community during the period. In the years immediately following the official recognition of the HIV virus, Burroughs' rewriting of queer death as a moment of transcendence, salvation, and freedom from oppression seems politically charged.[17] If, as Murphy notes, the Red Night trilogy suggests that the writer can produce "alternative scripts that undermine and even replace the transcendent script of the law," then Burroughs' attempts to imagine a queer afterlife could be read as a fantastic response to AIDS that constitutes in its very hyperbole an implicit critique of heterosexual apathy and ignorance.[18]

From this perspective, the use of the fantastic in *The Western Lands* reads like an indictment of the American health authorities, as if Burroughs were saying "your provisions have been so appallingly inadequate as to make fantasy our only recourse."

However, in many respects, Burroughs' vision of death and afterliving also seems willfully blind to the suffering caused by the AIDS crisis. On one level, at least, the "retroactive fantasy" which the texts produce seems an inadequate response to the reality of the gay community's suffering throughout the 1980s. The retroactive utopia of afterliving is quite out of touch with the proactive strategies employed by many sections of the gay community (including other gay novelists and artists).[19] In addition, Burroughs' writing of this period also seems out of step with AIDS literature, if only because it consistently evades recognition of the crisis.[20]

Although AIDS demands that all gay writing of the 1980s must inevitably be read with reference to the epidemic, the extent of Burroughs' silence about the issue is particularly surprising given his fascination with viruses and disease and his membership in two of the communities most at risk from the virus (as gay man and former junkie). In many respects, such reticence is indicative of the extent to which the fantasy of afterliving that the Red Night trilogy establishes is best understood in terms of Burroughs' previous concerns with heterosexual regulation and gay male autonomy. The AIDS crisis certainly remains a point of reference throughout the trilogy—in particular *The Western Lands*—but is only ever incidental. In fact, the distrust of the body that Burroughs displays throughout the trilogy and later texts is an extension of that body horror that we have repeatedly seen in the earlier novels.

Burroughs' representation of the gay male body is in stark contrast to the erotic investment in the physical upon which the majority of gay literature is predicated. Consider, for instance, the example of John Rechy, one of the few gay authors Burroughs is on record as admiring.[21] Rechy's novels—*City of Night* (1963), *Numbers* (1967), and *The Sexual Outlaw* (1977)—found widespread popularity during the years between gay liberation and the advent of AIDS and in many respects form an interesting counterpoint to

Burroughs' later Red Night trilogy.[22] Both novelists are explicitly interested in forms of gay masculinity, although the extreme imaginary of Burroughs' texts owes more to the genres of fantasy and science fiction than Rechy's work (which predominantly belongs to the social realist tradition of American gay literature).[23] What is so intriguing in the comparison between Rechy's and Burroughs' texts is the marked difference in their presentation of the gay male body. Although both employ a simplistic political discourse regarding the relationship between sex and salvation, they offer two very different readings of the role of the gay male body within the movement toward liberation.

Before the official recognition of the HIV virus in the United States in the early 1980s, mainstream gay literature had been centered on a deliberate policy of solidifying the sociopolitical gains made by the Gay Liberation movement. Rechy's documentary journal/novel *The Sexual Outlaw* was typical of this strategy, offering a supposedly confessional account of the author's sexual life while emphasizing the gay subculture's production of a lifestyle in which sex was divorced from social institutions such as marriage and used for personal fulfillment. In many ways, Rechy's text forms a neat summary of the revolution in gay subjectivity that occurred between Stonewall and the AIDS crisis, capturing in a "documentary" account, the sudden shift toward defiant, masculine paradigms of identity. According to Rechy, promiscuity—the "numbers" alluded to in the title of one of his texts—signaled the salvation of the gay subject since it indicated the extent to which gay men had left the closet and embraced their sexuality, their desires, and, most importantly, their role as members of a (sexual) community. In Rechy's text, hypermasculine sex is a revolutionary act (sex=salvation). Promiscuity becomes the defining aesthetic and ethic of resistance: "Promiscuous homosexuals (outlaws with dual identities—tomorrow they will go to offices and athletic fields, classrooms and construction sites) are the shock troops of the sexual revolution."[24] He continues: "In the sex moments pressurized into high intensity by life-crushing strictures challenged, the sexual outlaw experiences to the utmost the rush of soul, blood, cum through every channel of his being into the physical and psychical discharge of the fully awakened, living, *defiant* body."[25]

The demands of such a political call to arms are great, as Rechy himself is keen to emphasize (and even romanticize). The sexual outlaw inhabits a world ruled by the violence inherent within the fetishized, masculine style: "Daily, nightly he confronts cops and maniacs."[26] No wonder that one of Armistead Maupin's characters, on considering the dangers of drugs, S/M, and the psychopaths that the hypermasculine scene attracted, laments that "It was almost enough to make you stick with Mary Tyler Moore."[27] As Rechy's protagonist plays a dangerously subversive game that leaves him simultaneously liberated and isolated, he is carried to "the pinnacle of sexual freedom—the high that only outlaw sex can bring—as well as to the abyss of suicide."[28] Just how important a resistance this is, for Rechy at least, is illustrated by the overblown revolutionary prose of the text's conclusion. With an obvious debt to theorists of the sexual revolution such as Norman O. Brown and Wilhelm Reich, Rechy exclaims:

> Televise it all, the kissing, the fucking, masturbating, sucking, rubbing, rimming, touching, licking, loving. Thousands of bodies stripped naked joined in a massive, *loving* orgy [. . .] Would the cops break ranks? Flee? Join? [. . .] Cum instead of blood. Satisfied bodies instead of dead ones. Death versus orgasm. Would they bust everyone? With cum-smeared tanks would they crush all?[29]

This reading of the physical realm as the site of resistance and of the masculine body as one possible weapon in the battle for sexual liberation becomes, in many ways, impossible in the post-AIDS environment. Rechy's naive utopianism is overly simplistic, while the unfettered "Sex Hunger" that his novels glamorize today seems frighteningly unsafe.

The erotic investment in the gay male body that Rechy's text displays owes much to the clone scene; its presentation of gay masculinity is clearly influenced by the post-Stonewall masculinization of the gay scene. *The Sexual Outlaw* focuses (to the exclusion of almost anything else) on pleasure, self-fulfillment, masculinity, and rough sex (although never S/M). Indeed, the text is so obsessive in its transcription of a gay macho style that it reads, today at least, like a parody of the clone ethos:

> He is stripped to sweat-faded cutoffs. His pectorals are already pumped from repetitions of dumbbell presses on a bench, inclined, flat, then declined; engorged further by dumbbell flyes extending the chest muscles into the sweeping spread below the collar. His "lats"—congested from set after set of chin ups—slow, fast, wide-grip, medium-grip weights strapped about his waist for added resistance that will allow him to do only half-chins as the muscles protest— flare from armpits to mid-torso. His legs are rigid from the squats held tense at half-point.
>
> Round, full, his arms are hard, hard from sets of curls, the dumbbell an appendage of strength and power in his hands. The horseshoe indention at his triceps is engraved sharply by repetitions of barbell extensions.[30]

The (dull) repetitions of the above paragraph simultaneously attempt to capture the physical endurance of the gym workout and to glorify the gay male body into a "rigid," "hard," "tense," "pumped," "congested" and (most importantly) "engorged" machine that epitomizes the physical ideal of the hypermasculine. Such adoration of the corporeal is re-emphasized through the sex act itself, creating a procession of mirror images:

> In the framed mirror, Jim saw his own cum spill in slow arcking spurts as the man directed the white liquid onto his clothed body, on the jockstrap, on his face, on his lips, over the open magazine, and on the photograph in it of a muscular man standing naked over a clothed man surrounded in bed by magazines of photographs of muscular nude bodies.[31]

This naive narcissism and self-glorification is admittedly alienating (particularly considering the fact that Jim is Rechy's alter ego). What is worth noting, however, is the way in which Rechy's text forms a watershed between the pre-AIDS gay scene and the post–1979 culture. While I do not want to suggest that Rechy's vision of the gay male body is the only representation that existed in the years before the AIDS crisis, it is useful to draw a comparison between its eroticism and the images of the body that can be seen in Burroughs' work of the 1980s.

The extreme physicality of Rechy's text is hardly out of step with gay literature, erotica, or pornography. The glorification of the masculine body that Rechy undertakes is—if we ignore the simplistic revolutionary and political program of which it is part—quite alien to Burroughs' oeuvre, for despite his reputation as a pornographer, the texts are actually lacking in any graphic descriptions of the gay *body* as the site of desire. Sex and the body, for Burroughs, are always reduced to a simple equation: penis and anus. Moments of gay sex that do not involve anal penetration or penis celebration are rare in Burroughs' work, and in general there is little erotic investment in the bodies of the gay heroes. The texts predominantly focus only on the genitals, ignoring the degenitalized mapping of the rest of the body that occurs in Rechy's gym scene.

Of course, such an obsession with the phallus is in keeping with the kind of gay sex with which Burroughs' texts present the reader. The masculinity that the queer sexual act bolsters in Burroughs' vision is, after all, based upon the role of the phallus as a dispenser of sex/gender identity. However, the absence of any lingering description of the flesh creates pornographic texts that are unusually "prudish" in their fastidious refusal to focus on the bodies of their characters. This lack of interest in the flesh is in many ways the starting point of the texts' desire to transcend the corporeal. Lacking an erotic investment in the masculine body upon which *The Sexual Outlaw* and the clone scene itself relied, the texts occupy a paradoxical position, simultaneously outlining a masculine identity while letting the gay male body disappear (or at best transmuting it into little more than a phallus-anus).

Burroughs' distrust of the physical realm is always closely related to his understanding of heterosexual regulation and queer autonomy. In many respects Burroughs reads the AIDS crisis as yet another example of the regulation of the homosexual body by the

heterosexual dominant. Since the general policy of the American
authorities was, as Simon Watney has claimed, to use AIDS as "a
pretext throughout the West to 'justify' calls for increasing legislation and regulation of those who are considered to be socially un-
acceptable," Burroughs' desire to escape the body (the site on
which, according to the texts, such legislation and regulation
would operate) and to resignify gay sex as offering a transcendence
of death and an escape from the heterosexual world into a utopian
queer afterlife seems politically motivated.[32]

Thus the texts are not a direct response to AIDS per se, but
rather a critique of the heterosexual regulation of marginal sexualities that had preoccupied Burroughs in his fiction since the 1950s.
The AIDS crisis underscores the extent to which such regulation
is still deployed through the legal and medical discourses of the
dominant. From this perspective the desire to escape the body becomes part of Burroughs' wider vision of autonomy; the escape to
a "spirit state" as a body of light is a utopian image of the individual who has escaped power's influence. As Burroughs explains in
an interview with Ginsberg:

> Ginsberg: Well, that is to say the anxiety of the invasion
> seems at the end to be dispersed by the dissolution of space
> and time, or the dissolution of time.
> Burroughs: Yes, it is. That was it. The dissolution was nec-
> essary in order to neutralize the conspiracy. From this comes
> the theme that the only future is to . . . enter into a spirit, a
> completely spirit state. So that any conspiracy that's based
> on . . .
> Ginsberg: Grasping for matter? There is a notion that
> most conspiracies are actually, in a sense, spiritual conspira-
> cies; in the sense of, power takeovers involving people's
> minds.[33]

Hence masculine autonomy can be achieved only without a
body. Burroughs' paranoid vision of control and regulation reaches
its "logical" conclusion as the body is voluntarily discarded. The invasion of the subject—by the feminine and effeminacy, as well as
HIV—is no longer possible. Even death is forestalled, since Bur-

roughs believes that it also operates like a virus, as his discussion of the Egyptian hieroglyphic for death illustrates: "Notice that the death glyph is a man splitting his own head with an axe [. . .] Death is here conceived as coming from within, as an implanted self-destruct mechanism."[34] In this manner, Burroughs' play with the transcendence of the body can be clearly linked with his continuing desire to delineate a masculine, gay identity. The masculine subject has no need of the feminine, vulnerable body.

Significantly, the discourses on AIDS produced throughout the 1980s frequently depicted the gay male body as feminized. The representations of the corporeal that emerged in discussions of AIDS were characterized by a desire to resignify the gay male body as Other. Reawakening discourses of morality, divine judgment, and sin, which had been increasingly silenced throughout the 1960s and 1970s, the heterosexual response to the AIDS crisis (in its most reactionary incarnation) was one that sought to stigmatize the gay male body as the tool of dangerous pleasures and desires. The connection between homosexuality and disease is, as Sandor Gilman suggests, well established in Western discourses on health. The AIDS crisis offered reactionary members of the heterosexual dominant the opportunity to reinstate such associations, focusing in particular on the relation between homosexuality, (feminized) promiscuity, and older sexually transmitted diseases such as syphilis.[35]

As Leo Bersani has suggested, the media attention given to the story of Gaetan Dugas—the French airline steward who was believed to be "Patient Zero" for the HIV virus in America—is indicative of attempts to marginalize the epidemic and its sufferers as irresponsibly promiscuous. Bersani argues that the story of Dugas is "sensationalized from the very start with the most repugnant image of homosexuality available: that of the irresponsible male tart who willfully spread the virus after he was diagnosed and warned of the dangers of his promiscuity to others."[36] This fear of what Bersani aptly calls the "male tart" indicates a link between representations of AIDS and misogynist discourses on sexual diseases, particularly the nineteenth century's representations of female prostitutes and syphilis. As Bersani suggests, the common theme is the belief that "Women and gay men spread their legs with an unquenchable appetite for destruction."[37] The implicit feminization of the body that this association proposes offers a further impetus to Burroughs to escape from the flesh. The patriarchal discourse on health and bodies that seeks to demonize the woman and the gay man is, for Burroughs, the mark of all that he has been reacting against since it not only feminizes the (gay male) body but also demands the regulation of that body, thereby robbing the subject of his autonomy. As commentators have frequently noted, such discourses on AIDS conflate pleasure, femininity, and infection.[38]

Faced with this destabilized contemporary gay male body, it seems no wonder that the texts should need to fantasize the transcendence of the physical realm. Since Burroughs' understanding of the masculine has always been based upon stability, rigidity, and sameness, he cannot afford to assimilate the fragmentation of the gay male body that occurs in the 1980s. The texts' fantasy of escaping the corporeal altogether is a response to the undermining of phallic stability that occurs as a result of AIDS, the continuing regulation of homosexuality under the guise of health concerns and queer/gender theory's interest in performative identities and the transformation of the masculine.

"WE ARE HERE TO GO":
REICH, ORGASM, AND TRANSCENDENCE

In many ways, Burroughs' distrust of the corporeal is epitomized by the contrast that the Red Night trilogy sets up between two kinds of bodies: rigid, mummified remains, and the more fluid, spirit forms of the post-corporeal bodies of light. The transition from rigidity to fluidity is the key concern of *The Western Lands;* the bodies of the Wild Boys and Johnsons—which have always been on the verge of becoming hypermasculine, rigid, and hard, like the clone—are finally replaced by transcendent bodies of "light" that are immune to the dangerous, viral influences of the feminine and to the regulation imposed by power. The body of light is transfigured in both its escape from the law and in its immutable nature. Lacking materiality, it can no longer be conditioned, drugged, or regulated by the heterosexual dominant.

What facilitates this escape from the flesh? A cursory reading of Burroughs' texts might well suggest that it is drugs that trigger the transcendental movement, particularly since the Burroughs myth has always relied upon a romanticized reading of the author as the granddaddy of heroin, a shadowy figure behind the counterculture of the 1960s, the punk era, and even today's club culture. This vision of Burroughs as a drug guru is, however, not completely accurate. As early as the 1960s, Burroughs was suggesting that liberating drug experiences ought to be replicated by other means. His attempts to discover non-chemical means of transcendence centered on the Scientology-inspired cut-up texts, films, and tape recorder experiments, as well as flirtations with all manner of what would now be termed "New Age" fads: orgone accumulators, sensory deprivation tanks, stroboscopic lights (linked with Brion Gysin's infamous "Dream Machine") and the Eastern disciplines of the martial arts and yoga.[39]

Although never a practicing Buddhist like Ginsberg, Burroughs was clearly interested in similar transcendental goals, but he was also more than happy to utilize a curious mixture of ancient practices (including Gysin's Moroccan-influenced magic) and modern technology (from the shotguns used to blast holes in some of his canvases, to the use of film and audiotape) to achieve them. However, more important than any of these practices is the role of gay sex. The novels foreground sex between masculine-identified men as *the* primary means of escaping from the flesh. While drugs force the subject back into a pattern of circular desire that is the "Algebra of Need," gay sex, the texts argue, unplugs him from the circuit boards of power entirely, and in a far quicker and more permanent way than any of the "New Age" methods. As "The Great Slastobitch" exclaims: "This is the space age and sex movies must express the longing to escape from the flesh through sex. The way out is the way through" (*WB*, 82). Entry into the "space" inhabited by the bodies of light is always through gay sex since "space is here. Space is where your ass is" (*PDR*, 305). In the sex scenes between Kim and Jerry, Burroughs playfully depicts the transcendental possibilities of gay sex as a challenge to NASA's more cumbersome space program:

> Kim sees himself spread on a pink launching pad like a soft rocket. His ass is the touchhole, Jerry's cock the light. Now it touches, enters in a blaze of light as they streak out over the river and trees . . . a wake of jism across the Milky Way. (*PDR*, 282)

This belief in the liberatory power of sex has much to do with Burroughs' interest in the theories of Wilhelm Reich. Whereas most scientists and psychologists of the time dismissed Reich as a charlatan, a misguided disciple of Freud who had bastardized the great man's work, Burroughs was always keen to point out Reich's role as the first person to demand research into sexual activity. Unlike Kinsey, who was concerned only with classification of sexual behavior, Reich was intrigued with investigating, even measuring orgastic potency in order to prove a link between sexual repression and neurosis. The fact that Reich was—according to Burroughs at least—harassed to death by the American authorities not only underlined Burroughs' conclusion that those in power want to restrict all new forms of knowledge, but also indicated that Reich's findings must have been correct: "You can almost judge the importance of a discovery by the efforts made to suppress it. Reich's Orgone Theory is an example of a discovery that was very viciously suppressed" (*Job*, 122).

The most extended study of the influence of Reich on the texts is Allan Johnston's essay "The Burroughs Biopathy: William S. Burroughs' *Junky* and *Naked Lunch* and Reichian Theory."[40] Interestingly, though, Johnston pays little attention to Burroughs' representations of sexual activity. Reich's influence on the novels is predominantly discussed in terms of Burroughs' stance on heroin addiction. Sex and sexuality are only secondary to this (principally because of the diminished libido of the heroin addict). The scope of Johnston's essay is limited to just two novels, both from the 1950s. Reich's influence on Burroughs, though, extends much further than this, right up into his final novels of the 1980s and 1990s, in which the theories of orgasm are extremely important.

Reich's work is in many ways one of the starting points for the philosophy of desire that finds its voice in Deleuze and Guattari, Foucault, and Lyotard. These postmodern philosophers, particularly Deleuze and Guattari, owe much to Reich's Oedipal break from Freud, the critique of many of his mentor's assumptions about the libido that eventually resulted in his "excommunication." Deleuze and Guattari, themselves performing a critique of Freud, are generous towards Reich in *Anti-Oedipus;* his attempts to develop a materialistic psychiatry leads straight into their concept of desiring machines: "The fact remains that Reich, in the name of desire, caused a song of life to pass into psychoanalysis. He denounced, in the final resignation of Freudianism, a fear of life, a resurgence of the ascetic ideal, a cultural broth of bad consciousness."[41]

Yet Reich is not simply a theorist of desire. While much of his later work reaches out toward the social sphere in an attempt to understand the allure of mass movements such as fascism, his earlier interest in "orgasm theory" seems to be more concerned with notions of pleasure. The difference between pleasure and desire is underlined by Foucault who, as mentioned in the previous chapter, is keen to promote pleasure as a new realm free from the discourse of (Freudian) psychoanalysis. Reich's understanding of the orgasm seems more concerned with *jouissance,* a liberating pleasure that transforms the individual subject. According to Reich, "*Orgiastic potency is the capacity to surrender to the flow of biological energy, free of any inhibitions; the capacity to discharge completely the damned-up sexual excitation through involuntary, pleasurable convulsions of the body.*"[42] He continues: "In the sexual act, free of anxiety, unpleasure and fantasies, the intensity of pleasure in the orgasm is dependent upon the amount of sexual tension concentrated in the genitals. The greater and steeper the 'drop' of the excitation, the more intense the pleasure."[43]

The "sexual tension" held in the genitals produces various physiological effects, the most important being the production of an "armored body." Those individuals who are neurotic are likely to

display this neurosis through their musculature. Tight, tense muscles indicate a mental and emotional rigidity, an inability to give,
to free the self from anxiety, to expand toward the world. The quality of the moment of orgasm is central in all of this. The neurotic
is unable to experience orgiastic potency and is thus unable to
achieve release through orgasm. As a result, bodily tension is not
released, and emotional life suffers: "You are afraid of falling and of
losing your 'individuality' when you should let yourself go."[44] For
Reich, such emphasis on the body is diametrically opposed to
Freud's Victorian impulse to dismiss the physical realm. In Reich's
theories of sex-economy, the body is central to the individual's
well-being, mediating between the self and the world. With the
exception of the concept of armoring, the main emphasis of Reich's
discussions of the body is on the genitals. A parallel emerges here
with Burroughs' genital-obsessed pornography.

Burroughs' appropriation of these theories of orgasm and the
armored body is apparent throughout his texts. As he advises in
Naked Lunch: "We see God through our assholes in the flash bulb
of orgasm. . . . Through these orifices transmute your body" (*NL,*
220). This, in essence, is the basis of the texts' desire to transcend
the physical, in order to reach a higher realm of conscious existence. It is in many ways a *release,* something emphasized in the
passages in the Nova trilogy, that demand: "Come out of your stupid body you nameless assholes" (*SM,* 149). This concept of orgasm as a potentially liberating moment is reiterated throughout
the Wild Boy and Red Night texts, culminating in the fantasy of
orgasm as a moment of entry into the queertopia of bodies of light
in *The Western Lands.* Much of this is, of course, directly related to
Burroughs' interest in Reich.

Like Reich, Burroughs is aware of the role that the body plays
in mediating between self and other. The mummies that populate
The Western Lands, unworthy vessels that are likely to fall apart or
be desecrated before the subject finishes his quest for immortality,
could thus be read in part as metaphorical examples of Reich's armored body. Indeed, Reich's illustrator in *Listen, Little Man!* por-
trays the armored body as a mummified person. The quotation

from the text that follows it is "Your biological aberration, in the form of rigidity, has lasted only six thousand years."[45] The armored body and the mummy must both be overcome before the Western Lands can be reached.

However, there is an important difference between Reich's and Burroughs' presentation of the transformative effects of orgasm. While Reich believed that orgasm is accompanied by a release of energy that facilitates the momentary loss of the self—what contemporary postmodern theorists style as *jouissance*—Burroughs considers its importance in terms of the "transmutation" referenced in the quotation from *Naked Lunch*. Rather than a loss of the self, orgasm offers the possibility of overcoming the body. Never keen to replace a stable masculine identity with anything less certain, Burroughs has no interest in *jouissance*. Although the transmigration experienced in much of the queer heroes' sex is presented as a welcome re-emphasis of the extent to which they are all "the same," it is ultimately limited in its appeal. As the Transmigrants in *Cities of the Red Night* illustrate, the interchanging of bodies during the moment of orgasm can often become part of a system of oppression and violence. The Transmigrants fail spectacularly to achieve liberation. What Burroughs argues for instead is a fantastic theory of orgasm that replaces transmigration with transmutation so that orgasm becomes a means of changing the individual from a physical being to an incorporeal "body" of light.

Furthermore, Burroughs' reworking of Reich's theories also challenges the latter's assertion of heterosexuality as the primary sexual event. Although Reich viewed homosexuality as "an aberration originating in conflicted childhood experiences," he was liberal enough to suggest that it was hypocritical of the heterosexual dominant to condemn homosexuality since the dominant itself was so far from optimum sexual and emotional health.[46] Indeed, a list of sexual rights and freedoms that Reich composed in the early 1930s included the call for the "abolition of all laws against abortion, birth control, and homosexuality."[47] Regardless of this tolerance, Reich's ideas about the function of orgasm were always placed within a heterosexual context. It is this that Burroughs overturns, making the central points of Reich's orgasm theory applicable only to homo-sexuals, since he claims that it is only between two members of the same (male) sex that an uninhibited orgasm can result, when there is no Other (that is, woman) present.

In *The Western Lands,* Burroughs' bizarre vision of gay sex as a means of allowing a fearless orgasm is outlined by Kim. Called into the District Supervisor's office, Kim is briefed on his new mission:

> "Your job now is to find the Western Lands. Find out how the Western Lands are created. Where the Egyptians went wrong and bogged down in their stinking mummies. Why they needed to preserve the physical body."
>
> Kim gives him the textbook answer: "Because they had not solved the equation imposed by a parasitic female Other Half who needs a physical body to exist, being parasitic on other bodies. So to maintain the Other Half in the style to which she has for a million years been accustomed, they turn to the reprehensible and ill-advised expedient of vampirism.
>
> "If, on the other hand, the Western Lands are reached by the contact of two males, the myth of duality is exploded and the initiates can realize their natural state. The Western Lands is the natural, uncorrupted state of all human males. We have been seduced from our biologic and spiritual destiny by the Sex Enemy."
>
> The D.S. turns to a Russian Commissar. "You see the man is well instructed."
>
> "Straight thinking," grates a five-star general. (*WL*, 74–75)

Whatever this may be, it is certainly not "straight" thinking, but instead an obviously queer and very personal resignification of Egyptian mythology and Reichian orgasm theory. Taking Reich's de-emphasis of the procreative aims of sexual activity as his starting point, Burroughs queers Reich's work to produce his vision of the gay male orgasm as a transcendent, liberating force that has the capacity to free the subject from the prison of the flesh and take him to the Western Lands, a queertopia of inter-stellar spirits.

This shift toward liberatory orgasm begins essentially with the development of the idea of alertness during sex. As we saw in the last chapter, Burroughs' concern with self-mastery (ascesis) emerges in the final orgy that ends *Port of Saints*. Burroughs describes the Wild Boy participants as remaining alert and aware of their purpose, even at the height of their pleasure. Indeed, pleasure takes a secondary place, turning the orgy into a ritual, a piece of Crowley-inspired sex magic that has one aim—the transcendence of the flesh. For Burroughs, the orgasm holds the key to this, but *only if* the subject uses the moment of orgasm to lose sight of his body while retaining a sense of his masculinity. Unlike the Foucauldian interest in degenitalizing gay male sex by opening up new sexual planes on the body, Burroughs presents the queer orgasm as a technique of *re*genitalizing the body; the Wild Boys' orgasms allow them to focus solely on the phallic signifier of their masculinity while the rest of the body is disregarded. Sex thus loses its procreative force and becomes instead a means of escape, a tool to be used in the battle for gay male autonomy and self-empowerment:

> The Mexican pulled him off the bed and bent him over the white chair. He put a throwing knife into the boy's hand.
> "Throw it when you go off."
> As the boy ejaculated, the Mexican pulled him straight with a hand across his stomach. With a sharp animal cry Jerry threw a knife straight into the bullseye.
> [...]
> The Boys are summoned before the skull and their training begins. The smell of the skull on first exposure precipitates sexual frenzies. The boys tear off their clothes ejaculating, the red skull rash burning in lips and nipples and crotch and rectum as the skull smell steams off their bodies. They will learn to draw, aim and fire in the moment of orgasm, to throw a knife and use rifle and tommy gun. They will learn to conceive plans in this moment. They will learn that *sex is power*. (*PoS*, 56–57)

Burroughs' desire to transcend the flesh separates his queer project from the extreme, physical masculinity of the clone scene. From a Reichian perspective, Rechy's *The Sexual Outlaw* and the accompanying vision of the "rigid," "defiant," "hard," and "pumped" body of his protagonist (or *alter ego*) smacks of unfulfilled desire, the inability to find pleasure in the release of sexual tension. Reich often recounted how the men who attended his sex-therapy sessions would make much of their potency, their ability to have a succession of orgasms. Such boasting, he claimed, often served to conceal guilt and dissatisfaction with sex. Rechy's promiscuous "outlaws" with their armored bodies seem very similar. By de-emphasizing the body, Burroughs is clearly distancing himself from the sociohistorical reality of gay masculinization during the 1970s and early 1980s.

While Foucault and other queer theorists valorize S/M as a physical practice that transforms the masculinity of the gay male participants, Burroughs seeks not *jouissance* but instead the end of the body. As the orgy sequence in *Port of Saints* makes clear, "purposeful abandonment" leads to "squirming quivering flesh faces bursting from the pressure riding the wild bucking loins" (*PoS*, 165). This dissolution of the body is to be differentiated from the loss of the self in *jouissance*. The distinction is crucial, for it forms the basis of the texts' understanding of a post-corporeal environment as always masculine. As will become apparent, the end of the body facilitates the overcoming of weakness, fear, and shame. Burroughs' texts suggest that masculinity is not something that can be signified simply by a male body, no matter how muscled and strong that body may be. In this manner, the Red Night trilogy proves to be as concerned (and paranoid) about issues of homosexuality and gender as Burroughs' work of the 1950s. The gender dynamics of the Western Lands fantasy can all be related to Burroughs' fears about effeminacy and it is these fears that lead into his mythology of the afterlife, orgasm, and the body of light.

AFTER GENDER:
THE END OF THE FLESH AND THE LAW

Burroughs' fantasy of queer male-masculine stability ultimately leads him to imagine a world in which the gay male body is no longer necessary. His paranoid (and, from our post-Foucauldian perspective, overly simplistic) reading of the relationship between the gay subject and the heterosexual dominant results in the suggestion that his queer heroes must transcend their flesh in order to escape regulatory control. As we have seen, Burroughs suggests that it is only through gay sex that this transcendence can be achieved. In *The Western Lands,* gay sex offers the opportunity for the male subject to reject both heterosexual regulation and the influence of the feminine. Furthermore, he is able to prove his masculine status as he confronts death and journeys through the purgatorial "Land of the Dead" to the utopian Western Lands. Clearly, this fantasy is partisan in the extreme, a combination of effeminophobia, misogyny, and an occult-inspired vision of a post-corporeal environment. It seems no wonder that critics have largely ignored the role of gender in Burroughs' treatment of transcendence.

Burroughs' plan of afterliving must always be read in relation to his fantasy of queer male separatism. The quest for immortality in the Western Lands is closely tied to this search for masculine identity. The texts present death as the final challenge to the subject's masculine status, and significantly, the journey through the "Land of the Dead" is one that only the truly masculine subject can complete. Survival of "Last Chance" (*WL,* 141–142) with its dueling, gunfights, and Russian roulette is the ultimate test; it is here that the program of deconditioning and training that the earlier novels delineated is employed: "Few pilgrims reach the town of Last Chance. Sloth, self-indulgence, alcohol, addictions, old age, stupidity, all are obstacles. But lack of a special courage is the only insuperable barrier—the courage to confront *your* opponent, *your* final enemy" (*WL,* 141). The Old West imagery that accompanies the description of this realm implicitly indicates that it is no place for women or effeminate men.

The exclusionary nature of Burroughs' fantasy is startlingly illustrated in his description of one of the mythical Seven Souls:

> The Ka, the double, takes the same chances you take in the Land of the Dead. If you die, he dies. If you are tortured, so is he. So your interests are absolutely synonymous. And that

is the only basis for absolute trust. He will be there when you need him and he will know when that is.

The male Ka acts as an agent designed to further male interests in the widest sense, with particular attention to immortality. [. . .]

Remember that as a man your Ka must be a male, so any female Ka is sure to be lethal impostor, happily embraced by an appalling percentage of idiotic and besotted males just aching to be turned into swine. Remember that the Egyptian glyph for poltroon is woman as man, that is, a female Ka taking over a male body.

Now, Kas is all a little different, but people who look alike, Ka alike. They may be viewed interchangeably. The basic Ka spirit, the male Ka, is in fact Imam. The quickest manner of contact is sexual. Sex is the basis of fear, how we got caught in the first place and reduced to the almost hopeless human condition. The Ka can be freed by the act of sex when there is no fear present. (*WL*, 200–201)

The effeminophobia that informs this vision is almost exactly the same as the one underpinning the Talking Asshole routine in *Naked Lunch*. The "poltroons" are set in opposition to Burroughs' vision of the masculine-identified male whose masculine essence is kept pure through his complete rejection of the feminine. The heterosexual or effeminate gay man is unable to free himself from the influence of the feminine and thus loses his autonomous status. Gay sex offers salvation, since, as the quotation suggests, it is the only sexual act (involving more than one subject) that allows the individual to experience pleasure without fear and without an encounter with the sexed body of the Other. The narcissistic elements of gay sex—the celebration of masculinity among men that such sex can promote—are thus styled as a redemptive movement toward transcendence.

Furthermore, gay sex, for Burroughs, constitutes a challenge to the binary structures that underpin the heterosexual dominant. As masculine-identified, anatomically male bodies come together, the (heterosexual) need for a female or feminine position is no longer paramount; thus the distinction between sex and gender is collapsed. In a situation in which both participants are male *and* masculine-identified, there is no need to treat sex and gender as separate factors. The anatomical sex of the participants is reflected in their gender identification, while their gender identification is reflected by their anatomical sex. The establishment of a masculine-focused gay identity offers the opportunity for gay sex to transgress the heterosexual matrix, since it no longer complies with the hierarchical structures of male/female, masculine/feminine, active/passive participants. Monogendered (masculine) sexual couplings, in which the relation between participants is fluid rather than fixed as active/passive, cannot be assimilated into the heterosexual matrix. As such, Burroughs suggests, masculine gay sex challenges the organization of the social field that heterosexual desire produces. Notions of "family," "domesticity," "partnership," and "love" are thrown into question as the texts attempt to demolish the binary logic that underpins the heterosexual monopoly and its "myth of duality" (*WL,* 75).

The Red Night trilogy's mythology clearly signifies Burroughs' continuing distrust of the binary structures that organize western thought, human biology and social/gender models. In *Cities of the Red Night,* Dr. Peterson asks whether the symptoms of the B–23 virus are not "simply the symptoms of what we are pleased to call 'love'?" (*CRN,* 25). He continues:

> Eve, we are told, was made from Adam's rib . . . so a hepatitis virus was once a healthy liver cell. If you will excuse me, ladies, nothing personal . . . we are all tainted with viral origins. The whole quality of human consciousness, as expressed in male and female, is basically a virus mechanism. I suggest that the virus, known as "the other half," turned malignant as a result of the radiation to which the Cities of the Red Night were exposed. (*CRN,* 25)

Such reasoning ends with the suggestion that "The whole human position is no longer tenable" (*CRN,* 25).[48] The belief that gender dualism is a crippling, unproductive force reverberates throughout Burroughs' writings. In the essay "Women: A Biologic

Mistake?" he considers the possibility that "the separation of the sexes" could be an arbitrary whim of evolutionary development rather than a necessity.[49] The creation of a masculine queer identity leads Burroughs to imagine what the final result of sex and gender separatism might be.

This reading of the texts as a challenge to the binary structures of western thought is far from original. As Wayne Pounds has suggested, Burroughs "sees history as determined by a primordial fall from an androgynous unity into a strife-ridden duality whose chief expressions are language and sexual difference."[50] Robin Lydenberg supports this in her assertion that sexual dualism is, for Burroughs, the "origin and model for all other forms of hierarchical domination."[51] However, such discussions are consistent in their attempt to style Burroughs' challenge to hierarchical binary structures as part of the post-structuralist tradition. Lydenberg, for instance, suggests that "While he may promote a kind of sexual indeterminacy by playing with castration and with the mother's body, by inventing images of androgyny and hermaphroditism, Burroughs envisions ultimately the explosion of *all* bodies in the constantly shifting gears of his writing machine."[52] This focus on "*all* bodies" leads her to suggest a similarity between Burroughs' vision and the "high-tech utopia of desire envisioned in *Anti-Oedipus* [in which] there are no monuments, no fixed identities or totalities which might impose a hierarchy or a center. Everything circulates, connections are broken and reformed in perpetual metamorphosis."[53]

However, as we have repeatedly seen, this approach to the texts does not fully explain their queer/gender dynamics. Considering the texts in terms of "becoming"—the dissolution of fixed identities—is problematic, since it ignores the monocentric nature of Burroughs' fantasy. He is not interested in *all* bodies, but only those of his queer heroes. He does not seek the dissolution of identities, but rather the establishment of one fixed identity, the queer masculine. Thus the texts' desire to challenge the binary structures that govern sex and gender does not lead to some radical indeterminacy but instead to the delineation of a stable, masculine iden-

tity. The impetus of Burroughs' project is not deconstructive because its negotiation of the "myth of duality" involves the creation
of a determinate identity that cuts across the interrelated binaries
of male/female, masculine/feminine, sex/gender. Upholding the
male-masculine half of the binary logic that underpins all discourses on sex and gender, Burroughs creates a monocentric fantasy in which all that is *not-masculine* and *not-male* is excluded.

Of course, this monocentricism is particularly startling since the
later texts claim to be in search of an alternative to the stultifying
limitations of the Judeo-Christian "One God Universe" (*WL*,
113). Yet what quickly becomes apparent is that this desire for
multiplicity does not extend into the sexual arena delineated by the
texts. The male-male desire that Burroughs plays with forms a
paradoxical counterpoint to his rants against monotheism, global-
ization, and conformity. In *Ghost of Chance*, Burroughs reveals the
full extent of his masculine monocentricism:

> A rift is built in the human organism, the rift or cleft between
> two hemispheres, so any attempt at synthesis must remain
> unrealizable in human terms. I draw a parallel between this
> rift separating the human body and the rift that divided
> Madagascar [the site of Mission's utopian commune] from
> the mainland of Africa. One side of the rift drifted into en-
> chanted timeless innocence. The other moved inexorably to-
> ward language, time, tool use, weapon use, war, exploitation
> and slavery.
>   It would seem that merging the two is not viable, and one
> is tempted to say, as Brion Gysin did, "*Rub out the word.*"
>   But perhaps "rub" is the wrong word. The formula is quite
> simple: reverse the magnetic field so that, instead of being
> welded together, the two halves repel each other like oppos-
> ing magnets. This could be a road to final liberation, as it
> were, a final solution to the language problem, from which all
> human "problems" stem. (*GC*, 49–50)

This strategy of repelling the other half is clearly the logic behind Burroughs' battle with the binary structure of sex and gender. His monogender, monosex plan strives to make the world

male-masculine, not by trying to explode all bodies into space, as Lydenberg asserts, but rather by fantasizing the post-corporeal, post-gender establishment of an identity that can *only be* male-masculine.

What is so interesting about Burroughs' vision of both sex and gender is the manner in which his understanding of the desired male-masculine identity is always based upon a set of essentialist assumptions that are in stark contrast to the theorization of sex and gender in contemporary queer and gender theory. For Judith Butler, the distinction between sex and gender is the crucial starting point for any discussion of bodies, sex and identity:

> Originally intended to dispute the biology-is-destiny formulation, the distinction between sex and gender serves the argument that whatever biological intractability sex appears to have, gender is culturally constructed: hence, gender is neither the casual result of sex nor as seemingly fixed as sex. The unity of the subject is thus already potentially contested by the distinction that permits of gender as a multiple interpretation of sex.[54]

As Butler's argument continues, this becomes more complex, beginning with the suggestion that "Gender ought not to be conceived merely as the cultural inscription of meaning on a pregiven sex (a juridical conception); gender must also designate the very apparatus of production whereby the sexes themselves are established."[55] The ultimate instability of the category of sex itself—finding expression in both Foucault's and Butler's work—centers upon those moments during which there is a rupture in the sexed body that threatens the supposed stability of the corporeal. In such moments of sex/gender disjunction, the bodies of the hermaphrodite, the transsexual, and the infant born with indeterminate primary sexual characteristics, are central.

Lydenberg's discussion of Burroughs' texts' "sexual indeterminacy" is clearly related to the postmodern notions of sex/gender instability to be found in the work of theorists like Butler.[56] However, as we have seen, Burroughs' understanding of both the sexed body and gender identity is always predicated on the assumption that there is a natural and authentic male-masculine body and identity. By presenting the sexed (male) body as a given reality, Burroughs' texts are clearly not interested in creating indeterminacy. In the course of the narratives this body may well be assimilated by alien species, dismembered, or rendered hermaphroditic, yet these events are presented as a defilement, pollution, and corruption of the sexed body's original purity of form. The texts foreground sex/gender indeterminacy as a nightmarish corruption of the stable, phallic male body and accuse the heterosexual dominant of producing such confusion in an attempt to marginalize gay subjects.

By exercising control over the space between the signifier (the male body) and the signified (a masculine identity), the heterosexual dominant can corrupt the "natural" link between the two. This moment of rupture—in which the male body comes to signify something other-than-masculine—is crucial to Burroughs' queer project, in that it is this weakness, this potential for disaster that leads to the call for the end of the body. Aware of the possibility that the sexed body serves as the base upon which (gender) identity is constructed, Burroughs notes throughout the texts of the 1950s and 1960s, the way in which gay gender identification is always constructed from without by social forces such as psychoanalysis, the law, the medical establishment, and the Church. By the time of the Red Night trilogy, of course, such social regulation had reached a peak unprecedented since the 1950s as the AIDS epidemic became an excuse for extensive heterosexual intervention in the gay community.

Burroughs thus dispenses with the body for two reasons: to escape the influence of power and regulatory control and, more importantly, because it is no longer necessary in his queertopia. Envisaging a future world that is solely queer, masculine, and male, Burroughs has no need of the body, since in an environment that is free from difference, in which each inhabitant is male and masculine, the body's role as a signifier of sexual difference is defunct.

However much the texts imagine the creation of a less-than-masculine male body in their visions of effeminate men, castrated subjects, and talking assholes, they consistently indicate a belief in an essential masculine identity, a given subjecthood that cannot be eliminated entirely (since deconditioning can reclaim it), only cut off from expression. At this point, if it were not already apparent, Burroughs diverges sharply from contemporary queer, gender, and postmodern theory. All men in the world of the texts are masculine; it is viral invasion, the influence of the feminine and social regulation, that makes some men lose control of their bodies and forget their masculine status.

The queer body is distrusted as a signifier of "maleness" because it can always be resignified through the regulation and production of meaning emanating from power. The fact that Burroughs is a gay man who experienced firsthand the fear and loathing of the 1950s, when homosexuality was considered a sickness, when the (moneyed, bourgeois) gay man went from one psychoanalyst's couch to the next, and when a McCarthyite policy of guilt by suspicion was a daily reality, should not be underestimated. Unlike many of those gay men too young to have been at Stonewall, too young even to have read about it in the next day's newspapers, Burroughs experienced the post–Gay Liberation Front emergence of the masculine paradigm from an ironic distance. As a result, he is not enamored of the clone scene's emphasis on the body as the site of masculinity, and he is skeptical of the radical claims of such a corporeal identity, having experienced the manner in which the corporeal became the site of repressive regulation in the years preceding gay liberation.

Yet similarly the texts do not suggest that the mitigated, post-AIDS understanding of masculinity as parody, of the butch stance as masquerade is a viable option either. Curiously, Burroughs' extraordinary position is that of an essentialist (a believer in an essence of maleness) who is more than happy to see the male body—which is, of course, *the* signifier of an essential sex/gender—disappear. However, the texts envisage this paradoxical disappearance in certain, strict terms. The male spirit, or male Ka, as it is finally termed, can be established only in a context that is free from power's influence once the subject has brought about the coincidence of this Ka with the flesh. The texts style the end of the body as the final act of liberation from oppression. This fantasy of freedom centers on the moment when the soul of the subject (his identity, his essence) is able to eject his fragile body (the signifier of sex and the site at which gender is made solid) in a moment of pure identification. The subject has achieved masculinity, maleness and has survived the physical dangers of Last Chance. Masculine identity has been proven, stability has been secured, and the body is abandoned so that no controlling power can ever again demand an effeminate resignification of that flesh and, concomitantly, that identity.

Burroughs is always wary of the manner in which the self and identity can easily be manipulated by external, controlling forces. Both are open to co-option and even external construction, a hall of mirrors in which the original, supposedly autonomous subject is no longer able to distinguish himself from the simulacra, the original from the copy. His vision of the Western Lands, then, is one in which gay sex offers a unity of self and body, a unity that proffers autonomy and wholeness.[57] Yet this is merely a means to an end; once this unity has been achieved, once signifier and signified converge to offer stable meaning, the body is no longer necessary—it can be dispensed with since the subject has reached the utopian Western Lands in which he is surrounded by other masculine gay men. The subject is no longer in a world of difference but one of sameness, a community of masculine selves who no longer need the body—nor indeed, the concept of masculinity—now that they have all become one.

However, such a fantastic strategy of exclusion, separatism, and essentialism is ultimately self-defeating. The "utopian" elements of the fantasy quickly unravel, suggesting that the queertopia of the Western Lands is as likely to collapse into dystopia as the Red Night cities. The sexual binary is one that always creates conflict, variation, and change in that it is based upon a difference that Burroughs' texts seemingly want to disavow. If the conflict between the sexes that the texts depict ends, then clearly all possibility of change will end as well, leaving the new queer order to stagnate slowly. Since masculinity is reliant on conflict, the utopian project is in many ways impossible, since it would mean an end to the masculine identifications that Burroughs prizes so dearly. The male-masculine needs conflict, needs the *not-male* in order to be able to define itself. Without this, it simply disappears into nothingness.

Significantly, *The Western Lands* ends without having created the queertopia that was promised. The possibility of achieving the desired queer autonomy is thrown into doubt, as is the usefulness of such autonomy. Burroughs' alter ego, the old writer of the novel's framing narrative, dies as a result of his Wishing Machine. The moral of the fairy tale is: "So think, before you wish out some rotten-weed wish" (*WL*, 249). In the final pages, the authorial voice asks: "How long does it take a man to learn that he does not, cannot want what he 'wants'?" (*WL*, 257). No salvation is promised us, the battle continues:

> There were moments of catastrophic defeat, and moments of triumph. The pure killing purpose. You find out what it means to lose. Abject fear and ignominy. Still fighting, without the means to fight. Deserted. Cut off. Still we wore the dandy uniform, like the dress uniform of a distant planet long gone out. Messages from headquarters. *What* headquarters? Every man for himself—if he's got a self left. Not many do. (*WL*, 253)

The reference to the "dandy uniform" and the fear of the loss of the self that underpins this passage suggest that the identity confusion brought about by the effeminate paradigm remains an important issue for Burroughs even after decades of masculine identification. Gay men are still forced to wear the uniform of femininity by straight culture, regardless of their preferences of gender identification. The peace that could possibly be found in the Western Lands is not yet achieved, and the novel closes with Burroughs having made his own preparations for sailing across the Duad. His readers are advised to make their own way.

The essentialism and separatism that underpin Burroughs' queer vision are ultimately the very qualities that prevent its fulfillment. Of course, much of this paradox could be worked out if Burroughs were prepared to relinquish his essentialist concerns and enter instead the postmodern sphere of gender play in which the creation of a body of light might signify entry into a realm of indeterminacy. As Zachary I. Nataf notes, the transgendered body represented as angel represents "an escape from sex and gender altogether, in that it transcends the body. The angelic entity is pure spirit. The sex of angels is often portrayed in art as an androgynous unity of the essences of both genders and so beyond sexual difference and duality as to be corporeally neuter."[58] But Burroughs' old-fashioned belief in masculinity as a determinate quality prevents him from making this leap, and so the bodies of light of his queer heroes never become androgynous, indeterminate or transfigured. Perhaps it is too much to expect of an author whose career as a gay novelist spans McCarthy, the Mattachine Society, Stonewall, the Gay Liberation Front, the clone scene, AIDS, and the emergence of the discourses of postmodernity.

AFTERWORD

Burroughs' position within the gay community has always been negligible, something quite appropriate considering the fact that the rent boys of Tangier dubbed him "*el hombre invisible.*"[1] Yet there are brief moments during which he steps into the mainstream of gay politics, culture, and discourse. One of these is the essay "Sexual Conditioning" which appeared in the 1973 *Gay Liberation Book*.[2] Of course, Burroughs' essay is quite different in tone and subject from any of the other texts besides which it stands. While the other essays seek to defend and justify gay lifestyles and identity, challenging the repressive tide of heterosexual comment, Burroughs sidesteps the whole issue of gay *identity,* drawing instead on his usual interest in science and behavioral conditioning to suggest that all desire, both hetero- and homosexual, is conditioned. Sexual morality is dead, he claims, since

> experiments have shown that sexual desire is a matter of stimulating certain brain areas and that such stimulation is *purely arbitrary.* Admittedly, homosexuals can be conditioned to react sexually to a woman—or to an old boot, for that matter. In the same way, heterosexual males can be conditioned to react sexually to other men. And who is to say that one is more desirable than the other?[3]

As always, Burroughs' misogyny remains problematic. However, what is interesting about the passage is the suggestion that conditioning techniques could be potentially liberating. Such a reworking of conditioning could, Burroughs claims, be the key to autonomy: "Recent experiments in electric brain stimulation have shown that sexual excitements can now be produced at push-button control. Experiments in autonomic shaping have shown that subjects can learn to control these responses and reproduce them at will, once they learn where the neural buttons are located."[4]

This is the essence of Burroughs' understanding of sexuality. It is always an issue of the relationship between social control and individual autonomy; "freedom" is possible only once the subject is released from the processes of conditioning (or gains knowledge of counter techniques of deconditioning). Although Burroughs clearly recognizes that such complete freedom is impossible, his understanding of power remains overly simplistic. Ultimately, this is the central problem of Burroughs' vision of gay liberation. It is as though the specter of McCarthyism and, more importantly, the widespread regulation of homosexuality during the postwar years, hovers over all of Burroughs' texts. Since he believes that effeminacy represents a loss of autonomy, Burroughs always outlines queer (masculine gay) identity as a fight for self-mastery against the influence of external social forces.

The gender dynamics of Burroughs' queer politics are as problematic as his paranoid vision of social regulation. By relentlessly pursuing a masculinist agenda of separatism and exclusion, Burroughs' texts produce fantasies of violent revolution that seem anachronistic in comparison with the gay liberation movement's attempts to effect real social change throughout the 1960s and 1970s. By the time of *The Western Lands* he seems aware of his own isolation: "So here I am in Kansas with my cats, like the honorary agent for a planet that went out light-years ago" (*WL,* 252).

Such isolation has become even more explicit since queer theory began to draw upon feminist understandings of the interrelation of sex and gender and employed strategies of play and parody in a subversive attempt to undermine the cultural inscriptions of masculine/feminine, male/female. Burroughs' quest for masculine stability is antithetical to such playful appropriations and reworkings. It is finally this desire for stability that marks Burroughs' exclusion from both contemporary queer and postmodern discourses on identity. His essentialist assumptions over issues of gender place him at odds with the prevalent trend of queer, gender, and postmodern theory. While this does not justify Burroughs' exclusion from the queer canon, it does indicate the extent to which his inclusion would be politically problematic and could only ever be regarded as a historical recuperation of a novelist whose work expresses desires that the contemporary gay movement has long since sought to distance itself from.

Notes

Introduction

1. Mailer, quoted by Victor Bockris in *With William Burroughs: A Report from the Bunker* (New York: Seaver Books, 1981), p. xix.
2. Burroughs appeared on the Internet as part of a benefit netcast entitled "Psychic Drag Queens Live on the Net" in February 1997 along with Allen Ginsberg and other literary luminaries. A report of this event by Steve Silberman entitled "Burroughs Pops On-line Cherry with Drag Queens" can be found at the *Wired News* site: http://www.wired.com/news/news/culture/story/2173.html. It is worth noting that Burroughs was not one of the "Psychic Drag Queens" himself.
3. The accusation of pedophilia was leveled in Graham Caveney's article "Pimp of the Perverse," *Arena* (November, 1997), p. 76, and in his biography *The "Priest," They Called Him: The Life and Legacy of William S. Burroughs* (London: Bloomsbury, 1998), p. 19.
4. Norman Mailer, quoted by Ted Morgan in *Literary Outlaw: The Life and Times of William S. Burroughs* (New York: Henry Holt, 1991), p. 581.
5. Burroughs' principal biographer has attempted to overturn this understanding of the author as "masculine," explaining his homosexuality in Oedipal terms: "Athletically inept, finding difficulty in making friends, rejected by his father from such male enclaves as the basement workshop, Burroughs fit the Kinsey Institute's definition of 'gender non-conformity' in childhood as the most important factor in future homosexuality. He was isolated from his father and his male peers, and his mother encouraged in subtle ways the feminine side of his nature." This seems a problematic, unnecessary, and insultingly slight attempt to excuse Burroughs' sexual orientation. See Morgan, p. 582. Furthermore, he claims

that the key to much of Burroughs' sexuality is a childhood incident involving the family governess, her boyfriend, and the young Burroughs. Apparently Burroughs was forced to perform fellatio, something that traumatized him throughout his life (the biographical critical school would no doubt attribute the almost total absence of fellatio from the texts' sexual scenarios to this story); see Morgan, p. 31. More evidence of Burroughs' "feminine" temperament emerges in the description of his affair with Allen Ginsberg: "Burroughs in the act of sex underwent an amazing transformation. This reserved, sardonic, masculine man became a gushing, ecstatic, passionate woman. The change was so extreme and startling that Allen was alarmed." Morgan, p. 230.

6. *Naked Lunch* (dir. David Cronenberg, 1991). Burroughs' accidental shooting of his common-law wife, Joan Vollmer, is discussed in Morgan, pp. 194–196.

7. Cronenberg in *Cronenberg on Cronenberg*, ed. Chris Rodley (London and Boston: Faber and Faber, 1992), p. 162.

8. The most interesting response to Cronenberg's film is Richard Dellamora's discussion in *Apocalyptic Overtures: Sexual Politics and the Sense of an Ending* (New Brunswick, NJ: Rutgers University Press, 1994), pp. 117–128. Dellamora notes the manner in which the film effectively heterosexualizes Burroughs' radical sexual politics.

9. See *Gay Sunshine* 21 (Spring 1974).

10. Burroughs, "Lee and the Boys" in *Interzone*, ed. James Grauerholz (New York: Penguin, 1989), pp. 35–36.

11. Gregory Woods, "William Seward Burroughs II" in Emmanuel S. Nelson, ed., *Contemporary Gay American Novelists: A Bio-Bibliographical Critical Sourcebook* (Westport, CT and London: Greenwood Press, 1993), p. 40.

12. Emmanuel S. Nelson in his introduction to *Contemporary Gay American Novelists*, p. xvii.

13. John Calder, "Introduction" in *A William Burroughs Reader* (London: Picador, 1982), p. 16.

14. Hassan, Ihab, "The Subtracting Machine: The Work of William Burroughs," in Jennie Skerl and Robin Lydenberg, eds., *William S. Burroughs: At the Front: Critical Reception, 1959–1989* (Carbondale and Edwardsville: Southern Illinois University Press, 1991), p. 55.

15. Timothy S. Murphy, *Wising Up the Marks: The Amodern William Burroughs* (Berkeley and Los Angeles: University of California Press, 1997), p. 60.

16. *Ibid.*, p. 60.
17. *Ibid.*, p. 61.
18. Even the most queer reading of Burroughs' texts—Richard Dellamora's discussion in *Apocalyptic Overtures*—is finally unsatisfactory. Using Burroughs to illustrate wider issues of apocalyptic male sexual dissidence, Dellamora frustratingly concludes with the comment that "What remains unaddressed is the significance of Burroughs' queerness to the history of sexual minorities." See Dellamora, p. 128.
19. "Body of light" is a term used by Aleister Crowley. Burroughs appropriates it in his texts of the 1970s and 1980s. See Crowley, *Magick in Theory and Practice* (1929; rpt. New York: Dover Publications, 1976), p. 88.

CHAPTER ONE

1. Burroughs, *The Letters of William S. Burroughs 1945–1959*, ed. Oliver Harris (1993; rpt. London: Picador, 1993), pp. 119–120. Hereafter cited parenthetically in the text as *Letters*.
2. In his exhaustive study of the gay subculture in New York from 1890 to 1940, George Chauncey notes a lexical shift in gay slang at the turn of the century: "men who identified themselves as different from other men primarily on the basis of their homosexual interest rather than their womanlike gender status usually called themselves 'queer' [. . .] Many queers considered *faggot* and *fairy* to be more derogatory terms, but they usually used them only to refer to men who openly carried themselves in an unmanly way." See Chauncey, *Gay New York: The Making of the Gay Male World 1890–1940* (New York: Basic Books, 1994), p. 101. Burroughs seems to be relying on exactly this shift in meaning.
3. Theo van der Meer notes the absence of the subject of fellatio in eighteenth-century legal discourses on sexual habits. He argues that fellatio was considered the "libertine's vice" and that it is possible that "the fellator was perceived as 'active' and perhaps even imposed his social superiority or at least his libertinism on an inferior." See "Sodomy and the Pursuit of a Third Sex in the Early Modern Period" in Gilbert Herdt, ed., *Third Sex, Third Gender: Beyond Sexual Dimorphism in Culture and History* (New York: Zone Books, 1994), pp. 160–162. In the twentieth century the active/passive alignments have been radically reversed, aided no

doubt by Freud's Oedipal reading of fellatio as a substitute for suckling at the mother's breast, an emasculating interpretation that denies the fellator active, masculine status. See Freud, "Some Psychical Consequences of the Anatomical Distinction Between the Sexes," *The Standard Edition of the Complete Psychological Works of Sigmund Freud* (hereafter *S.E.*) vol. 19, ed. James Strachey in collaboration with Anna Freud (London: The Hogarth Press, 1953–74), pp. 251–252.

4. Judith Butler, *Gender Trouble: Feminism and the Subversion of Identity* (New York and London: Routledge, 1990), p. 122.

5. Burroughs, "The Finger" in *Interzone*, p. 17.

6. *Ibid.*, p. 17.

7. Harris, p. xxi.

8. For a more detailed history of this period and the trials of publication, see Burroughs' letters to Ginsberg and Kerouac during spring 1952 (*Letters*, p. 105*ff*).

9. Burroughs considered the original publication with *Narcotic Agent* "an appalling idea" (*Letters*, p. 143), although on reading Helbrant's book he decided that "He does not sound like an overly obnoxious character" (*Letters*, p. 187). The two covers for these novels indicate the problems that Solomon faced with *Queer*. Both offer aggressively heterosexual images of men attacking or arresting "bad" women. The cover of *Junkie* shows a man grappling with a female addict; the cover of *Narcotic Agent* has a similar addict being handcuffed by police as she sits stoned in her negligée. Such pulp packaging with its typical reliance on eroticized violence and bondage would have no doubt been hard pushed to find a suitable cover for *Queer*. Helbrandt inscribes his novel "To Anne, Of Course" underlining his heterosexuality, while Burroughs cryptically inscribes *Junkie* "To A.L.M.," the initials of Adelbert Lewis Marker (who would later appear as Eugene Allerton in *Queer*).

10. Morgan discusses the belated publication of *Queer* in his biography; see Morgan, p. 597. As Oliver Harris has pointed out, the "exceptional contingency" of *Queer* renders any attempt to discuss its historical position within the Burroughs corpus problematic. The introduction to the text was added in the 1980s, and there are also "sections of new text, added to the original manuscript in the editorial process, including passages taken from contemporary letters." See Harris, "Can You See a Virus? The Queer Cold War of William Burroughs" *Journal of American Studies* 33.2 (1999), 248 and 248*n*20 respectively.

NOTES

197

11. Burroughs' dismissal of *Queer* can be seen—among other places—in his interview with Phillippe Mikriammos; see "The Last European Interview" *Review of Contemporary Fiction* (Spring 1984), 13.

12. Burroughs, *Junkie* (New York: Ace Books, 1953), p. 84. Hereafter cited parenthetically in the text as *J*. When this text was revised and republished by Penguin in the 1970s the spelling was updated to "Junky." In order to maintain textual coherence, I have referred to the original 1953 edition of the text—"Junkie"—when referencing this work.

13. Burroughs, Introduction to *Queer* (New York: Viking, 1985), p. xii. Hereafter cited parenthetically in the text as *Q*.

14. The organization of gay relationships in terms of the heterosexual matrix of masculine-feminine, active-passive, and the role of the "occasional homosexual" is discussed by Jamie Gough in "Theories of Sexual Identity and the Masculinization of the Gay Man" in Simon Shepherd and Mick Wallis, eds., *Coming on Strong: Gay Politics and Culture* (London: Unwin, 1989), pp. 119–136. One might suggest that the shift from *Junkie* to *Queer* is one in which Lee changes from "occasional homosexual" (as the references to his wife in the former emphasize) to confirmed homosexual. Interestingly, Burroughs himself had made such a shift during the space between the composition of the two novels following the shooting of his common-law wife Joan Vollmer.

15. "Effeminophobia" is a term used by Eve Kosofsky Sedgwick; see "How to Bring Your Kids Up Gay: The War on Effeminate Boys" in *Tendencies* (London: Routledge, 1994), pp. 154–164.

16. David Savran, *Taking It Like a Man: White Masculinity, Masochism and Contemporary American Culture* (Princeton: Princeton University Press, 1998), p. 88.

17. *Ibid.*, p. 52.

18. Murphy, p. 65.

19. *Ibid.*, p. 65.

20. *Ibid.*, p. 66.

21. Harris, p. 259.

22. *Ibid.*, p. 258.

23. Burroughs and Ginsberg, *The Yage Letters* (San Francisco: City Light Books, 1963), pp. 44–46. Hereafter cited parenthetically in the text as *YL*.

24. See John Marks, *The Search for the "Manchurian Candidate": The CIA and Mind Control* (London: Allen Lane, 1979) for an exhaustive account of the CIA's MKULTRA program.

25. Michel Foucault, *The History of Sexuality, Volume One: An Introduction* 1976, trans. Robert Hurley (1978; rpt. London: Penguin, 1990), p. 43. As Elaine Showalter notes, the term "homosexual" was coined by Hungarian writer Karoly Benkert in 1869 and entered the English language with the translation of Krafft-Ebing's *Psychopathia Sexualis* in the 1890s. See Showalter, *Sexual Anarchy: Gender and Culture at the Fin de Siècle* (New York: Viking, 1990), p. 171.

26. Showalter surveys the two dominant modes of gay identity that emerged at the end of the nineteenth century; she terms one the "paradigmatic *fin de siècle* model of inversion" citing Ulrichs, Hirschfeld, Carpenter, and J.A. Symonds as its main theorists. The other is the pro "gender differentiation" model, which argues for manly men and feminine women. Significantly she omits to give a list of theorists for this second model, managing only to footnote a quote from Friedländer. This remarkable lack of examples is symptomatic of the way in which the effeminate paradigm came to dominate all theorization of homosexual identity until the middle of the twentieth century. The masculine models that the sexologists suggested and that Friedländer espoused so radically have been generally ignored and silenced. See Showalter, pp. 172–173.

27. Gert Hekma, "'A Female Soul in a Male Body': Sexual Inversion as Gender Inversion in Nineteenth-Century Sexology" in Herdt, p. 239.

28. Alan Sinfield, *The Wilde Century: Effeminacy, Oscar Wilde and the Queer Moment* (London and New York: Cassell, 1994), pp. 11–12. Showalter offers the interesting suggestion that the Wilde trials effectively de-aestheticized male-male love. Homosexuality had been regarded as aesthetically pleasing by the *fin-de-siècle* decadents because it dispensed with (reproductive) function and became a sexual manifestation of "Art for Art's Sake." However, the trials' emphasis on the mundane reality of stained bedsheets robbed homosexuality of its decadent aesthetic credentials. See Showalter, p. 177.

29. Freud, "The Psychogenesis of a Case of Homosexuality in a Woman" (1920) in *S.E.*, 18, p. 170.

30. *Ibid.*, p. 171.

31. Freud, "Psycho-analytic Notes on an Autobiographical Account of a Case of Paranoia (Dementia Paranoides)" (1911) in *S.E.*, 12, pp. 3–82.

32. *Ibid.*, p. 20.

33. *Ibid.*, p. 17.

34. Chauncey, p. 9.

35. Freud, "Letter to an American Mother" (1935). Reprinted in Paul Friedman's essay "Sexual Deviations" in Silvano Arieti, ed., *The American Handbook of Psychiatry*, Vol. 1 (New York: Basic Books, 1959), pp. 606–607. Cited by Ronald Bayer, *Homosexuality and American Psychiatry: The Politics of Diagnosis* (New York: Basic Books, 1981), p. 27.

36. Bayer, p. 29. Incidentally, American psychoanalysts continued to regard homosexuality as a disease until 1973, when pressure from the Gay Liberation Front finally led them to reconsider their terms; only then did the board of trustees of the American Psychiatric Association delete homosexuality from the DSM (Diagnostic and Statistical Manual of Mental Disorders). Simon LeVay discusses the politics of the event in his *Queer Science: The Use and Abuse of Research into Homosexuality* (Cambridge, MA: MIT Press, 1996), pp. 211–230.

37. Sandor Rado, *The Psychoanalysis of Behavior: Collected Papers*, Vol. 1 (New York and London: Grune and Stratton, 1956), p. 206.

38. See Colin Spencer, *Homosexuality: A History* (1995; rpt. London: Fourth Estate, 1996), p. 354.

39. *Ibid.*, p. 349.

40. John D'Emilio, *Sexual Politics, Sexual Communities: The Making of a Homosexual Minority in the United States, 1940–1970* (Chicago and London: University of Chicago Press, 1983), p. 17.

41. Spencer, pp. 347–348. The time-consuming process of checking the third sign of deviance appears to have been regularly skipped; Spencer documents the account of a gay teenager who went through the screening and was simply asked whether or not he liked girls. The psychiatrist apparently failed to read his bleached blond curly hair and the "sissy S" in his voice as subcultural markers.

42. D'Emilio, pp. 44–45.

43. Remarkably, Burroughs' attempts to find a position with the forces during the war all failed. The navy turned him down after he flunked the physical exam (flat feet and myopia). The Office of Strategic Services (OSS) rejected him after one of the interviewers remembered him from his student days at Harvard (where he had refused to join any clubs and kept a ferret in his room). The Glider Corps turned him down because of his eyesight. In early 1942 Burroughs apparently volunteered for service at the Jefferson Barracks in St. Louis, Missouri. To his surprise he was accepted. However, his experience of infantry life as a private was not what he had hoped for. After complaining about the army to his parents

Burroughs was examined—at his mother's request—by Dr. David Rioch (then resident at Washington University in St. Louis). Burroughs alerted Rioch to his psychiatric history (in particular the amputation of his little finger with a pair of shears after his tumultuous love affair with Jack Anderson ended) and was given a "blue discharge"—like many other gay men and women during this period. See Morgan, p. 82 and Barry Miles, *William Burroughs: El Hombre Invisible* (London: Virgin Books, 1992), pp. 29–30. I am extremely grateful to James Grauerholz for clarifying the nature of Burroughs' military experience and discharge.

44. See D'Emilio, pp. 46–47.

45. The sad irony being, of course, that both Hoover and McCarthy were gay themselves. In his autobiography Duberman writes: "'Hell hath no fury,' went a common underground quip, 'like a closeted gay'." See Martin Duberman, *Cures: A Gay Man's Odyssey* (1991; rpt. London: Penguin, 1991), p. 47. The most important discussion of the intersection of homosexuality and the politics of the McCarthy period is Robert J. Corber's *In the Name of National Security: Hitchcock, Homophobia and the Political Construction of Gender in Postwar America* (Durham: Duke University Press, 1993) and also his *Homosexuality in Cold War America: Resistance and the Crisis of Masculinity* (Durham and London: Duke University Press, 1997).

46. A. C. Kinsey, W. B. Pomeroy, and C. Martin, *Sexual Behavior in the Human Male* (Philadelphia: Saunders, 1948). Burroughs had actually met Kinsey in the 1940s and been one of the thousands of subjects upon whom Kinsey based his data on American sexual behavior. As Morgan notes, "[Burroughs] may be the only writer of renown to have his sexual history on file, including his penis size soft and erect, at the Kinsey Institute for Research in Sex, Gender and Reproduction in Bloomington, Indiana. Unfortunately for the biographer, the file is closed." Morgan, p. 122.

47. See Bayer's discussion of Ford and Beach and Hooker, pp. 46–66; and Clellan Ford and Frank Beach, *Patterns of Sexual Behavior* (New York: Harper Brothers, 1951).

48. Mattachine Society, "The Mattachine Society Today" mimeographed (Los Angeles, 1954), 3. Cited by Bayer, p. 70.

49. D'Emilio, p. 113.

50. Bayer, p. 72. The quotation he cites is from *Mattachine Review* (August 1956), 48.

51. "Response to R.L.M." *ONE* (September 1953), 13; and Lyn Pedersen [James Kepner], "The Importance of Being Different" *ONE* (March 1954), 4–6. Both articles cited by D'Emilio, p. 114.

52. In his introduction to the writings of Hay, Will Roscoe notes that the Mattachine Society was named after the French folk dance *Les Mattachines* (The Society of Fools) which was "performed in Renaissance France by fraternities of clerics (i.e., unmarried men), called *sociétés joyeuses,* whose public performances satirized the rich, powerful, high and holy." They protected themselves from retaliation by wearing masks. See Hay, *Radically Gay: Gay Liberation in the Words of Its Founder,* ed. Will Roscoe (Boston: Beacon Press, 1996), p. 4.

53. Donald Webster Cory [pseud. for Edward Sagarin], *The Homosexual in America: A Subjective Approach* (New York: Greenburg, 1951), pp. 92–93. Cory later argues that effeminacy serves a purpose as a means of negotiating male-to-male relations, a coded set of signifiers that signal a willingness to engage in a same-sex encounter (p. 117). Effeminacy thus switches from an essential, "out" identity to a strategic role that can be assumed at will. While modern understandings of camp and effeminacy acknowledge the performative nature of such roles, Cory predominantly argues that effeminacy is a mode of being rather than a subcultural style.

54. *Ibid.,* p. 152.

55. See Michael Barry Goodman, *Contemporary Literary Censorship: The Case History of Burroughs'* The Naked Lunch (London and Metuchen, NJ: The Scarecrow Press, 1981), for an in-depth discussion of the novel's place in the history of American literary censorship.

56. Burroughs, *Naked Lunch* (Paris: Olympia Press, 1959), pp. 131–134. Hereafter cited parenthetically in the text as *NL.* "Berger" is presumably an ironic take on Edmund Bergler the American psychoanalyst whose lay text *Homosexuality: Disease or Way of Life?* (New York: Hill and Wang, 1956) was published shortly before *Naked Lunch.* Bergler followed typically American psychoanalytic readings of homosexuality, emphasizing the neurosis of homosexuals and the possibility of curing them. Burroughs' negative presentation of the doctor (echoed in the presentation of Dr. Benway as arch-controller, swindler, and criminal) suggests his antipathy to the medical establishment of the 1950s. Ironically, one of Burroughs' critics briefly used Bergler's work on homosexuality as "an analytic tool" in his discussion of the role of women in Burroughs' fiction (without, presumably, being aware of Burroughs' satirical attack on him in *Naked Lunch*). See Neal Oxenhandler, "Listening to Burroughs' Voice" in Skerl and Lydenberg, p. 140.

57. See Spencer, pp. 351–353. Burroughs later fantasizes revenge in the story "Electricals," in which a group of gay teenagers harness the power of electric shock therapy to attack their homophobic enemies. See Burroughs, *Exterminator!* (1973; rpt. London: Calder and Boyars, 1974), pp. 144–148. Hereafter cited parenthetically in the text as *EX.*

58. Spencer cites the experiments in Czechoslovakia by Doctors Srnec and Freund who used emetics and slides of naked men in their aversion therapies (Spencer, p. 353). Burroughs makes a lame joke about such treatment in a letter to Ginsberg in 1957: "Did I tell you about the rat who was conditioned to be queer by the shock and cold water treatment every time he makes a move at a female? He says: 'Mine is the love that dare not squeak its name'"(*Letters,* 371). The gay laboratory rats reappear in *Naked Lunch* in Benway's experiments (*NL,* 40).

59. Benway's method is the reverse of the "talking cure." Rather than listening to Carl, Benway talks *at* him incessantly. Earlier in *Naked Lunch,* the Professor of Interzone advises us, *"You can find out more about someone by talking than by listening,"* explicitly linking this with both Coleridge's Ancient Mariner and psychoanalysis (*NL,* 84). The appropriation of this method by Benway underscores the fact that it is Benway who is *creating* or, in contemporary terms, *constructing* Carl's gay identifications.

60. Hay in Roscoe ed., pp. 60–61.

61. Robin Lydenberg, *Word Cultures: Radical Theory and Practice in William S. Burroughs' Fiction* (Urbana and Chicago: University of Illinois Press, 1987), p. 20.

62. It is interesting to note that the two voices of the passage (the carny man and the asshole) are oppositional in their registers; the carny man's only line is indicative of an upper-class, English identity— "Oh I say, are you still down there, old thing?"—whereas the asshole speaks with a voice that is, in comparison, coarse and uncouth, "Nah, I had to go relieve myself" (*NL,* 127). Such alignment of class and gender roles—the asshole's working class, coarse and masculine voice offset against the carny man's effeminate, genteel tones—is the opposite of that intersection of sexual identity and class espoused by Ginsberg, who makes a distinction between the "populist, humanist, quasi-heterosexual, Whitmanic, bohemian, free-love, homosexual tradition" and the "privileged, exaggeratedly effeminate, gossipy, moneyed, money-style-clothing conscious, near-hysterical queen." David Savran notes the intersection here of sexuality, gender identification and class and goes on to suggest

that Burroughs' work follows a similar pattern of "masculine, universalized proletarian" and "feminized, minoritized campy bourgeois." The talking asshole routine suggests that for Burroughs, the role of class in gender identification is not so clear cut, for here it is the masculine carny man who is genteel, the feminine anus that is signified "proletariat." See Savran, pp. 70–71 and Ginsberg's interview with Allen Young, *Gay Sunshine Interview* (1973; rpt. Bolinas: Grey Fox Press, 1974), p. 19.

63. See for example, the cinematic representations of homosexuality assessed in Vito Russo's *The Celluloid Closet: Homosexuality in the Movies* (New York: Harper & Row, 1981). Amongst the many examples that Russo discusses is Cary Grant's "drag" scene in the thirties screwball comedy *Bringing Up Baby* (dir. Howard Hawks, 1938); when asked why he is wearing a women's nightgown, Grant screams, "I just went gay all of a sudden!" Such a moment is indicative of the regulation of gay identities by the censor, especially the introduction of the Hays Code in the 1930s. Grant's camp is ambivalent in its play: does it suggest that the character's insanity throughout the film includes his descent into sexual insanity (transvestism/homosexuality), or is it indicative of the attempts by filmmakers during the period to create some (albeit marginal and coded) degree of gay visibility in the cinema? Russo claims that Grant's ad-libbing is the only time the word "gay" was used (at least in reference to homosexuality) during the Hays Code years and it is not, significantly, to be found in any of the extant versions of the film's script. See Russo, p. 47. Burroughs offers his own gay rewrite of Hollywood narrative in *Naked Lunch*'s story of Lucy Bradshinkel, Brad, and Jim (*NL*, 123–125).

64. Butler, *Gender Trouble*, p. 31.

65. Guy Hocquenghem, *Homosexual Desire*, trans. Daniella Dangoor (1972; rpt. London: Allison and Busby, 1978), p. 87.

66. Abram Kardiner, *Sex and Morality* (Indianapolis and New York: Bobbs-Merrill, 1954), p. 174.

67. *Ibid.*, p. 175.

68. *Ibid.*, pp. 172–173.

69. The image of the baboon dressed as a woman also occurs in a skit accredited to Brion Gysin in *The Third Mind* entitled "*The Naked Lunch:* Fragment of a Scenario." Benway offers the advice about offering up one's Sugar Bum as a means of self-preservation but is then replaced by a baboon named Violet who is dressed as a "Marlene-type diseuse" in a 1920s nightclub. She sings a 12–verse song for her audience; verses 10 and 11 read: "I'm not uptight / I don't

wanna fight / I got no reason to fight / None at all! / Oh I'm a baboon / Won't join your platoon / One and all! / I'll take your attack / Lying flat on my back / Or bracing myself / On a wall, any wall / Any old wall / At all, at all, at all!" See Burroughs and Gysin, *The Third Mind* (1978; rpt. London: John Calder, 1979), pp. 155–158.

70. Burroughs to J. E. Rivers, in "An Interview with William S. Burroughs" *Resources for American Literary Study* 10.2 (Autumn 1980), 158. See also Burroughs' rant against the "dubious metaphysical concepts" of ego, super ego and id in his essay "On Freud and the Unconscious" in Burroughs, *The Adding Machine: Collected Essays* (London: John Calder, 1985), pp. 88–96.

71. Hugh David recounts the story of "Nicolas," a gay Cambridge undergraduate in the late 1950s who received Pavlovian aversion therapy at the Maudsley Hospital in London. Interestingly, the drug apomorphine was used to facilitate his treatment. Burroughs was successfully treated with apomorphine by Dr. Dent in London in 1956 as part of a heroin addiction cure. He was so impressed that he publicized apomorphine in the U.S. edition of *Naked Lunch* and throughout the 1960s. In the Nova trilogy the drug assumes semi-mythical status as Burroughs claimed that it allows the subject to escape from addiction/control. He may not have been aware of its simultaneous use as part of the heterosexual dominant's regulation of homosexuals, although he does quite explicitly state in a much later text that "*Apomorphine is not an aversion treatment*" (*Job*, 153). For the story of "Nicolas," see Hugh David, *On Queer Street: A Social History of British Homosexuality 1895–1995* (London: Harper Collins, 1997), pp. 181–182.

72. Burroughs, "On Freud and the Unconscious" in *Adding Machine*, p. 90.

Chapter Two

1. See Gysin, "Cut-Ups: A Project for Disastrous Success" in *Third Mind*, p. 44.

2. Burroughs' relation to the countercultural movement is one that is more often taken for granted by critics than actually examined in any detail. The Merry Pranksters' overriding enthusiasm for new technology—which seems a direct parallel to Burroughs' concerns with both film and audio experimentation throughout the

decade—is apparent in Tom Wolfe's account of their history. The Acid Tests themselves read like something out of the Nova trilogy (minus the gay sex). Indeed, Wolfe claims that *Nova Express* was amongst the acidheads' reading material. See Tom Wolfe, *The Electric Kool-Aid Acid Test* (1968; rpt. London: Black Swan, 1998), p. 281. Despite the similarities between his work and that of the emergent youth culture, Burroughs was never really a fan of psychedelics and, when introduced to psilocybin by Leary experienced nothing but bad trips; Leary recalls him announcing: "I'm not feeling too well. I was struck by juxtaposition of purple fire mushroomed from the pain banks. Urgent warning. I think I'll stay here in shriveling envelopes of larval flesh. I'm going to take some apomorphine. One of the nastiest cases ever processed by this department." See Morgan, p. 377. Kerouac—who was, as always, committed to alcohol—was similarly unimpressed with psychedelics. It was only Ginsberg who managed the transformation from "beat" to "hippie," becoming an important countercultural spokesman in the process.

3. Morgan, p. 321.

4. Indeed, both Burroughs and Gysin have always been keen to associate themselves with this fabulous company into which they had contrived to stumble. See, for instance, Burroughs' comments on Tzara in "The Cut-Up Method of Brion Gysin" in *Third Mind*, p. 29.

5. Burroughs, *The Job: Interviews with William S. Burroughs* (1969; rpt. New York: Grove Press, 1974), p. 28. Hereafter cited parenthetically in the text as *Job*.

6. See Morgan, p. 323.

7. John Willett, "UGH . . ." *Times Literary Supplement* 3220 (14 November 1963), 919. Reprinted in Skerl and Lydenberg, p. 44.

8. The Balch/Burroughs/Gysin/Sommerville collaboration lasted throughout the 1960s, producing several films that made deliberate use of the cut-up method such as *Towers Open Fire* and *The Cut Ups.* These short works have been subsequently released on videocassette as *Towers Open Fire and Other Short Films* (Mystic Fire Video, 1990).

9. As Oliver Harris has noted, Burroughs' trilogy "has to be the most bizarre trilogy ever written: three different titles, indeed, but *six* different texts! [. . .] So garbled is the history of these texts that the first title—*The Soft Machine* (1961)—has become the last text (1968), and the last title—*Nova Express*—has ended up the earliest text (1964)." The difficulties faced by critics approaching the

multiple texts and revisions of the trilogy are outlined in Harris' discussion of John Watters' article "The Control Machine: Myth in *The Soft Machine* of W. S. Burroughs" *Connotations* 5.2–3 (1995/96), 284–303 and the work of Jennie Skerl and Robin Lydenberg. See Harris, "A Response to John Watters, 'The Control Machine: Myth in *The Soft Machine* of W. S. Burroughs'" *Connotations* 6.3 (1996/97), 340. In order to maintain coherence, I have focused only on the final, most popular versions of the texts.

10. Burroughs, *The Ticket That Exploded* (1962; rpt. New York: Grove Press, 1967, revised edition), pp. 54–55. Hereafter cited parenthetically in the text as *TTE*.

11. Burroughs, *Nova Express* (1964; rpt. New York: Grove Black Cat, 1965), p. 13. Hereafter cited parenthetically in the text as *NE*.

12. Tony Tanner, "Rub Out the Word" in Skerl and Lydenberg, p. 107 and p. 105 respectively.

13. Lydenberg, p. 48.

14. *Ibid.*, p. 63.

15. Burroughs, "Unfinished Cigarette" (1963). Reprinted in *The Burroughs File* (San Francisco: City Light Books, 1984), p. 29.

16. Lydenberg, p. 44

17. Discussions of Korzybski's influence on Burroughs have been more forthcoming than ones of Hubbard (presumably the suspect nature of Scientology is to blame). The most informed consideration of the influence of General Semantics is David Ingram's essay "William Burroughs and Language" in A. Robert Lee, ed., *The Beat Generation Writers* (London and Chicago: Pluto Press, 1996), pp. 95–113.

18. See Burroughs' "Reactive Agent Tape Cut by Lee The Agent in Interzone" and Gysin's cut-up of "Calling all re active agents" in Sinclair Beiles, William Burroughs, Gregory Corso, and Brion Gysin, *Minutes To Go* (1960; rpt. San Francisco: Beach Books, 1968), pp. 26–28 and 29–31 respectively.

19. Burroughs, like many gay men in the 1940s and 1950s, had had firsthand experience of psychoanalysis. In letters to Ginsberg and Kerouac during the 1956–1957 period, he occasionally claimed that he had been cured: "I feel myself closer and closer to resolution of my queerness which would involve a solution of that illness. For such it is, a horrible sickness. At least in my case. I have just experienced emergence of my non-queer persona as a separate personality" (*Letters*, 369). Such comments are indicative of the influence of the sickness theory of homosexuality that was omnipresent during the 1950s. As he abandoned psychoanalysis, this

confusion disappeared. The most fascinating account of the gay experience of psychoanalysis in America during this period is queer historian Martin Duberman's autobiographical *Cures: A Gay Man's Odyssey*. As is frequently remarked, it is telling that there are no comparable texts written by "cured" homosexuals who achieved the heterosexual "normality" that the analysts were promising.

20. For Burroughs' interest in General Semantics see his letter to Ginsberg in 1949 (*Letters*, 44) and Morgan, pp. 71–72.

21. Korzybski, *Science and Sanity* (1933; rpt. Connecticut: The International Non-Aristotelian Library, 1973, 4th edition), p. xxvi.

22. *Ibid.*, p. 35.

23. *Ibid.*, p. 34. Thirty years later Burroughs repeated such thinking almost verbatim: "There are certain formulas, word-locks, which will lock up a whole civilization for a thousand years. Now another thing is Aristotle's *is* of identity: this *is* a chair. Now, whatever it may be, it's not a chair, it's not the word chair, it's not the label chair." (*Job*, 49).

24. Korzybski, p. 21

25. *Ibid.*, p. 501.

26. *Ibid.*, p. 481.

27. *Ibid.*, p. 12.

28. See Burroughs' interview with Conrad Knickerbocker in *Third Mind*, p. 4. This interview was first printed in *Paris Review*, then reprinted in its *Writers at Work* series and in *The Third Mind*, a clear indication of its importance as an explanation of the significance of the cut-up technique. See "William Burroughs: An Interview" *Paris Review* 10.35 (Spring 1966), 13–49 and *Writers at Work: The "Paris Review" Interviews*, 3rd series, ed. Alfred Kazin (New York: Viking, 1967), pp. 143–174.

29. Burroughs to Knickerbocker, *The Third Mind*, pp. 5–6.

30. This interest in bodily freedom is reiterated in Burroughs' references to a "*sanity drug*" named apomorphine (*NE*, 14). In 1956 Burroughs had taken the apomorphine cure for heroin addiction in Dr. John Yerbury Dent's London clinic. Dent used the morphine derivative as a metabolic and psychic regulator, normalizing the subject's disturbed metabolism so that drugs were no longer craved. Although the treatment did not guarantee that the addict would never use narcotics again, the success rate was high and Burroughs himself was so impressed that he spent the next two decades publicizing Dent's research and demanding that it be approved by the American Medical Association (*Job*, 60–61). The Nova trilogy—as well as other texts, such as the 1965 *Health Bulletin, APO–33: A*

Metabolic Regulator (New York: Fuck You Press, 1965)—mythologizes the drug so that it becomes, like the cut-up technique itself, a weapon of the partisans: "Apomorphine is the only agent that can disintoxicate you and cut the enemy beam off your line" (*NE*, 14). Similarly, apomorphine's role as a metabolic regulator acts to return bodily control to the ex-addict, regulating the action of the hypothalamus *without* being addictive. This short-lived, non-addictive regulation of the body in order to allow the subject time to recompose himself and then regain control of his body and mind is what Burroughs took as the main virtue of apomorphine. Significantly, Burroughs ignored the fact that apomorphine was simultaneously being used in aversion therapy in order to cure homosexuals, something he would surely have been aware of.

31. Albert I. Berger notes the influence of Korzybski's work on a range of science fiction authors, including Heinlein and Asimov. See Berger, "Towards a Science of the Nuclear Mind: Science-Fiction Origins of Dianetics" *Science-Fiction Studies* 16 (1989), 128–129.

32. *Ibid.*, 123. Hubbard's original essay appeared *Astounding Stories* (May 1950).

33. *Ibid.*, 124.

34. L. Ron Hubbard, *Dianetics: The Modern Science of Mental Health* (1950; rpt. East Grinstead: New Era Publication, 1997, with different title of *Dianetics: The Power of the Mind over the Body*), p. 60. Hereafter cited parenthetically in the text as *D*.

35. See Roy Wallis, *The Road to Total Freedom: A Sociological Analysis of Scientology* (London: Heinemann, 1976), p. 33 and Jeff Jacobsen, "Dianetics: From Out of the Blue?" *The Arizona Skeptic* 5.2 (September/October 1991), 2.

36. Jacobsen, 2.

37. Morgan, p. 440. Burroughs joined the organization just as it was becoming an increasingly popular subject of government hysteria in the United Kingdom. In the summer of 1968, the *Times* quoted the Minister of Health's belief that Scientology is "socially harmful" and that "its authoritarian principles and practices are a potential menace to the personality and well-being of those so deluded as to become its followers." *Times* (26 July 1968). The fact that the Church of Scientology still has a street-level office on London's Tottenham Court Road today (as well as in many other cities around the world) would seem to indicate the continuing international power wielded by the organization, even after the death of Hubbard in 1986.

38. Burroughs, "Burroughs on Scientology" *Los Angeles Free Press,* 6 March 1970. Reprinted in Burroughs, *Ali's Smile/Naked Scientology* (Bonn: Expanded Media Editions, 1972), p. 72 and p. 70.
39. *Ibid.,* p. 71.
40. Burroughs, review of *Inside Scientology* by Robert Kaufman (Paris: Olympia Press, 1972) *Rolling Stone* (9 November 1972). Reprinted in *Ali's Smile/Naked Scientology,* p. 87.
41. Burroughs, "Open Letter to Mister Gorden Mustain" *The East Village Other* 5.31 (7 July 1970). Reprinted in *Ali's Smile/Naked Scientology,* p. 79. George Wallace was a right wing politician, governor of Alabama from 1962–1966 and an independent presidential candidate in 1968. His bid for the presidency failed and he campaigned again in the early 1970s with the Democrats, but was shot at a rally and partly paralyzed. The homophobia inherent in Hubbard's denunciation of "Godless practices of subversion" was also a problem that Burroughs had to face up to. In *Dianetics,* Hubbard claims that "the sexual pervert" is one who indulges in "homosexuality, lesbianism, sexual sadism, etc., and all down the catalog of Ellis and Krafft-Ebing" (*D,* 149).
42. See Burroughs, review of *Inside Scientology Rolling Stone* (9 November 1972). Reprinted in *Ali's Smile/Naked Scientology,* p. 83.
43. The extent of Burroughs' indebtedness to Hubbard's work deserves serious study. The science fiction background that Hubbard wove around his theories of mental health were largely derived from his original career as a pulp novelist. Burroughs, also a fan of the golden age of American science fiction, clearly borrows heavily from Hubbard's work while composing the Nova trilogy. In *Scientology: A History of Man,* for instance, Hubbard tells the story of mankind's original intergalactic divine nature and our battles with "the Martian Fourth Invader Force" who employed such torture methods as "the Jack-in-the-Box" and the "Coffee-Grinder." Comparisons with the "ovens" of *Nova Express* seem obvious. Many of the science fiction narratives Hubbard uses within Scientology seem to have caught Burroughs' imagination. In *Have You Lived Before this Life?* Hubbard explains how Dianetic therapy can help us recover our past lives. He recounts the hypnotic regression of one Scientologist who returns to a time "55,000,000,000,000,000,000 years" before the twentieth century. After his spaceship crashes on Earth the Scientologist is cast adrift without a body. After centuries of wandering he "arrives in error on a planet which is being taken over by 'Black Magic operators' who are very low on the ethical scale." These villains deceive

him by using hypnosis and "pleasure implants" into a love affair with "a robot decked out as a beautiful red-haired girl who receives all of his confidences." The content and tone of this narrative seem very similar to Burroughs' science fiction fantasies. The "operators" who are "low on the ethical scale" even echoes Burroughs' street slang argot, while the story of the crashed spaceship, bodiless existence, and the deceptive female match much of Burroughs self-consciously pulp science fiction scenarios. See Hubbard, *Scientology: A History of Man* (Los Angeles: Bridge Publications, 1994) and Hubbard, *Have You Lived Before This Life? A Scientific Survey* (East Grinstead: The Department of Publications Worldwide [The Church of Scientology], 1968), pp. 156–157.

44. Just how serious Burroughs is as he advocates General Semantics and Dianetics to his readers is a moot point. In his letters to Ginsberg in 1959, for instance, Burroughs promotes Hubbard's work with apocalyptic gravity: "So once again and most urgently (believe me there is not much time), I tell you: 'Find a Scientology Auditor and have yourself run'." (*Letters,* 434). Yet in the same letter he also seems somewhat skeptical about the Scientology *movement:* "Southern California camouflage seemingly necessary" (*Letters,* 432). A year later, Burroughs seems to be suggesting that Dianetic therapy, or at least his own cut-up version of it, is the best antidote to Ginsberg's post-*yagé* breakdown. Ginsberg, following Burroughs' example, had gone off into the Amazon to sample the hallucinogen. The effects of the drug terrified him, prompting a lengthy letter to Burroughs: "I don't know how all this sounds to you but you know me reasonably well, so write, fast, please." Burroughs' reply suggests the extent of his immersion in Dianetics/Scientology: the date on the letter reads "June 21 1960 Present Time Pre-Sent Time"; in place of the reassurance that Ginsberg seems to need, Burroughs advises him to make a cut-up of the letter: "You want 'Help.' Here it is." The cut-up method becomes a literal self-help therapy which, Burroughs implies, will restore Ginsberg's psychic stability after his bad trip. See *The Yage Letters*, p. 55 and p. 59.

45. Burroughs, "Open Letter" in *Naked Scientology*, p. 80.

46. Burroughs repeatedly suggests that "self-help" is an affront to power/control. See, for instance, his discussion of the need for heroin addicts to bypass psychoanalysis in favor of apomorphine treatment (*Job*, 153–154) and his belief that a vitamin-A-based cold-cure would never be allowed on the market since the American Medical Association "is opposed to self-medication" (*Job*, 60).

47. Burroughs, *The Soft Machine* (1961; rpt. London: Calder and Boyars, 1968, 3rd revised edition), p. 56. Hereafter cited parenthetically in the text as *SM*.

48. "Program Empty Body" is simultaneously the invaders plan to remove the original (masculine) identity from the humans that they attack and their attempt to set up a control system that will run itself without supervision. The empty bodies of the human victims are used as vessels through which power can organize itself; the invaders operate through these bodies without exposing themselves to capture or danger. See, for instance, the example of "Genial" (*TTE*, 13–21). As one of the policemen notes, "Yes we know the front men and women in this organization but they are no more than that . . . a façade . . . tape recorders . . . the operators are *not there . . .*" (*TTE*, 21).

49. The extent to which the effeminate paradigm becomes a production of discourse and communication suggests the possibility of reading Burroughs' queer politics and paranoia in relation to the postwar interest in cybernetics. David Porush offers the most illuminating discussion of Burroughs' relation to communication theory in his *The Soft Machine: Cybernetic Fiction* (New York and London: Methuen, 1985). The development of a reading of Burroughs' sexual politics from this vantage point has been suggested by both Harris in "Can You See a Virus? The Queer Cold War of William Burroughs" and Dellamora in *Apocalyptic Overtures.*

50. Ian Sommerville, "William Burroughs and Brion Gysin" (diptych), ca. 1962 in William S. Burroughs Papers, University Libraries, Special Collection, Arizona State University, Tempe. Reproduced in Robert A. Sobieszek, *Ports of Entry: William S. Burroughs and the Arts* (Los Angeles: Los Angeles County Museum of Art and Thames & Hudson, 1996), p. 54. The "marked erotic reaction" (*TTE*, 163) that Burroughs claims accompanies such experiments might well be related to this loss of the self, an element of *jouissance.* Of course, the political importance of the cut-up is simply a question of who uses it; in the hands of the heterosexual dominant it is a weapon of destruction, but when used by the partisans it is depicted as liberating and transformative.

51. Burroughs repeatedly discusses Mayan civilization in the context of control techniques, telepathy, and conditioning throughout his writing; much of this is based on the courses he took in Mayan and Mexican archaeology at Mexico City College in 1949. See Morgan, p. 173.

52. In the "Public Agent" section of *The Soft Machine* (*SM*, 22–25), Burroughs offers a vision of the subject, who is rendered schizophrenic by the influence of the mass media: "So I am a public agent and don't know who I work for, get my instructions from street signs, newspapers and pieces of conversation" (*SM*, 22). Intriguingly, the Agent is represented as a repressed homosexual, whose homophobic violence suggests a link between him and the similarly schizophrenic Vigilante in *Naked Lunch* (*NL*, 13). These are the only two examples in Burroughs' fiction of a latent homosexual, masculine character whose frustration leads him to assault other gay men. The suggestion seems to be that the discourses of the heterosexual dominant can not only leave the gay man possessed by a feminine identity, but also can result in the gay subject being overtaken by violent, homophobic impulses. Queer genocide—as in the Countessa di Vile's plans in *The Ticket That Exploded*—occasionally emerges in the texts as a secondary strategy employed by the dominant (the primary strategy being the deployment of the effeminate model). The fact that the agent is a "public" one only underscores the extent to which he is actually closeted and latent.

53. Ginsberg to Allen Young, pp. 38–39.

54. James Steakley, *The Homosexual Emancipation Movement in Germany* (New York: Arno Press, 1975), p. 54.

55. Ginsberg, "Howl" in *Collected Poems, 1947–1980* (New York: Harper & Row, 1984), p. 128.

56. The Satyrs are briefly mentioned in Simon LeVay and Elisabeth Nonas, *City of Friends: A Portrait of the Gay and Lesbian Community in America* (Cambridge, MA, and London: MIT Press, 1995), p. 178. The all-male motorcycle gang was the site of many hetero- and homosexual desires during the postwar period. As Mark Thompson notes, there were many gay motorcycle clubs established in the 1950s and 1960s; he lists the Oedipus in Los Angeles, and the Warlocks and Californian Motorcycle Club in San Francisco. See Mark Thompson, "Introduction" in *Leatherfolk: Radical Sex, People, Politics and Practice* (Boston: Alyson Publications, 1991), p. xv. A decade later the release of *Scorpio Rising* (dir. Kenneth Anger, 1963) and *The Leather Boys* (dir. Sidney J. Furie, 1964) defiantly queered the subculture. The Hell's Angels, who were the focus of widespread media hysteria in the mid–1960s, were somewhat offended by the association that the press releases drew between their outlaw status and that of Anger's queer bikers. As one Angel put it, "Shit, did you see the way those punks were

dressed? And those silly junk-wagon bikes? Man, don't tell me that has any connection with us." Ironically, such bitchy fashion-consciousness on the part of the Angels sounds vaguely in keeping with camp stereotypes. See Hunter S. Thompson, *Hell's Angels* (1966; rpt. London: Penguin, 1967), p. 95.

57. James Baldwin, *Giovanni's Room* (New York: The Dial Press, 1956), p. 39.

58. Gore Vidal, *The City and the Pillar* (1948; revised edition 1965; rpt. London: Abacus, 1997), p. 97. Significantly, Vidal would later write the screenplay for *Ben-Hur* (dir. William Wyler, 1959). The film's macho posturing was inevitably queered by Vidal's script. Aware of the lack of any real motivation for the characters, Vidal and Wyler decided to create a gay subtext for the relationship between Messala (Stephen Boyd) and Ben-Hur (Charlton Heston). Fearing that Heston might "fall apart" if alerted to the real meaning of his scenes the screenwriter and director left him in a state of ignorance, while Boyd—who was somewhat less conservative—played the enraptured lover to perfection. As Vidal describes it, "So Heston thinks he's doing his Francis X. Bushman in a silent version; his head is always constantly on high like this and like this. And Stephen Boyd is acting to pieces; there are looks that he gives him that are so clear." See Vidal's interview in the documentary film made of Vito Russo's text, *The Celluloid Closet* (dir. Rob Epstein and Jeffrey Friedman, 1995).

59. Murphy, p. 146.

60. There were important links between the social phenomenon of the Beat Generation and the new gay radicalism. D'Emilio notes Ginsberg's role as a "bridge between a literary *avant-garde* tolerant of homosexuality and an emerging form of social protest indelibly stamped by the media as sexually deviant." Burroughs was in Paris and London during this period and played no epic role in the liberation movement outside of the fantasies of resistance and revolution that his texts were delineating. See D'Emilio, p. 181.

61. Ginsberg, quoted in *Village Voice* 3 July 1969. Cited by D'Emilio, p. 232. Burroughs was not present at the riots or their aftermath. However, a note of continuity was struck by the fact that Stonewall occurred on the tenth anniversary of *Naked Lunch*'s publication. The day after the riots, the *Village Voice*'s description of the scene suggested that "Sheridan Square [. . .] looked like something from a William Burroughs novel as the sudden specter of 'gay power' erected its brazen head." Cited by James Martin in "Burroughs' Fiction" *Gay Sunshine* 21 (Spring 1974), 3.

62. GLF, "Statement of Purpose, July 1969," published in *RAT* (12 August 1969). Cited by D'Emilio, p. 234.

63. D'Emilio suggests that such demands had already found currency among researchers such as Evelyn Hooker. By 1967 Hooker was chairing a committee on homosexuality organized by the National Institute of Mental Health; the committee's report called for social tolerance and a redefinition of the concept of homosexuality in terms other than those of the sickness theory. See D'Emilio, pp. 176–195 and Bayer, p. 53.

64. An amusing story to cheer the heart of the doctoral student arises out of this episode. As the demonstrators clashed with police, Genet (who was in America illegally without a visa, having been smuggled across the Canadian border by a group of Quebec separatists) fled. Rushing blindly through unfamiliar streets, with the riot police immediately behind him, Genet ran into an apartment building and knocked on a door at random, crying "*C'est monsieur Genet.*" The bemused tenant opened the door and gave him safe haven before explaining that he was a postgraduate student writing a thesis on the author's work. The veracity of this incident, given the infamous nature of its protagonist's lies, is a moot point. See Morgan, p. 446.

65. Unlike Ginsberg, Burroughs never followed the shift from beat to hippie and thus eschewed the flower-power ethos of passive demonstration. His personal position on anti-establishment protest is summed up in his claim, "The only way I like to see cops given flowers is in a flower pot from a high window" (*Job*, 74).

66. Burroughs, *Cities of the Red Night* (1981; rpt. London: John Calder, 1981), p. 70. Hereafter cited parenthetically in the text as *CRN*.

67. Burroughs, *The Place of Dead Roads* (New York: Holt, Rinehart and Winston, 1984), p. 73 Hereafter cited in parenthesis in the text as *PDR*.

68. Burroughs, *The Wild Boys: A Book of the Dead* (1971; rpt. New York: Grove Press, 1992), p. 26. Hereafter cited parenthetically in the text as *WB*.

69. Catherine R. Stimpson, "The Beat Generation and the Trials of Homosexual Liberation" *Salmagundi* 58–59 (1982–1983), 392. Burroughs does not acknowledge that his presentation of lesbians as butch male pretenders replays the same Ulrichian logic that produces the effeminate paradigm of male homosexuality. One wonders if his antipathy is towards all lesbians, or merely those who are gender-deviant; the fact that the texts seem unable to

conceive of a *femme* mode of lesbian identity (the equivalent of the masculine gay male identity he is in search of) is telling.

70. Burroughs, *Port of Saints* (1973; rpt. Berkeley: Blue Wind Press, 1980), p. 104. Hereafter cited parenthetically in the text as *PoS*.

71. For a more detailed discussion of the intersection between Hassan i Sabbah and Burroughs' work, see Murphy, pp. 120–130.

72. Burroughs, *Ah Pook is Here and Other Texts* (London: John Calder, 1979), p. 56. Hereafter cited parenthetically in the text as *APH*.

73. Of course, the fact that the texts are so rarely regarded as gay/queer novels—and thus reach a much larger and much straighter audience than most queer novels—makes them particularly subversive in this respect. Burroughs' reversal of the subordinate/dominant hierarchy is part of a strategy frequently adopted by gay literature in its attempt to deal with the signification of gay lives and experience as falling somewhere between the oppositional poles of "different" or "same" in relation to heterosexuality. Jonathan Dollimore notes that any strategy of creating "the authentic as oppositional" is an essentialist one that has a considerable (although by no means exclusive) tradition in lesbian fiction as evidenced in his discussion of Rita May Brown's *Rubyfruit Jungle* and, more importantly, Monique Wittig's work. See Dollimore, *Sexual Dissidence: Augustine to Wilde, Freud to Foucault* (Oxford: Clarendon Press, 1991), pp. 52–55.

74. As already mentioned, such an emphasis on queer childhood has led at least one commentator to suggest that Burroughs' work displays the sexual desire of the pedophile; see Caveney, p. 19. Interestingly, Burroughs wrote a preface to *William's Mix*, a novel by the self-confessed pedophile C. J. Bradbury Robinson. Burroughs discusses the novel in terms of the "basic contradiction in interest between any sexual image stuck in past time and the interests of any living approximation of this image," suggesting that his admiration for Bradbury Robinson goes much further than simple sexual fantasy. Burroughs' introduction is from June 1971, printed with prefatory remarks by Patrick J. Kearney in Rupert Loydell ed., *My Kind of Angel: i.m. William Burroughs* (Exeter: Stride Publications, 1998), pp. 51–56. Robinson's novel remains unpublished.

75. See John Z. Guzlowski, "The Family in the Fiction of William S. Burroughs" *Midwest Quarterly* 30.1 (1988), 13–14.

76. Burroughs, "Lee and the Boys" in *Interzone*, pp. 35–36.

77. Bockris notes that the subtitle was later removed from the jacket and title page. Could it have been because parents might have been misled as to the contents? See Bockris, p. 32. Significantly,

the old writer in the Red Night trilogy is William Seward Hall. While he is clearly an authorial *alter ego*, we might also read his name as an allusion to G. Stanley Hall, the turn-of-the-century American sociologist whose most famous work was on adolescence. See G. Stanley Hall, *Adolescence: Its Psychology and Its Relations to Physiology, Anthropology, Sociology, Sex, Crime, Religion and Education* 2 vols. (New York and London: Appleton, 1904).

78. The section entitled "Seeing Red" in *Exterminator!* also invokes the destructive force of the fairy tale. Lee's pictures (the contents of which remain unknown, although it seems feasible to assume that they are pieces of gay pornography) kill off the customs agents and policemen who look at them: "The Piper pulled down the sky" (*EX*, 142). This idea of an image so potent that it produces violent death is a recurring one through the texts; see, for instance, "Short Trip Home" (*EX*, 15–16) in which the spectacle of two boys having sex causes the sheriff, his deputies and the Anti-Obscenity League to start "flopping around shitting and pissing on the ground . . ." (*EX*, 16). The latter episode is an apt example of Burroughs' hatred of those obsessed with minding other people's business.

79. Dave Wallis, *Only Lovers Left Alive* (London: Blond, 1964), and J. G. Ballard, *Running Wild* (London: Hutchinson, 1988).

80. Burroughs, *The Cat Inside* (1986; rpt. New York: Viking, 1992), p. 33. Hereafter cited parenthetically in the text as *CI*.

81. Geoff Ward, "William Burroughs: A Literary Outlaw?" *Cambridge Critical Quarterly* 22.4 (1993), 343.

82. Leslie A. Fiedler, "Come Back to the Raft Ag'in, Huck Honey!" *Partisan Review* 15.6 (June 1948), 664–671.

83. See Charles B. Harris' discussion of the essay's reception in his introduction to the second edition of *Love and Death in the American Novel* (1960; rpt. Normal, Illinois: Dalkey Archive Press, 1997), p. vi. All subsequent references to Fiedler's text are from this edition.

84. Fiedler, *What Was Literature? Class, Culture and Mass Society* (New York: Simon and Schuster, 1982), p. 15.

85. Fiedler, *Love and Death*, p. 370.

86. *Ibid.*, p. 26.

87. *Ibid.*, p. 339.

88. *Ibid.*, p. 182. Burroughs' own later use of the term "boys' book" is significant here. For more background on the American tradition of the boys' book see Marcia Jacobsen, *Being a Boy Again: Autobi-*

ography and the American Boy Book (Tuscaloosa and London: University of Alabama Press, 1994).

89. Of course, much of this, as Fiedler suggests, is a response to fears about miscegenation. This issue has little relevance to Burroughs' use of the male-male relationship (although his texts do replicate the interracial nature of the affairs).

90. In this manner, the logic is clearly similar to what we have seen displayed in American culture during the postwar period. The homoerotic play of the heterosexual—or even the "occasional homosexual"—is never treated with the same condemnation as the actions and desires of the confirmed homosexual.

91. Fiedler, "Come Back to the Raft Ag'in Huck, Honey!," 665.

92. Implicit within Fiedler's analysis of American literature and his comments on American youth culture is the association of homosexuality with adolescent and political immaturity. For Fiedler, heterosexuality represents not only the assumption of a position of genital maturity, but also one of social responsibility. In this manner, Fiedler replicates a well-established discourse on innocence, immaturity, and male development that was frequently rehearsed during the Cold War, particularly by former Marxist intellectuals (such as Fiedler) who had gravitated toward a liberal position. As Corber notes, there was a precedent in such discourse for associating far-left politics with homosexuality and a certain immaturity of vision. The most interesting site of this conflict is the postwar readings of "Billy Budd," in particular the venomous, homophobic, and personal attack undertaken by Richard Chase on F. O. Matthiesen. In his discussion of this incident Corber suggests, "As a gay fellow traveler, Matthiesen could be said [by Chase] to suffer from arrested sexual development. His homosexuality could be seen as proof that a commitment to left-wing politics did indeed represent a continuation of the negative Oedipus complex into adulthood. Moreover, his tragic suicide shortly before he was to appear before the House Un-American Activities Committee in 1950 could be interpreted as a 'fatally passive' act that duplicated Billy's passive submission to authority." See Corber, *Homosexuality in Cold War America*, pp. 171–172. As Corber also argues, the common lament of liberal critics that they were a dying breed probably had much to do the "mixed legacy" that they had left behind the sixties progressives—in particular their increasingly reactionary politics. See Corber, *In the Name of National Security*, p. 249 *n.* 15. In *The Soft Machine* Burroughs replays the Billy Budd

story with a significant twist; on hanging the passive innocent, the ship's crew discovers that he is actually a transvestite lesbian—a "foul and unnatural act whereby a boy's mother take over his body and infiltrate her horrible old substance right onto a decent boat and with bare tits hanging out, unfurls the nastiest colors of the spectroscope." (*SM*, 155).

93. References to Fiedler's attack on the Beat Generation frequently appear in commentaries on this period; see, for instance Savran, pp. 65–67 and Corber, *In the Name of National Security*, pp. 165–166. However, while the predominant emphasis of these discussions is on the differences between Fiedler and the Beat Generation, I want to highlight the similarities between the queer masculine desires of Burroughs' texts and the sex/gender politics of Fiedler's own position.

94. Fiedler, "The New Mutants" *Partisan Review* 32.4 (Fall 1965), 517.

95. *Ibid.*, 520.

96. Fiedler, "The Un-Angry Young Men: America's Post-War Generation." This essay originally appeared in *Encounter* (January 1958) and has subsequently been reprinted in *The Collected Essays of Leslie Fiedler, Volume One*, 2 vols. (New York: Stein and Day, 1971), p. 406.

97. Fiedler, "The New Mutants," 516.

98. *Ibid.*, 516.

99. The doubleness of the Burroughs/Fiedler relationship cuts both ways. Fiedler's notoriety—in particular the banning of his short story "Nude Croquet" by officials in Knoxville, Tennessee, in 1957 and the arrest of himself, his wife, and his son in 1967 under suspicion of hosting a drug-addled hashish party in his home—could be interpreted as signifying a *potential* role as one of the beats/hipsters that he inveighs against. This reading is flawed, however. Regardless of his conservative sex/gender politics, Fiedler's reaction to the drug arrest—in his 1969 text *Being Busted*—betrays the "straight" (as opposed to "hip") sensibility of the liberal academic/intellectual outraged by his firsthand experience of surveillance, misrepresentation, and guilt by association. *Being Busted* is less an audacious attempt to style himself as a controversial, anti-establishment figure than a desperate attempt to clear his smeared name and prove his "straight" innocence. See *Being Busted* (New York: Stein and Day, 1969).

100. Fiedler, "The New Mutants," 517.

101. *Ibid.*, 519.

102. This antagonism between Fiedler and Burroughs resurfaced once or twice in the following decades. In the 1970s, for instance, Burroughs turned down a teaching position at the University of Buffalo because Fiedler—whom he considered "a martinet"—was the head of the English department. See Morgan, p. 477. In 1980, Fiedler and Burroughs crossed swords at a D. H. Lawrence conference, where Fiedler is said to have remarked to Burroughs, "I always thought you were more influenced by Edgar Rice Burroughs than by Lawrence." See Morgan p. 561.

103. Eric Mottram, *The Algebra of Need* (1971; rpt. London: Marion Boyars, 1977), p. 169.

104. Anthony E. Rotundo discusses the nineteenth-century concern about the state of American youth and cites one commentator who described the wild adolescents as "the race of boys." See Rotundo, *American Manhood: Transformations in American Masculinity from the Revolution to the Modern Era* (New York: Basic Books, 1993), pp. 31–40.

105. Burroughs and Ginsberg discuss the battle between European and Native American spiritual ideals in "Interview with Allen Ginsberg." See Burroughs, *Three Novels* (New York: Grove Press, 1980), p. 190.

106. Historical documentation of the sexual lives of turn-of-the-century cowboys is rare, although by no means nonexistent. In the all-male world of mining camps, the wilderness, and the trails, homosexuality was, it seems, widely tolerated. Colin Spencer discusses the letters of an early nineteenth-century cowboy who recalled how his trail boss would encourage the men to pair off during the long, cold nights on the plains: "At first pairing they'd solace each other gingerly and, as bashfulness waned, manually. As trust in mutual good will matured, they'd graduate to the ecstatically comforting 69 . . . Folk know not how cock-hungry men get." In a separate account, a gold miner recalls how the Vaseline kept in the first-aid kit was frequently the first item to be exhausted. See Spencer, p. 332.

107. In "Thanksgiving Day, Nov. 28, 1986" Burroughs undertakes a similarly subversive reinscription of a hallowed part of American culture—the thanksgiving prayer—in order to expose the inequalities of the American system: "thanks for the KKK, for nigger-killing / lawmen feeling their notches, for decent / church-going women with their mean, pinched, / bitter, evil faces—/ thanks for "Kill a Queer for Christ" stickers—/ thanks for laboratory AIDS [. . .] / thanks for the last and greatest betrayal of the last and

greatest of human dreams." The prayer appeared in *Tornado Alley* (Cherry Valley Editions, 1989), pp. 7–8 and was made into a short film by Burroughs and Gus Van Sant, *Thanksgiving Prayer* (dir. Gus Van Sant, 1990).

108. David Glover, "Burroughs' Western" in Skerl and Lydenberg, pp. 211–212.

109. That Norman Mailer would later endorse Burroughs as masculine despite his sexuality—"Burroughs may be gay, but he's a man"—is indicative of the paradoxical position created by the texts' appropriation of the masculine. Dismissed by Fiedler as queer and accepted by Mailer as masculine, the texts are always trapped within the inconsistent logic of the dominant.

CHAPTER THREE

1. See *William Burroughs* (dir. Howard Brookner, 1983). This sentiment contrasts markedly with that given in Burroughs' interview with *Gay Sunshine* magazine in the early 1970s, in which, when asked if revolutionary movements (for all minorities, including gay men and women) were still viable in the post–1968 world, he states: "I don't like to seem pessimistic, but it is my feeling that no revolutionary movement in the West has any real chance of success." See Laurence Collinson and Roger Baker, "An Interview with William Burroughs" *Gay Sunshine* 21 (1974), 1.

2. In the immediate post-Stonewall period, of course, such statements of violent intent were frequently heard amongst gay radicals. For example, Jim Fouratt (one of the leading activists of the Gay Liberation movement) is on record as arguing for the total commitment of gay men to direct action: "We have got to radicalize . . . Be proud of what you are . . . And if it takes riots or even guns to show them what we are, well, that's the only language that the pigs understand." See Martin Duberman, *Stonewall* (1993; rpt. London: Plume, 1994), p. 211.

3. The texts of the 1950s and the Nova trilogy were not complicated by this kind of extremism since they were predominantly concerned with creating a space in which the masculine model could flourish, rather than delineating its dynamics. The hyperbolic, vaguely camp tone of the 1950s routine gives way to the equally hyperbolic but partisan masculinity of the post-Stonewall novels.

4. The general oscillation of the texts between these two poles has been frequently noted by critics. Steven Shaviro argues that Burroughs' Red Night trilogy indicates the fact that "when the forces of metamorphosis are unleashed, nobody can hope to stabilize or control the outcome." Shaviro's comment is to some extent a neat summary of the Red Night trilogy's utopian/dystopian wavering; as he himself suggests, "The utopian impulse, like that of nostalgia, is a movement never to be consummated, but also, in its perpetual incompletion, recurrent and unavoidable." See Shaviro, "Burroughs' Theater of Illusion: *Cities of the Red Night*" in Skerl and Lydenberg, p. 201 and p. 206 respectively. In a similar fashion, Skerl has read the Wild Boys as "a metaphorical concept made up of private and public fantasies." Thus, as Glover succinctly suggests, it is "through them [that] utopias and dystopias battle for supremacy." See Skerl, *William S. Burroughs* (Boston: Twayne Publishers, 1985), p. 78 and Glover in Skerl and Lydenberg, p. 212.

5. Thomi Wroblewski, "Wild Boys" (1988), reproduced in Sobieszek, *Ports of Entry*, p. 160. Interestingly, Dolce and Gabbana's spring 1999 run of advertisements for their "masculine" and "feminine" perfumes have taken Wroblewski's picture as a point of reference. The nude bodies are arranged in exactly the same circular pattern. The only difference being that, of course, the D&G ads use "purified" men *and women* whose bodies are toned and tanned rather than daubed with the symbols of oppression.

6. See Thomas Clark, "Allen Ginsberg: An Interview," *Paris Review* 10.37 (Spring 1966), 32.

7. Burroughs in interview with Robert Palmer, *Rolling Stone* (11 May 1972), 38.

8. *Ibid.*, 38. Murphy suggests that this separatist policy is a gay male parallel of that displayed in Wittig's *Les Guérillères* (1969) and Joanna Russ' *The Female Man* (1975). See Murphy, p. 147. In addition, an interesting parallel could be drawn with Valerie Solanas' *SCUM Manifesto* (1967). Solanas' radical separatism reads like a female version of Burroughs' concerns with experimental surgery, genetics, artificial reproduction, and single-sex communities. For Solanas, "The male is a biological accident: the Y (male) gene is an incomplete X (female) gene, that is, has an incomplete set of chromosomes. In other words, the male is an incomplete female." See *SCUM Manifesto* (1967; rpt. San Francisco and Edinburgh: AK Press, 1996), p. 1. The similarities between this and Burroughs' belief that "Women may well be a biological mistake" are

obvious. See Burroughs, "Women: A Biological Mistake?" in *Adding Machine,* p. 125. Solanas calls for the total eradication of men in a violent female revolution. Her vision of social reorganization includes "Turd sessions," gatherings at which "every male present will give a speech beginning with the sentence: 'I am a turd, a lowly, abject turd,' and then proceed to list all the ways in which he is." See Solanas, p. 39.

9. Palmer, 38.
10. Rivers, 166.
11. Murphy offers an insightful discussion of the role of *The Book of the Dead* in Burroughs fiction. See Murphy, pp. 147–150.
12. The phrase is used by Skerl to describe the novels of the 1980s. See Skerl, "Freedom through Fantasy in the Recent Novels of William S. Burroughs" in Skerl and Lydenberg, pp. 189–196.
13. Murphy, p. 153.
14. *Ibid.,* p. 153.
15. *Ibid.,* p. 173.
16. *Ibid.,* p. 199.
17. *Ibid.,* p. 199.
18. Murphy, for instance, reads them as a parallel of "the radical student movements of the sixties" rather than Stonewall rioters. See Murphy, p. 168.
19. Martin P. Levine, *Gay Macho: The Life and Death of the Homosexual Clone,* ed. Martin S. Kimmel (New York and London: New York University Press, 1998), p. 7.
20. *Ibid.,* p. 27.
21. Spencer, p. 374.
22. Levine, p. 79.
23. *Ibid.,* p. 95.
24. Burroughs claimed that his reputation as an author who is interested in sadism is misconceived: "There's not that much sadism. While I have that reputation, I don't think I dwell very much on torture with a sexual connotation. It certainly is nothing that interests me personally; beating people, being beaten, all that just seems to me terribly dull and unpleasant" (*Job,* p. 115).
25. Jeffrey Weeks appropriates a phrase used by Dick Hebidge—"semiotic guerrilla warfare"—to characterize the multiplication of signifiers that the clone scene produced. Bandannas and keychains, for example, were used to signify the wearer's sexual preferences; their meaning altered depending on their color and their positioning on the body of the wearer. See Jeffrey Weeks, *Sexuality and Its Discontents: Meanings, Myths and Modern Sexualities*

(London and New York: Routledge, 1985), p. 191 and Hebidge, *Subculture: The Meaning of Style* (London: Methuen, 1979). For an in-depth explanation of the erotic proclivities signified by the bandannas, see Levine, p. 66, table 3.3.

26. Levine, pp. 46–47. Consider, for instance, the comparison with Jerry's all-male family in *Port of Saints,* as discussed in chapter two.

27. Gough, in Shepherd and Wallis, eds., p. 122.

28. Dennis Altman, "What Changed in the Seventies" in *Homosexuality: Power and Politics,* ed. Gay Left Collective (London and New York: Allison and Busby, 1980), p. 59.

29. *Ibid.,* p. 52.

30. *Ibid.,* p. 61.

31. *Ibid.,* p. 53.

32. Spencer, p. 375.

33. Seymour Kleinberg, "The New Masculinity of Gay Men and Beyond" in Michael Kaufman, ed., *Beyond Patriarchy: Essays By Men on Pleasure, Power and Change* (New York and Toronto: Oxford University Press, 1987), p. 123.

34. Richard Dyer, "Getting Over the Rainbow: Identity and Pleasure in Gay Cultural Politics" in George Bridges and Rosalind Brunt, eds., *Silver Linings: Some Strategies for the Eighties* (London: Lawrence and Wishart, 1981), pp. 60–61.

35. Murray Healy, *Gay Skins: Class, Masculinity and Queer Appropriation* (London and New York: Cassell, 1996), p. 202. Interestingly, Levine recounts the story told to him by an aging clone that many of the men in his community had, just a few years before, been effeminate in dress and manner: "Just look at these clones, dear. With their pumped up bodies and thick mustaches, they all look so 'butch.' But I remember them when everyone was 'nelly.' What a joke!" See Levine, p. 55.

36. Leo Bersani, "Is the Rectum a Grave?" *October* 43 (1987), Special Book Issue: *AIDS: Cultural Analysis/Cultural Activism,* ed. Douglas Crimp (London and Cambridge, MA: MIT Press, 1988), 207.

37. *Ibid.,* 207–208.

38. Bersani, *Homos* (Cambridge, MA and London: Harvard University Press, 1995), p. 66

39. Bersani, "Loving Men" in Maurice Berger, Brian Wallis and Simon Watson, eds., *Constructing Masculinity* (London and New York: Routledge, 1995), p. 118.

40. Earl Jackson Jr., *Strategies of Deviance: Studies in Gay Male Representation* (Bloomington and Indianapolis: Indiana University Press, 1995), p. 17.

41. *Ibid.,* p. 19.
42. As Burroughs has often pointed out, the noun "Johnson" comes from Jack Black's novel *You Can't Win* (1927), which was an auto-biographical account of life among the bums and thieves of 1920s America. A Johnson was an honorable criminal who maintained certain ethical standards while breaking the law. Burroughs comments on the influence of Black in "The Johnson Family" in *Adding Machine,* pp. 74–77. He also wrote the foreword to the 1988 republication of the text; see Black, *You Can't Win: The Autobiography of Jack Black* (1927; rpt. New York: Amok Press, 1988).
43. Burroughs, "The Revised Boy Scout Manual" *RE-Search 4/5: Special Book Issue: William S. Burroughs, Brion Gysin and Throbbing Gristle,* ed. V. Vale and Andrea Juno (San Francisco: RE-Search Books, 1982), 5.
44. Unlike the majority of Burroughs' characters, sadly Captain Everhard never reappears in the texts. His name is both a symbol of the fantastic gay male body (the penis that is always erect) and a pun on New York's all-night bathhouse, the "Everard Baths" (1888–1977), a well-known location for those looking for casual sex (and a frequent haunt of Burroughs, Ginsberg, and even—on occasion—Jack Kerouac). Burroughs' use of the Huntsmen is interesting in that it is one of the few literary references (of the 1950s) to the burgeoning but still underground macho gay culture.
45. Wayne Pounds notes that, throughout *The Place of Dead Roads,* Burroughs deliberately uses the same language to describe pistols and penises. See Pounds, "The Postmodern Anus: Parody and Utopia in Two Recent Novels by William S. Burroughs" in Skerl and Lydenberg, p. 225.
46. See his comments in *Word Virus: The William S. Burroughs Reader,* ed. James Grauerholz and Ira Silverberg (New York: Grove Press, 1998), p. 360.
47. The fact that the boys transform into dogs is perhaps worth emphasizing, given Burroughs' repeated assertion that dogs (especially in comparison to cats) are vicious beasts: "I am not a dog hater. I do hate what man has made of his best friend. [. . .] But a dog's snarl is *ugly,* a redneck lynch-mob Paki-basher snarl . . . snarl of someone got a 'Kill a Queer for Christ' sticker on his heap, a self-righteous occupied snarl. When you see that snarl you are looking at something that has no face of its own. A dog's rage is not his. It is dictated by his trainer. And lynch-mob rage is dictated by conditioning" (*CI,* 63). This association of the dog with

racists and homophobes suggests that the transformation of the Wild Boys into dogs is a moralistic comment on them; their violent pursuit of pleasure reduces any heroic status they might otherwise have attained.

48. Krup is an allusion to Friedrich Alfred Krupp, the gay German industrialist who was one of the first victims of the "outing" process in the early years of the twentieth century. Exposed by Brand's *Gemeinschaft der Eigenen,* Krupp later committed suicide. The outing process was appropriately dubbed *Weg über Leichen* ("path over corpses"). See Simon LeVay, *Queer Science: The Use and Abuse of Research into Homosexuality* (Cambridge, MA and London: The MIT Press, 1996), p. 34.

49. James Grauerholz has informed me that Kim's song is a parody of an old S. A. song that Burroughs heard on the streets of Salzburg, Austria in July 1936 when he attended the Salzburg festival. Kim's version of the song replaces "Jewish blood" with the blood of (Nazi) "shits."

50. Burroughs' choice of Kit/Kim Carsons as the name of his protagonist is particularly apt. Christopher "Kit" Carson (1809–1868) was a prominent trapper, guide, Indian agent, and army officer on the American frontier. His twentieth-century biographers have made great claims for his heroism and modesty, frequently canonizing him as an honest, racially tolerant, self-reliant individual who, according to one biographer "did not drink, swear nor use coarse language." Burroughs clearly has much fun with this supposed purity in his association of Carson with the profane and obscene. See M. Morgan Ettergreen, *Kit Carson: A Portrait in Courage* (Norman: University of Oklahoma Press, 1962), p. xviii. For a similar presentation of Carson, see also Thelma S. Guild and Harvey L. Carter, *Kit Carson: A Pattern for Heroes* (Lincoln and London: University of Nebraska Press, 1984), pp. 285–295 in particular.

51. Kendra Langeteig, "*Horror Autotoxicus* in the Red Night Trilogy: Ironic Fruits of Burroughs's Terminal Vision," *Configurations* 5 (1997), 159.

52. Foucault, *The History of Sexuality, Volume One,* p. 101.

53. The "Queen's 69th" is fittingly ambiguous, for while the "69" position overturns notions of active/passive sexual couplings, the fact that Everhard was in the "Queen's" regiment could be read as a statement on his gender identifications as well as his sexuality.

54. Burroughs, *The Western Lands* (1987; rpt. London: Picador, 1988), p. 26. Hereafter cited parenthetically in the text as *WL.*

55. Van der Meer, p. 185.
56. With the arrival of the Johnsons, such "sameness" seems to be only strengthened further; the name signifies the end of diversity almost as succinctly as if they had been called "the Smiths."
57. Jackson, p. 20.
58. Burroughs, quoted by Bockris, p. 60.
59. Healy, p. 108.
60. *Ibid.*, p. 108.
61. Jackson, p. 19.
62. *Ibid.*, pp. 33–34.
63. *Ibid.*, p. 33.
64. Foucault, "Le Gai savoir (I)," *Mec Magazine* 5 (June 1988), 34. Cited by David Halperin, *Saint Foucault: Towards a Gay Hagiography* (New York and Oxford: Oxford University Press, 1995), p. 90. The translation used by Halperin is an unpublished one by Michael West; see Halperin, p. 215*n*.
65. Halperin reads "queer" as "*whatever* is at odds with the normal, the legitimate, the dominant. *There is nothing in particular to which it necessarily refers.* It is an identity without an essence." See Halperin, p. 62.
66. *Ibid.*, p. 88.
67. Foucault, "Le Gai Savoir (II)," *Mec Magazine* 6–7 (July-August 1988), 32. Cited by Halperin, p. 94, using a translation by David Macey.
68. *Ibid.*, p. 94.
69. Bob Gallagher and Alexander Wilson, "Michel Foucault. An Interview: Sex, Power and the Politics of Identity," *The Advocate* 400 (7 August 1984), 28.
70. Foucault cited by David Macey, *The Lives of Michel Foucault* (London: Hutchinson, 1993), p. 364. Cited also by Halperin, p. 95.
71. Halperin, p. 85.
72. *Ibid.*, p. 99. The extent of this social reorganization is charted in Gayle Rubin's account of the 1970s gay "leather" scene and, in particular, the famous parties held in "The Catacombs." See Rubin, "The Catacombs: A Temple of the Butthole" in *Leatherfolk: Radical Sex, People, Politics and Practice,* ed. Mark Thompson (Boston: Alyson Publications), pp. 119–141.
73. Heterosexual masculinity, of course, cannot cope with the feminization inherent within the penetrative sexual practices of S/M nor the stereotypically "feminine" social gatherings of bake sales.
74. Foucault, *The History of Sexuality: Volume Two, The Use of Pleasure,* trans. Robert Hurley (1984; rpt. London: Penguin, 1992), p. 74.

75. Foucault, *Technologies of the Self: A Seminar with Michel Foucault*, ed. Luther H. Martin, Huck Gutman, and Patrick H. Hutton (London: Tavistock Publications, 1988), p. 19.

76. Foucault, *The History of Sexuality, Volume Two*, pp. 85–86.

77. *Ibid.*, pp. 82–83.

78. *Ibid.*, p. 85.

79. *Ibid.*, p. 85.

80. Foucault in Raul Fornet-Betancourt *et al.*, "The Ethic of Care for the Self as a Practice of Freedom: An Interview with Michel Foucault on January 20, 1984," trans. J. D. Gauthier, *Philosophy and Social Criticism* 12.2–3 (Summer 1987), 113. Cited by Halperin, pp. 76–77.

81. Foucault in Jean Le Bitoux *et al.*, eds., "De l'amitié comme mode de vie: Un Entretien avec un lecteur quinquagénaire," *Le Gai Pied* 25 (April 1981), 39 and 38 respectively. Cited by Halperin, p. 78 and 81. In addition see "Friendship as a Way of Life" trans. John Johnston in Sylvère Lotringer, ed., *Foucault Live: Interviews 1966–1984* (New York: Semiotext(e), 1989), pp. 203–211.

82. Halperin, p. 109.

83. *Ibid.*, p. 110.

84. Foucault, *The History of Sexuality, Volume Two*, p. 253.

85. Halperin, p. 79.

86. Burroughs' advocation of non-chemical means of altering consciousness—*"learn to make it without any chemical corn"* (*NE*, 13)—notably occurred after the explosion of drug use (particularly LSD) during the 1960s. Such calls to use drug experience as a springboard for self-transformation were, of course, typical during the period; even Ken Kesey, of all people, eventually urged the counterculture to move into the next phase of enlightenment *sans* hallucinogens. Burroughs, though, was never a great advocate of hallucinogens. As it later emerged that the CIA had experimented with LSD on unsuspecting American citizens throughout the 1950s (spiking the drinks of clients in specially established brothels) Burroughs no doubt considered his avoidance of acid culture a lucky escape and a vindication of his earlier paranoia over the intelligence services' interest in mind control. On the CIA's experiments with LSD, see Martin A. Lee and Bruce Shlain, *Acid Dreams: The Complete Social History of LSD, the CIA, the Sixties and Beyond* (1985; rpt. New York: Grove Press, 1992). For Kesey's advocation of alternatives to LSD, see Wolfe, *The Electric Kool-Aid Acid Test*.

87. Significantly, as we will see in the following chapter, Burroughs' vision of the gay male body is predominantly limited to the genitals.

88. Klaus Theweleit, *Male Fantasies, Volume 2: Male Bodies: Psychoan-alyzing the White Terror,* trans. Chris Turner and Erica Carter in collaboration with Stephen Conway (1974; rpt. Cambridge: Polity Press, 1989), pp. 248–249.
89. Jackson, p. 32.
90. Theweleit, p. 7.

CHAPTER FOUR

1. The web memorial can be found on Malcolm Hulmes' William Burroughs Internet site at http://www. hyperreal.org/wsb/
2. The rumor that the post–Red Night trilogy texts were partly ghostwritten is perhaps in this instance, more of a compliment than the criticism it was intended to be, since it highlights Bur-roughs' central theme of the 1980s and 1990s texts: the creation of a post-corporeal realm. Who needs a body to write with anyway? The "ugly rumor" is noted by Roger Clarke in his obituary for Burroughs in the *Sunday Telegraph* (10 August 1997), 7. Dennis Cooper claims that "It's been a well-known secret that beginning with his 'comeback' novel *Cities of the Red Night* (1981), Bur-roughs' prose was a product of partial ghostwriting, and that his involvement in his books diminished to the point where there seemed to be nothing but textual smoke and mirrors." See Cooper, *All Ears: Cultural Criticism, Essays and Obituaries* (New York: Soft Skull Press, 1999), pp. 145–146. Grauerholz has fervently denied these accusations. See Jamie Russell, "Digging Burroughs: An In-terview with James Grauerholz," *Gay Times* 270.
3. An eyewitness account of the ceremony (by Patricia Elliott) is to be found on Levi Asher's Beat Generation homepage, "Literary Kicks" at http://www.charm.net/~ brooklyn/SlicedBardo/index.html.
4. Lydenberg, p. 71.
5. *Ibid.,* p. 72.
6. Gregory Stephenson, "The Gnostic Vision of William S. Bur-roughs," *Review of Contemporary Fiction* (Spring 1984), 40.
7. *Ibid.,* 49.
8. Burroughs, "Civilian Defense" in *Adding Machine,* p. 82.
9. Crowley, p. 88.
10. *Ibid.,* p. 144.
11. *Ibid.,* p. 143. This "body of light" can also be found in Hubbard's theories. Hubbard believed that thought had mass and that the

engram-riddled subject experienced a heaviness that blocked the electrical currents of the E-meter. The post auditing subject frequently reported a physical improvement in which the "body feels clearer (more relaxed) and *lighter*" (my emphasis). Such physical improvements were closely linked to Scientology's mythology of the "thetan," an immortal soul or spirit encased within the body and that could be released into space. The exteriorization of this "body of light" was the overriding goal of Scientology's program of training. See Hubbard, *Have You Lived Before This Life?*, p. 31. For an excellent discussion of Gnosis (including its relationship to Scientology) see Erik Davies, *Techgnosis: Myth, Magic and Mysticism in the Age of Information* (New York: Harmony Books, 1998).

12. Such sex magic is a recurrent issue in the texts. See, for instance, Kim's attack on Judge Farris (*PDR*, 19–20) and Clem Snide's 'occult' ceremony with Jim (*CRN*, 77–78).

13. Burroughs, "Silver Boys" (1987). Reproduced in Sobieszek, *Ports of Entry*, p. 133.

14. Burroughs notes his appropriation of Mailer's work in *The Western Lands* (*WL*, 5). He takes the *mise en scène*, character names and central themes from Mailer's text, but significantly queers them in the process. The central character of *Ancient Evenings* is a member of the Pharaoh's court who has successfully reincarnated himself four times (a method of survival reminiscent of the Transmigrants in Burroughs' earlier *Cities of the Red Night*). Interestingly, in Mailer's text, anal sex is part of the power matrix of Egyptian society. In the Pharaoh's court, the penetrated man loses his claim to masculinity, even if he is made sexually submissive by the divine Pharaoh himself. In Burroughs' vision, anal sex is, of course, resignified as liberating rather than humiliating. See Norman Mailer, *Ancient Evenings* (Boston: Little Brown, 1983).

15. Burroughs' interest in extraterrestrial contact culminated in his 1989 meeting with Whitley Strieber. After reading Strieber's autobiographical account of alien abduction, Burroughs struck up a friendship with the author and, according to journalist Roger Clarke, "spent several afternoons wandering Strieber's 100-acre wooded estate looking for alien action. But there were no visitations. Later Burroughs was informed by Strieber that the aliens had not appeared as they were *already familiar with William Burroughs.*" There are few authors who can claim such intergalactic fame. See Roger Clarke, "Interview with William Burroughs," *The Independent*, Weekend Supplement (23 September 1995), 3. In

addition, see Strieber's *Communion: A True Story Encounter with the Unknown* (New York: Beech Tree Books, 1987).

16. Murphy, p. 156.

17. There are many accounts of the beginnings of the AIDS crisis in America. Sandor L. Gilman, for instance, documents the emergence of the virus in 1979 in a series of unexplained deaths. It took until early 1982 for the sudden rise in deaths among gay and bisexual men to prompt the health authorities to issue warnings about what they called GRIDS (Gay Related Immune Deficiency Syndrome). Only as non-gay members of the population (such as hemophiliacs and I.V. drug users) began to suffer similar symptoms and deaths did the authorities begin to properly address the issue since it was clearly no longer simply a "gay disease." The acronym "AIDS" (Acquired Immune Deficiency Syndrome) was coined in late 1982. See Gilman, *Disease and Representation: Images of Illness from Madness to AIDS* (Ithaca and London: Cornell University Press, 1988), pp. 245–272.

18. Murphy, p. 176.

19. ACT-UP (AIDS Coalition to Unleash Power) is illustrative of the radical strategies employed by AIDS activists during the late 1980s and 1990s. Since its formation in New York in 1987, ACT-UP has staged demonstrations throughout the United States, offering a consistently strident condemnation of the heterosexual dominant's refusal to properly react to the epidemic. Disrupting court cases, television shows and even the New York Stock Exchange, ACT-UP initiated a politicized discourse of anger and activism that refused to be suppressed since, as the legend declared "SILENCE=DEATH." See Douglas Crimp and Adam Rolston, *AIDS DemoGraphics* (Seattle Bay Press, 1990). Crimp and Rolston's informative account of activist artwork, including the omnipresent SILENCE=DEATH logo, is reprinted as "AIDS Activist Graphics: A Demonstration" in Ken Gelder and Sarah Thornton, eds., *The Subcultures Reader* (London and New York: Routledge, 1997), pp. 436–444.

20. Burroughs' interview with David Ehrenstein, "Burroughs: On Tear Gas, Queers, *Naked Lunch,* and the Ginsberg Affair," *The Advocate* 581 (16 July 1991) briefly discusses AIDS, and critiques reactionary heterosexual responses to the epidemic: "an enormous number of people believe that homosexual intercourse can cause AIDS even if neither party had the virus! Now that's an immaculate conception!" Such discussion of the virus by Burroughs is, however, a rare occurrence. His most extended fic-

tional engagement with the crisis is in *Ghost of Chance* in which he challenges the heterosexual dominant's discourse on AIDS by imagining a "Christ Sickness." Emerging from Africa, the disease rampages across the globe, infusing sufferers with rabid religious zeal. Even in this moment he never actually names the epidemic itself. See *Ghost of Chance* (1991; rpt. London and New York: Serpent's Tail, 1995), p. 32*ff.* Hereafter cited parenthetically in the text as *GC*.

21. See Burroughs' conversation with Lou Reed in Bockris, p. 18.

22. The comparison between Rechy and Burroughs is one that has been noted previously by Stephen Adams, who reads both authors as progenitors of "terminal sex," couplings that simultaneously glorify the homosexual as "outlaw" and attempt to negate the body and self through sex: "Rechy's heroes communicate only with themselves, while Burroughs wants to break free of the self altogether, to escape into a psychic nowhere." Adams is quite scathing about the status of both authors in relation to the liberation movement, suggesting that neither is politically committed in any progressive sense. He accuses Burroughs, in particular, of offering "no hope or model for reshaping existing patterns of identity, only the injunction to destroy all patterns of constricting moulds, to release the entrapped spirit to some netherworld that lies, necessarily, beyond the scope of definition." As we will see, Burroughs' "netherworld" is never a "psychic nowhere" but always defined as masculine. Adams, *The Homosexual as Hero in Contemporary Fiction* (London: Vision Press, 1980), p. 104.

23. Parts of Burroughs' *Cities of the Red Night* read like a fantastic reworking of Rechy's *City of Night;* the sprawl of urban environments and queer hedonism are strangely similar. In addition, Rechy and Burroughs share an apprehension about the limits of hypermasculine identity, although Rechy is far more explicit in his condemnation of the links between the hypermasculine, fascism, and misogyny. The gay neo-Nazi in *City of Night* expounds—in an eerie echo of Burroughs' texts—his misogynist vision: "Women are vampires! Vicious, draining bloodsuckers!" As the text undermines his position, he is characterized as pathetic, weak, and ultimately masochistic. In his final moment he is discovered executing his aging cat while wearing an SS uniform in a ludicrous yet disturbing attempt to fulfill his violent fantasies. See Rechy, *City of Night* (1963; rpt. London: MacGibbon and Kee, 1964), p. 259 and p. 270 respectively. Burroughs later used much the same material in his discussion of SS initiation ceremonies and cat torture (*CI*, 33).

24. John Rechy, *The Sexual Outlaw: A Documentary: A Non-fiction Account, With Commentaries, of Three Days and Nights in the Sexual Underground* (1977; rpt. London: W. H. Allen: 1978), p. 299.

25. *Ibid.,* p. 300.

26. *Ibid.,* p. 300.

27. Armistead Maupin, *Tales of the City* (1978; rpt. London: Black Swan, 1997), p. 86

28. Rechy, p. 300.

29. *Ibid.,* p. 301.

30. *Ibid.,* p. 21.

31. *Ibid.,* p. 95.

32. Simon Watney, *Policing Desire: Pornography, AIDS and the Media* (Minneapolis: University of Minnesota Press, 1987), p. 3.

33. See Ginsberg's interview in *Three Novels,* p. 190.

34. Burroughs, *The Book of Breeething* (Berkeley: Blue Wind Press, 1975), no pagination.

35. Gilman, pp. 246–247.

36. Bersani, "Is the Rectum a Grave?," 202*n*. See also Randy Shilts, *And the Band Played On* (New York: St. Martin's Press, 1987).

37. Bersani, 211. Gilman discusses AIDS in relation to historical discourses on other illnesses in *Disease and Representation.*

38. See, for instance, Lee Edelman's discussion of the ideological structures governing AIDS discourses (both straight and gay), in particular the interplay of activism/passivity, pleasure/destruction, and the dangers of ratifying a cultural inscription of passivity "predisposed to observe and condemn the 'ass' in 'passive'." See Edelman, "The Mirror and the Tank: 'AIDS,' Subjectivity, and the Rhetoric of Activism" in *Writing AIDS: Gay Literature, Language and Analysis,* ed. Timothy F. Murphy and Suzanne Poirier (New York: Columbia University Press, 1993), p. 26.

39. The Dream Machine, a rotating cylinder with a flashing light source inside, was invented by Gysin (with Ian Sommerville's help) in order to facilitate trancelike states. Patented by Gysin, it never aroused a great deal of interest, despite his talents for self-promotion. In recent times, it has seen a revival of interest, most notably in connection with Kurt Cobain's death in 1994. An American "cult organization" called "Friends Understanding Kurt" issued statements after Cobain's death which claimed that "Kurt obtained a machine and was using it for up to 72 hours at a time. The machine was found 20 feet from his body but neither the police nor the coroner's office had any idea of its significance." Cobain had collaborated with Burroughs on the album *The Priest*

They Called Him (Tim/Kerr Records, 1993). See the article "Dream On" *New Music Express* (1 July 1995), 3. James Grauerholz has suggested to me in correspondence that this rumor was a hoax devised by one of the Dream Machine's latter-day manufacturers in the hope of boosting sales.

40. Allan Johnston, "The Burroughs Biopathy: William S. Burroughs' *Junky* and *Naked Lunch* and Reichian Theory," *Review of Contemporary Fiction* (Spring 1984), 107–120.

41. Gilles Deleuze and Felix Guattari, *Anti-Oedipus: Capitalism and Schizophrenia,* trans. Robert Hurley, Mark Seem and Helen R. Lane (1972; rpt. London: The Athlone Press, 1984), p. 119.

42. Wilhelm Reich, *The Function of the Orgasm: Sex-Economic Problems of Biological Energy,* trans. Vincent R. Carfagno (1942; rpt. London: Souvenir Press, 1983), p. 102.

43. *Ibid.,* p. 102.

44. Wilhelm Reich, *Listen, Little Man!* trans. Theodore P. Wolfe (1948; rpt. New York: Farrar, Straus and Giroux, 1972), p. 115.

45. See illustration and caption in *Listen, Little Man!* p. 42.

46. See W. Edward Mann and Edward Hoffman, *The Man Who Dreamed of Tomorrow: A Conceptual Biography of Wilhelm Reich* (Los Angeles: JP Tarcher, 1980), p. 59.

47. *Ibid.,* pp. 53–54.

48. This final comment might be the starting point for a re-emphasis of Burroughs' project in terms of a wider concern with the "human condition," which stretches beyond the narrow focus on masculine-identified gay men. At other points Burroughs demonstrates a similar desire to offer a broader vision; defending himself against accusations of misogyny in his essay "Women: A Biological Mistake?" he claims "Women may well be a biological mistake [. . .] but so is everything else I see around here." This attempt to replace misogyny with misanthropy is rather half-hearted and indicates little more than Burroughs' own awareness that his misogynist vision is not to everyone's taste. Burroughs may well distrust the division of the sexes, but it is always women who are made to suffer for this evolutionary mistake, the implication being that humanity would not be caught in such an impasse if it had remained male-masculine. See "Women: A Biological Mistake?" in *Adding Machine,* p. 125.

49. *Ibid.,* p. 126.

50. Pounds in Skerl and Lydenberg, p. 224.

51. Lydenberg, pp. 161–162.

52. *Ibid.,* p. 173.

53. *Ibid.*, p. 176.
54. Butler, p. 6.
55. *Ibid.*, p. 7
56. Lydenberg, p. 173.
57. Of course, feminist theory would suggest that Burroughs' vision of the body of light is part of a much wider, masculine discourse on light as part of the process of en*light*enment. The transformation of Burroughs' heroes into light might thus be read as indicative of his essentialism; the search for masculine stability is closely bound to the search for truth, knowledge and reason. For a discussion of the manner in which Western thought privileges "light" as part of the masculine relation to truth, see Cathryn Vasseleu, *Textures of Light: Vision and Touch in Irigaray, Levinas and Merleau-Ponty* (London and New York: Routledge, 1998).
58. Nataf, Zachary, I. "Skin-Flicks" in Sue Golding, ed., *The Eight Technologies of Otherness* (London and New York: Routledge, 1997), p. 173.

AFTERWORD

1. See Morgan, p. 261.
2. Burroughs, "Sexual Conditioning" in Len Richmond and Gary Noguera, eds., *The Gay Liberation Book* (San Francisco: Ramparts Press, 1973), pp. 194–195.
3. *Ibid.*, p. 194.
4. *Ibid.*, p. 195.

Works Cited

Adams, Stephen. *The Homosexual as Hero in Contemporary Fiction.* London: Vision, 1980.

Altman, Dennis. "What Changed in the Seventies?" In Gay Left Collective, eds. *Homosexuality: Power and Politics.* London: Allison and Busby, 1980, pp. 52–63.

Anger, Kenneth, dir. *Scorpio Rising.* Puck Film Productions, 1963.

Anon. "Response to R.L.M." *ONE* (September 1953), 13.

Arieti, Silvano, ed. *The American Handbook of Psychiatry, Volume One.* New York: Basic Books, 1959.

Asher, Levi, "Literary Kicks." Website: www.charm.net/~brooklyn/Lit-Kicks.html.

Balch, Anthony, dir. *Towers Open Fire.* 1963. With the collaboration of William Burroughs, Brion Gysin, and Ian Sommerville. Released on videocassette as *Towers Open Fire and Other Short Films.* Mystic Fire Video, 1990.

Baldwin, James. *Giovanni's Room.* New York: The Dial Press, 1956.

Ballard, J. G. *Running Wild.* London: Hutchinson, 1988.

Bayer, Ronald. *Homosexuality and American Psychiatry: The Politics of Diagnosis.* New York: Basic Books, 1981.

Berger, Albert I. "Towards a Science of the Nuclear Mind: Science-Fiction Origins of Dianetics." *Science-Fiction Studies* 16 (1989): 123–144.

Berger, Maurice, Brian Wallis, and Simon Watson, eds. *Constructing Masculinity.* London and New York: Routledge, 1995.

Bergler, Edmund. *Homosexuality: Disease or Way of Life?* New York: Hill and Wang, 1956.

Bersani, Leo. *Homos.* Cambridge, MA and London: Harvard University Press, 1995.

———. "Is the Rectum a Grave?" *October* 43 (1987): 197–222. Special Book Issue. *AIDS: Cultural Analysis/Cultural Activism.* Ed. Douglas Crimp. London, and Cambridge, MA: MIT Press, 1988.

———. 'Loving Men.' In Maurice Berger, Brian Wallis, and Simon Watson, eds. *Constructing Masculinity.* London and New York: Routledge, 1995, pp. 115–123.

Black, Jack. *You Can't Win: The Autobiography of Jack Black.* 1927. New York: Amok Press, 1988.

Bridges, George, and Rosalind Brunt, eds. *Silver Linings: Some Strategies for the Eighties.* London: Lawrence and Wishart, 1981.

Brookner, Howard. *William Burroughs.* Citifilmworks, 1983.

Burroughs, William S. *The Adding Machine: Collected Essays.* London: John Calder, 1985.

——. *Ah Pook Is Here and Other Texts.* London: John Calder, 1979.

——. *Ali's Smile/Naked Scientology.* Bonn: Expanded Media Editions, 1972.

——. *The Book of Breeething.* Berkeley: Blue Wind Press, 1975.

——. *The Burroughs File.* San Francisco: City Light Books, 1984. Second printing, 1991.

——. "Burroughs on Scientology." *Los Angeles Free Press* (6 March 1970). Reprinted in Burroughs, *Ali's Smile/Naked Scientology.* Bonn: Expanded Media Editions, 1972, pp. 63–77.

——. *The Cat Inside.* 1986. London: Viking, 1992. Revised edition.

——. *Cities of the Red Night.* 1981. London: John Calder, 1981.

——. *The Exterminator.* San Francisco: Auerhahn Press, 1960.

——. *Exterminator!* 1973. London: Calder and Boyars, 1974.

——. *Ghost of Chance.* 1991. London and New York: Serpent's Tail, 1995.

——. *Health Bulletin: APO–33, A Metabolic Regulator.* New York: Fuck You Press, 1965.

——. "Interview with Allen Ginsberg." In *Three Novels.* New York: Grove Press, 1980.

——. *Interzone.* Ed. James Grauerholz. New York: Viking, 1989.

——. "Introduction." In Black *You Can't Win: The Autobiography of Jack Black.* 1927. New York: Amok Press, 1988, pp. 54–56.

——. "Introduction to *William's Mix.*" In Rupert Loydell, ed. *My Kind of Angel: i.m. William Burroughs.* Exeter: Stride, 1998, pp. 54–56.

——. [using pseud. William Lee] *Junkie.* New York: Ace Books, 1953.

——. *The Letters of William S. Burroughs 1945–1959.* Ed. Oliver Harris. 1993. London: Picador, 1993.

——. *My Education: A Book of Dreams.* 1995. London Picador, 1995.

——. *Naked Lunch.* Paris: Olympia Press, 1959.

——. *Nova Express.* 1964. Grove Black Cat, 1965.

——. "Open Letter to Mister Gorden Mustain." *The East Village Other* 5.31 (7 July 1970). Reprinted in Burroughs, *Ali's Smile/Naked Scientology.* Bonn: Expanded Media Editions, 1972, pp. 78–82.

——. *The Place of Dead Roads.* New York: Holt, Rinehart and Winston, 1984.

————. *Port of Saints*. 1973. Berkeley: Blue Wind Press, 1980.

————. *Queer*. New York: Viking, 1985.

————. "Review of *Inside Scientology*." *Rolling Stone* (9 November 1972). Reprinted in *Ali's Smile/Naked Scientology*, pp. 83–89.

————. "The Revised Boy Scout Manual (excerpts from a novel of three one-hour tape recordings)." *RE-Search 4–5: Special Book Issue: William S. Burroughs, Brion Gysin, and Throbbing Gristle*. Ed. V. Vale and Andrea Juno. (San Francisco: RE-Search, 1982): 5–11.

————. "Sexual Conditioning." In Len Richmond and Gary Noguera, eds. *The Gay Liberation Book*. San Francisco: Ramparts Press, 1973, pp. 194–195.

————. *The Soft Machine*, 1961. 1966. Second Revised Edition. London: Calder and Boyars, 1968. Third Revised Edition.

————. *The Ticket That Exploded*. 1962. New York: Grove Press, 1967. Revised Edition.

————. *Three Novels: The Soft Machine, Nova Express, The Wild Boys*. Grove Press: New York, 1980.

————. *Tornado Alley*. Cherry Valley Editions, 1989.

————. *The Western Lands*. 1987. London: Picador, 1988.

————. *The Wild Boys: A Book of the Dead*. 1971. New York: Grove Press, 1992.

————. *A William S. Burroughs Reader*. Ed. John Calder. London: Picador, 1982.

————. *Word Virus: The William S. Burroughs Reader*. Ed. James Grauerholz and Ira Silverberg. New York: Grove Press, 1998.

Burroughs, William S., and Victor Bockris. *With William Burroughs: A Report from the Bunker*. New York: Seaver Books, 1980.

Burroughs, William S., and Roger Clarke. "An Interview with William Burroughs." *The Independent*. Weekend Supplement (23 September 1995): 3.

Burroughs, William S., and Kurt Cobain. *The "Priest" They Called Him*. Tim/Kerr Records, 1993.

Burroughs, William S., and Laurence Collinson, and Roger Baker. "An Interview with William Burroughs." *Gay Sunshine* 21 (1974): 1–2.

Burroughs, William S., and Allen Ginsberg. *The Yage Letters*. San Francisco: City Light Books, 1963.

Burroughs, William S., and Brion Gysin, Sinclair Beiles, and Gregory Corso. *Minutes To Go*. 1960. San Francisco: Beach Books, 1968.

Burroughs, William S., and Brion Gysin. *The Third Mind*. 1978. London: John Calder, 1979.

Burroughs, William S., and Conrad Knickerbocker. "William Burroughs: An Interview." *Paris Review* 10.35 (Spring 1966): 13–49.

Burroughs, William S., and Daniel Odier. *The Job: Interviews with William S. Burroughs*. 1969. New York: Grove Press, 1974.

Burroughs, William S., and Robert Palmer. "Interview." *Rolling Stone* 108 (11 May 1972): 34–39.

Burroughs, William S., and Claude Pélieu and Carl Weissner. *So Who Owns Death TV?* San Francisco: Beach Books, 1967.

Burroughs, William S., and J. E. Rivers. "An Interview with William Burroughs." *Resources for American Literary Study* 10.2 (Autumn 1980): 154–166.

Burroughs, William S., and Gus Van Sant. *Thanksgiving Prayer*. Island Video, 1990.

Butler, Judith. *Gender Trouble: Feminism and the Subversion of Identity*. New York and London: Routledge, 1990.

Calder, John. "Introduction." *A William Burroughs Reader,* pp. 7–24.

Caveney, Graham. "Pimp of the Perverse." *Arena* (November 1997): 76.

———. *The "Priest" They Called Him: The Life and Legacy of William S. Burroughs*. London: Bloomsbury, 1998.

Chauncey, George. *Gay New York: The Making of the Gay Male World 1890–1940*. New York: Basic Books, 1994.

Clarke, Roger. "William Burroughs." *Sunday Telegraph*. (August 10 1997): 7.

Cooper, Dennis. *All Ears: Cultural Criticism, Essays and Obituaries*. New York: Soft Skull Press, 1999.

Corber, Robert J. *Homosexuality in Cold War America: Resistance and the Crisis of Masculinity*. Durham and London: Duke University Press, 1997.

———. *In the Name of National Security: Hitchcock, Homophobia and the Political Construction of Gender in Postwar America*. Durham: Duke University Press, 1993.

Cory, Donald Webster [pseud. for Edward Sagarin]. *The Homosexual in America: A Subjective Approach*. New York: Greenburg, 1951.

Crimp, Douglas, ed. *October* 43 (1987). Special Book Issue. *AIDS: Cultural Analysis/Cultural Activism*. London and Cambridge, MA: MIT Press, 1988.

Crimp, Douglas, with Adam Rolston. *AIDS DemoGraphics*. Seattle Bay Press, 1990.

———. "AIDS Activist Graphics: A Demonstration." In Ken Gelder and Sarah Thornton, eds. *The Subcultures Reader*. London and New York: Routledge, 1997, pp. 436–444.

Cronenberg, David, dir. *Naked Lunch*. Twentieth Century Fox, 1991.

Crowley, Aleister. *Magick in Theory and Practice*. 1929. New York: Dover Publications, 1976.

David, Hugh. *On Queer Street: A Sociological History of British Homosexuality 1895–1995*. London: HarperCollins, 1997.

Erik Davies. *Techgnosis: Myth, Magic and Mysticism in the Age of Information*. New York: Harmony Books, 1998.

Deleuze, Gilles and Félix Guattari. *Anti-Oedipus: Capitalism and Schizophrenia*. 1972. Trans. Robert Hurley, Mark Seem, and Helen R. Lane. 1977. London: The Athlone Press, 1984.

Dellamora, Richard. *Apocalyptic Overtures: Sexual Politics and the Sense of an Ending*. New Brunswick, NJ: Rutgers University Press, 1994.

D'Emilio, John. *Sexual Politics, Sexual Communities: The Making of a Homosexual Minority in the United States 1940–1970*. Chicago and London: University of Chicago Press, 1983.

Dollimore, Jonathan. *Sexual Dissidence: Augustine to Wilde, Freud to Foucault*. Oxford: Clarendon Press, 1991.

Duberman, Martin. *Cures: A Gay Man's Odyssey*. 1991. London: Penguin, 1991.

———. *Stonewall*. 1993. London: Plume, 1994.

Dyer, Richard. "Getting Over the Rainbow: Identity and Pleasure in Gay Cultural Politics." In George Bridges and Rosalind Brunt, eds. *Silver Linings: Some Strategies for the Eighties*. London: Lawrence and Wishart, 1981, pp. 53–67.

Edelman, Lee. "The Mirror and the Tank: 'AIDS,' Subjectivity, and the Rhetoric of Activism." In Timothy F. Murphy and Suzanne Poirier, eds. *Writing AIDS: Gay Literature, Language and Analysis*. New York: Columbia University Press, 1993, pp. 9–38.

Ehrenstein, David. "Burroughs: On Tear Gas, Queers, *Naked Lunch*, and the Ginsberg Affair." *The Advocate* 581 (16 July 1991): 40–45.

Epstein, Rob and Jeffrey Friedman, dirs. *The Celluloid Closet*. Columbia Tristar, 1995.

Ettergreen, M. Morgan. *Kit Carson: A Portrait in Courage*. Norman: University of Oklahoma Press, 1962.

Fiedler, Leslie A. *Being Busted*. New York: Stein and Day, 1969.

———. *The Collected Essays of Leslie Fiedler*. Two volumes. (New York: Stein and Day, 1971).

———. "Come Back to the Raft Ag'in, Huck Honey!" *Partisan Review* 15.6 (June 1948): 664–671.

———. *Love and Death in the American Novel*. New York: Criterion Books, 1960.

———. *Love and Death in the American Novel*. Normal, Illinois: Dalkey Archive Press, 1997. Second Edition.

———. "The New Mutants." *Partisan Review* 32.4 (Fall 1965): 505–525.

————. "The Un-Angry Young Men." In *The Collected Essays of Leslie Fiedler, Volume One,* pp. 389–407.

————. *What Was Literature? Class Culture and Mass Society.* New York: Simon and Schuster, 1982.

Ford, Clellan, and Frank Beach. *Patterns of Sexual Behavior.* New York: Harper Brothers, 1951.

Fornet-Betancourt, Raul, *et al.,* eds. "The Ethic of Care for the Self as a Practice of Freedom: An Interview with Michel Foucault on January 20, 1984." Trans. J. D. Gauthier. *Philosophy and Social Criticism* 12.2–3 (Summer 1987): 112–131.

Foucault, Michel. "De l'amitié comme mode de vie: Un Entretien avec un lecteur quinquagénaire," *Le Gai Pied* 25 (April 1981), 38–39. Translated as "Friendship as a Way of Life" by John Johnston in Lotringer, ed. *Foucault Live: Interviews 1966–1984.*

————. "Le Gai savoir (I)." *Mec Magazine* 5 (June 1988): 32–36.

————. "Le Gai savoir (II)." *Mec Magazine* 6–7 (July-August 1988): 30–33.

————. *The History of Sexuality, Volume One: An Introduction.* 1976. Trans. Robert Hurley. 1978. London: Penguin, 1990.

————. *The History of Sexuality, Volume Two: The Use of Pleasure.* 1984. Trans. Robert Hurley. 1985. London: Penguin, 1992.

————. *Technologies of the Self: A Seminar with Michel Foucault.* Ed. Luther H. Martin, Huck Gutman, and Patricia H. Hutton. London: Tavistock Publications, 1988.

Freud, Sigmund. "Letter to an American Mother." 1935. Reprinted in Paul Friedman, "Sexual Deviations" in Silvano Arieti, ed. *The American Handbook of Psychiatry, Volume One.* New York: Basic Books, 1959, pp. 606–607

————. "Psycho-analytic Notes on an Autobiographical Account of a Case of Paranoia (Dementia Paranoides) [The Schreber Case]." 1911. In Freud, *The Standard Edition of the Complete Psychological Works of Sigmund Freud.* Translated and edited by James Strachey with the collaboration of Anna Freud. 24 volumes. London: The Hogarth Press, 1953–1974, vol. 12, pp. 3–82.

————. "The Psychogenesis of a Case of Homosexuality in a Woman." 1920. In Freud, *The Standard Edition of the Complete Psychological Works of Sigmund Freud.* Translated and edited by James Strachey with the collaboration of Anna Freud. 24 volumes. London: The Hogarth Press, 1953–1974, vol. 19, pp. 145–172.

————. "Some Psychical Consequences of the Anatomical Distinction Between the Sexes." 1925. In Freud, *The Standard Edition of the Complete Psychological Works of Sigmund Freud.* Translated and edited by

James Strachey with the collaboration of Anna Freud. 24 volumes. London: The Hogarth Press, 1953–1974, vol. 19, pp. 241–258.

———. *The Standard Edition of the Complete Psychological Works of Sigmund Freud.* Translated and edited by James Strachey with the collaboration of Anna Freud. 24 volumes. London: The Hogarth Press, 1953–1974.

Friedman, Paul. "Sexual Deviations." In Silvano Arieti, ed. *The American Handbook of Psychiatry, Volume One.* New York: Basic Books, 1959, pp. 606–607.

Furie, Sidney J., dir. *The Leather Boys.* Allied Artists, 1964.

Gallagher, Bob, and Alexander Wilson. "Michel Foucault: An Interview: Sex, Power and the Politics of Identity." *The Advocate* 400 (August 7 1984): 26–30, 58.

Gay Left Collective, eds. *Homosexuality: Power and Politics.* London: Allison and Busby, 1980.

Gay Liberation Front. "Statement of Purpose." *RAT* (12 August 1969).

Gelder, Ken and Sarah Thornton, eds. *The Subcultures Reader.* London and New York: Routledge, 1997.

Gilman, Sander L. *Disease and Representation: Images of Illness from Madness to AIDS.* Ithaca and London: Cornell University Press, 1988.

Ginsberg, Allen. "Howl," 1955–1956. In *Collected Poems: 1947–1980.* London and New York: Penguin, 1987, pp. 126–133.

Ginsberg, Allen, and Thomas Clark. "Allen Ginsberg: An Interview." *Paris Review* 10.37 (Spring 1966): 13–61.

Ginsberg, Allen, and Allen Young. *Gay Sunshine Interview.* 1973. Bolinas: Grey Fox Press, 1974.

Glover, David. "Burroughs' Western." In Jennie Skerl and Robin Lydenberg, eds. *William S. Burroughs: At the Front: Critical Reception, 1959–1989.* Carbondale and Edwardsville: Southern Illinois University Press, 1991, pp. 209–215.

Golding, Sue, ed. *The Eight Technologies of Otherness.* London and New York: Routledge, 1997.

Goodman, Michael Barry. *Contemporary Literary Censorship: The Case History of Burroughs' Naked Lunch.* London and Metuchen, NJ: The Scarecrow Press, 1981.

Gough, Jamie. "Theories of Sexual Identity and the Masculinization of the Gay Man." In Simon Shepherd and Mick Wallis, eds. *Coming On Strong: Gay Politics and Culture.* London: Unwin, 1989, pp. 119–136.

Guild, Thelma S., and Harvey L. Carter. *Kit Carson: A Pattern for Heroes.* Lincoln and London: University of Nebraska Press, 1984.

Guzlowski, John Z. "The Family in the Fiction of William Burroughs." *Midwest Quarterly* 30.1 (1988): 11–26.

Hall, G. Stanley. *Adolescence: Its Psychology and Its Relations to Physiology, Anthropology, Sociology, Sex, Crime, Religion and Education.* 2 vols. New York and London: Appleton, 1904.

Halperin, David. *Saint Foucault: Towards a Gay Hagiography.* New York and Oxford: Oxford University Press, 1995.

Harris, Charles B. "Introduction." In Fiedler, *Love and Death in the American Novel.* 1960. Normal, Illinois: Dalkey Archive Press, 1997, pp. v-xii.

Harris, Oliver. "Can You See a Virus? The Queer Cold War of William Burroughs." *Journal of American Studies* 33.2 (1999): 243–266.

―――. "A Response to John Watters, 'The Control Machine: Myth in *The Soft Machine* of W. S. Burroughs.' " *Connotations* 6.3 (1996/97): 337–353.

Hawks, Howard, dir. *Bringing Up Baby.* RKO Radio Pictures, 1938.

Hay, Harry. *Radically Gay: Gay Liberation in the Words of Its Founder.* Ed. Will Roscoe. Boston: Beacon Press, 1996.

Healy, Murray. *Gay Skins: Class, Masculinity and Queer Appropriation.* London and New York: Cassell, 1996.

Hebidge, Dick. *Subculture: The Meaning of Style.* London: Methuen, 1979.

Hekma, Gert. " 'A Female Soul in a Male Body': Sexual Inversion as Gender Inversion in Nineteenth-Century Sexology." In Gilbert Herdt, ed. *Third Sex, Third Gender: Beyond Sexual Dimorphism in Culture and History.* New York: Zone Books, 1994, pp. 213–239.

Helbrandt, Maurice. *Narcotic Agent.* New York: Ace Books, 1953.

Herdt, Gilbert, ed. *Third Sex, Third Gender: Beyond Sexual Dimorphism in Culture and History.* New York: Zone Books, 1994.

Hocquenghem, Guy. *Homosexual Desire.* 1972. Trans. Daniella Dangoor. London: Allison and Busby, 1978.

Hubbard, L. Ron. *Dianetics: The Modern Science of Mental Health.* 1950. Reprinted as *Dianetics: The Power of the Mind Over the Body.* East Grinstead: New Era, 1997.

―――. *Have You Lived Before This Life? A Scientific Survey.* 1968. East Grinstead. The Department of Publications Worldwide [The Church of Scientology].

―――. *Scientology: A History of Man.* Los Angeles: Bridge Publications, 1994.

Hulmes, Malcolm, "The William S. Burroughs Web-Memorial." Website: www.hyperreal.org/wsb.

Ingram, David. "William Burroughs and Language." In A. Robert Lee, ed. *The Beat Generation Writers.* London and Chicago: Pluto Press, 1996, pp. 95–113.

Jackson, Earl, Jr. *Strategies of Deviance: Studies in Gay Male Representation.* Bloomington and Indianapolis: Indiana University Press, 1995.

Jacobsen, Jeff. "Dianetics: From Out of the Blue?" *The Arizona Skeptic* 5.2 (September/October 1991): 1–5.

Jacobsen Marcia, *Being a Boy Again:* Autobiography and the American Boy Book. Tuscaloosa and London: University of Alabama Press, 1994.

Johnston, Allan. "The Burroughs Biopathy: William S. Burroughs' *Junky* and *Naked Lunch* and Reichian Theory." *Review of Contemporary Fiction* (Spring 1984): 107–120.

Kardiner, Abram. *Sex and Morality.* Indianapolis and New York: Bobbs-Merrill, 1954.

Kaufman, Michael, ed. *Beyond Patriarchy: Essays By Men on Pleasure, Power and Change.* New York and Toronto: Oxford University Press, 1987.

Kaufman, Robert. *Inside Scientology.* Paris: Olympia Press, 1972.

Kazin, Alfred, ed. *Writers At Work: The "Paris Review" Interviews.* Third Series. New York: Viking, 1967.

Kearney, Patrick J. "An Unpublished Introduction by William S. Burroughs: Prefatory Remarks." In Rupert Loydell, ed. *My Kind of Angel: i.m. William Burroughs.* Exeter: Stride, 1998, pp. 51–53.

Kinsey, A. C., W. B. Pomeroy, and C. Martin. *Sexual Behavior in the Human Male.* Philadelphia: Saunders, 1948.

Kleinberg, Seymour. "The New Masculinity of Gay Men and Beyond." In Michael Kaufman, ed. *Beyond Patriarchy: Essays By Men on Pleasure, Power and Change.* New York and Toronto: Oxford University Press, 1987, pp. 120–138.

Korzybski, Count Alfred. *Science and Sanity: An Introduction to Non-Aristotelian Systems and General Semantics.* 1933. Connecticut: The International Non-Aristotelian Library, 1973. Fourth Edition.

Langeteig, Kendra. "*Horror Autotoxicus* in the Red Night Trilogy: Ironic Fruits of Burroughs' Terminal Vision." *Configurations* 5 (1997): 135–169.

Lee, A. Robert, ed. *The Beat Generation Writers.* London and Chicago: Pluto Press, 1996.

Lee, Martin A., and Bruce Shlain. *Acid Dreams: The Complete Social History of LSD, the CIA, the Sixties and Beyond.* 1985. Revised edition. New York: Grove Press, 1992.

LeVay, Simon. *Queer Science: The Use and Abuse of Research into Homosexuality.* Cambridge, MA and London: The MIT Press, 1996.

LeVay, Simon, and Elisabeth Nonas. *City of Friends: A Portrait of the Gay and Lesbian Community in America.* Cambridge, MA: MIT Press, 1995.

Levine, Martin P. *Gay Macho: The Life and Death of the Homosexual Clone.* Ed. Michael S. Kimmel. New York and London: New York University Press, 1998.

Lotringer, Sylvère, ed. *Foucault Live: Interviews 1966–1984.* New York: Semiotext(e), 1989.

Loydell, Rupert, ed. *My Kind of Angel: i.m. William Burroughs.* Exeter: Stride, 1998.

Lydenberg, Robin. *Word Cultures: Radical Theory and Practice in William S. Burroughs' Fiction.* Urbana and Chicago: University of Illinois Press, 1987.

Macey, David. *The Lives of Michel Foucault.* London: Hutchinson, 1993.

Mailer, Norman. *Ancient Evenings.* Boston: Little Brown, 1983.

Mann, W. Edward, and Edward Hoffman. *The Man Who Dreamed of Tomorrow: A Conceptual Biography of Wilhelm Reich.* Los Angeles: J.P. Tarcher, 1980.

Marks, John. *The Search for the "Manchurian Candidate": The CIA and Mind Control.* London: Allen Lane, 1979.

Martin, James. "Burroughs' Fiction." *Gay Sunshine* 21 (Spring 1974): 3.

Mattachine Society. *Mattachine Review.* (August 1956).

———. "The Mattachine Society Today." Mimeographed (Los Angeles, 1954).

Maupin, Armistead. *Tales of the City.* 1978. London: Black Swan, 1997.

Van der Meer, Theo. "Sodomy and the Pursuit of A Third Sex in the Early Modern Period." In Gilbert Herdt, ed. *Third Sex, Third Gender: Beyond Sexual Dimorphism in Culture and History.* New York: Zone Books, 1994, pp. 137–212.

Metcalf, Andy, and Martin Humphries, eds. *The Sexuality of Men.* London: Pluto Press, 1985.

Mikriammos, Philippe. "The Last European Interview." *Review of Contemporary Fiction* (Spring 1984): 12–18.

Miles, Barry. *William Burroughs: El Hombre Invisible.* London: Virgin Books, 1992.

Morgan, Ted. *Literary Outlaw: The Life and Times of William S. Burroughs.* New York: Henry Holt, 1988.

Mottram, Eric. *William Burroughs: The Algebra of Need.* 1971. London: Marion Boyars, 1977.

Murphy, Timothy F., and Suzanne Poirier, eds. *Writing AIDS: Gay Literature, Language and Analysis.* New York: Columbia University Press, 1993.

Murphy, Timothy S. *Wising Up the Marks: The Amodern William Burroughs.* Berkeley, Los Angeles: University of California Press, 1997.

Nataf, Zachary I. "Skin-flicks." In Sue Golding, ed. *The Eight Technologies of Otherness.* London and New York: Routledge, 1997, pp. 172–189.

Nelson, Emmanuel S., ed. *Contemporary Gay American Novelists: A Bio-Bibliographical Critical Sourcebook.* Westport, CT and London: Greenwood Press, 1993.

New Music Express. "Dream On." *New Music Express* (July 1 1995): 3.

Oxenhandler, Neal. "Listening to Burroughs' Voice." In Jennie Skerl and Robin Lydenberg, eds. *William S. Burroughs: At the Front: Critical Reception, 1959–1989.* Carbondale and Edwardsville: Southern Illinois University Press, 1991, pp. 133–147.

Pedersen, Lyn [pseud. for James Kepner]. "The Importance of Being Different." *ONE* (March 1954): 4–6.

Porush, David. *The Soft Machine: Cybernetic Fiction.* New York and London: Methuen, 1985.

Pounds, Wayne. "The Postmodern Anus: Parody and Utopia in Two Recent Novels by William Burroughs." In Jennie Skerl and Robin Lydenberg, eds. *William S. Burroughs: At the Front: Critical Reception, 1959–1989.* Carbondale and Edwardsville: Southern Illinois University Press, 1991, pp. 217–232.

Rado, Sandor. *The Psychoanalysis of Behavior: Collected Papers.* 2 vols. New York and London: Grune and Stratton, 1956/1962.

Rechy, John. *City of Night.* 1963. London: MacGibbon and Kee, 1964.

———. *Numbers.* New York: Grove Press, 1967.

———. *The Sexual Outlaw: A Documentary; A Non-Fiction Account, with Commentaries, of Three Days and Nights in the Sexual Underground.* 1977. London: W. H. Allen, 1978.

Reich, Wilhelm. *The Function of the Orgasm: Sex-Economic Problems of Biological Energy.* 1942. Trans. Vincent R. Carfagno. London: Souvenir Press, 1983. Second Edition.

———. *Listen Little Man!* 1948. Trans. Theodore P. Wolfe. New York: Farrar, Straus and Giroux, 1972.

Richmond, Len, and Gary Noguera, eds. *The Gay Liberation Book.* San Francisco: Ramparts Press, 1973.

Rodley, Chris, ed. *Cronenberg on Cronenberg.* Boston and London: Faber and Faber, 1992.

Rotundo, E. Anthony. *American Manhood: Transformations in Masculinity from the Revolution to the Modern Era.* New York: Basic Books, 1993.

Rubin, Gayle. "The Catacombs: A Temple of the Butthole." In Mark Thompson, ed. *Leatherfolk: Radical Sex, People, Politics and Practice.* Boston, Alyson Publications, 1991, pp. 119–141.

Russ, Joanna. *The Female Man.* New York: Bantam Books, 1975.

Russell, Jamie. "Digging Burroughs: An Interview with James Grauerholz." *Gay Times* 270 (March, 2001): 80.

Russo, Vito. *The Celluloid Closet: Homosexuality in the Movies.* New York: Harper & Row, 1981.

Savran, David. *Taking It Like a Man: White Masculinity, Masochism and Contemporary American Culture.* Princeton, NJ: Princeton University Press, 1998.

Sedgwick, Eve Kosofsky. *Tendencies.* London: Routledge, 1994.

Shaviro, Steven. "Burroughs's Theater of Illusion: *Cities of the Red Night.*" In Jennie Skerl and Robin Lydenberg, eds. *William S. Burroughs: At the Front: Critical Reception, 1959–1989.* Carbondale and Edwardsville: Southern Illinois University Press, 1991, pp. 197–208.

Shepherd, Simon, and Mick Wallis, eds. *Coming On Strong: Gay Politics and Culture.* London: Unwin, 1989.

Shilts, Randy. *And the Band Played On.* New York: St. Martin's Press, 1987.

Showalter, Elaine. *Sexual Anarchy: Gender and Culture at the Fin de Siècle.* New York: Viking, 1990.

Silberman, Steve. "Burroughs Pops On-Line Cherry With Drag Queens." *Wired News* (20 February 1997).Http://www.wired.com/news/news/culture/story/2173.html.

Sinfield, Alan. *The Wilde Century: Effeminacy, Oscar Wilde and the Queer Moment.* London and New York: Cassell, 1994.

Skerl, Jennie. "Freedom Through Fantasy in the Recent Novels of William S. Burroughs." In Jennie Skerl and Robin Lydenberg, eds. *William S. Burroughs: At the Front: Critical Reception, 1959–1989.* Carbondale and Edwardsville: Southern Illinois University Press, 1991, pp. 189–196.

———. *William S. Burroughs.* Boston: Twayne Publishers, 1985.

Skerl, Jennie and Robin Lydenberg, eds. *William S. Burroughs: At the Front: Critical Reception, 1959–1989.* Carbondale and Edwardsville: Southern Illinois University Press, 1991.

Sobieszek, Robert A. *Ports of Entry: William S. Burroughs and the Arts.* Los Angeles: L.A. County Museum of Art and Thames and Hudson, 1996.

Solanas, Valerie. *SCUM Manifesto.* 1967. Edinburgh, San Francisco: AK Press, 1997.

Spencer, Colin. *Homosexuality: A History.* 1995. London: Fourth Estate, 1996.

Steakley, James D. *The Homosexual Emancipation Movement in Germany.* New York: Arno Press, 1975.

Stephenson, Gregory. "The Gnostic Vision of William S. Burroughs." *Review of Contemporary Fiction* (Spring 1984): 40–48.

Stimpson, Catherine R. "The Beat Generation and the Trials of Homosexual Liberation." *Salmagundi* 58–59 (1982–1983): 373–392.

Strieber, Whitley. *Communion: A True Story Encounter with the Unknown.* New York: Beech Tree Books, 1987.

Tanner, Tony. "Rub Out the Word." In Jennie Skerl and Robin Lydenberg, eds. *William S. Burroughs: At the Front: Critical Reception, 1959–1989.* Carbondale and Edwardsville: Southern Illinois University Press, 1991, pp. 105–113.

Theweleit, Klaus. *Male Fantasies, Volume Two: Male Bodies: Psychoanalyzing the White Terror.* 1978. Trans. Chris Turner and Erica Carter in Collaboration with Stephen Conway. Cambridge: Polity Press, 1989.

Thompson, Hunter S. *Hells Angels.* 1966. London: Penguin, 1967.

Thompson, Mark, ed. *Leatherfolk: Radical Sex, People, Politics and Practice.* Boston, Alyson Publications, 1991.

———. "Introduction." In Thompson, ed. *Leatherfolk: Radical Sex, People, Politics and Practice.* Boston, Alyson Publications, 1991, pp. xi–xx.

Cathryn Vasseleu. *Textures of Light: Vision and Touch in Irigaray, Levinas and Morleau-Ponty.* London and New York: Routledge, 1998.

Vidal, Gore. *The City and the Pillar.* 1948. Revised and unexpurgated edition, 1965. London: Abacus, 1997.

Wallis, Dave. *Only Lovers Left Alive.* London: Blond, 1964.

Wallis, Roy. *The Road to Total Freedom: A Sociological Analysis of Scientology.* London: Heinemann, 1976.

Ward, Geoff. "William Burroughs: A Literary Outlaw?" *Cambridge Critical Quarterly* 22.4 (1993): 339–354.

Watters, John G. "The Control Machine: Myth in *The Soft Machine* of W. S. Burroughs." *Connotations* 5.2–3 (1995/96): 284–303.

Weeks, Jeffrey. *Sexuality and Its Discontents: Meanings, Myths and Modern Sexualities.* London and New York: Routledge, 1985.

Willett, John. "UGH . . ." *Times Literary Supplement* 3220 (14 November 1963): 919. Reprinted in Jennie Skerl and Robin Lydenberg, eds. *William S. Burroughs: At the Front: Critical Reception, 1959–1989.* Carbondale and Edwardsville: Southern Illinois University Press, 1991, pp. 41–44.

Wittig, Monique. *Les Guérillères.* Paris: Les Editions de Minuit, 1969.

Wolfe, Tom. *The Electric Kool-Aid Acid Test.* 1968. London: Black Swan, 1998.

Woods, Gregory. "William Seward Burroughs II." In Emmanuel S. Nelson, ed. *Contemporary Gay American Novelists: A Bio-Bibliographical Critical Sourcebook.* Westport, CT and London: Greenwood Press, 1993, pp. 37–45

Wyler, William, dir. *Ben-Hur.* MGM, 1959.

INDEX